Kaffe Fassett's QUILTS IN ITALY

20 designs from Rowan for patchwork and quilting

featuring

Judy Baldwin

Sally Davis

Corienne Kramer

Liza Prior Lucy

Brandon Mably

Julie Stockler

The Taunton Press

First published in the USA in 2016 by

The Taunton Press, Inc., 63 South Main Street,
PO Box 5506, Newtown, CT 06470-5506
email: tp@taunton.com

Reprinted 2017

Created and produced by Westminster Fibers, Inc
3430 Toringdon Way, Suite 301
Charlotte, NC 28277
USA

Patchwork designs	Kaffe Fassett, Liza Prior Lucy, Brandon Mably, Judy Baldwin, Sally Davis, Corienne Kramer, Julie Stockler
Project coordination and quilt making	Heart Space Studios
Designer	Anne Wilson
Editors	Katy Denny, Sarah Hoggett
Technical editor	Lin Clements
Quilting	Judy Irish, Mary-Jane Hutchinson
Art direction/styling	Kaffe Fassett
Location photography	Debbie Patterson
Stills photography	Steven Wooster
Illustrations	Heart Space Studios
Publishing consultant	Susan Berry

Library of Congress Cataloging-in-Publication Data
in progress
ISBN 978-1-63186-708-8

Color reproduction	XY Digital, London

Printed in China

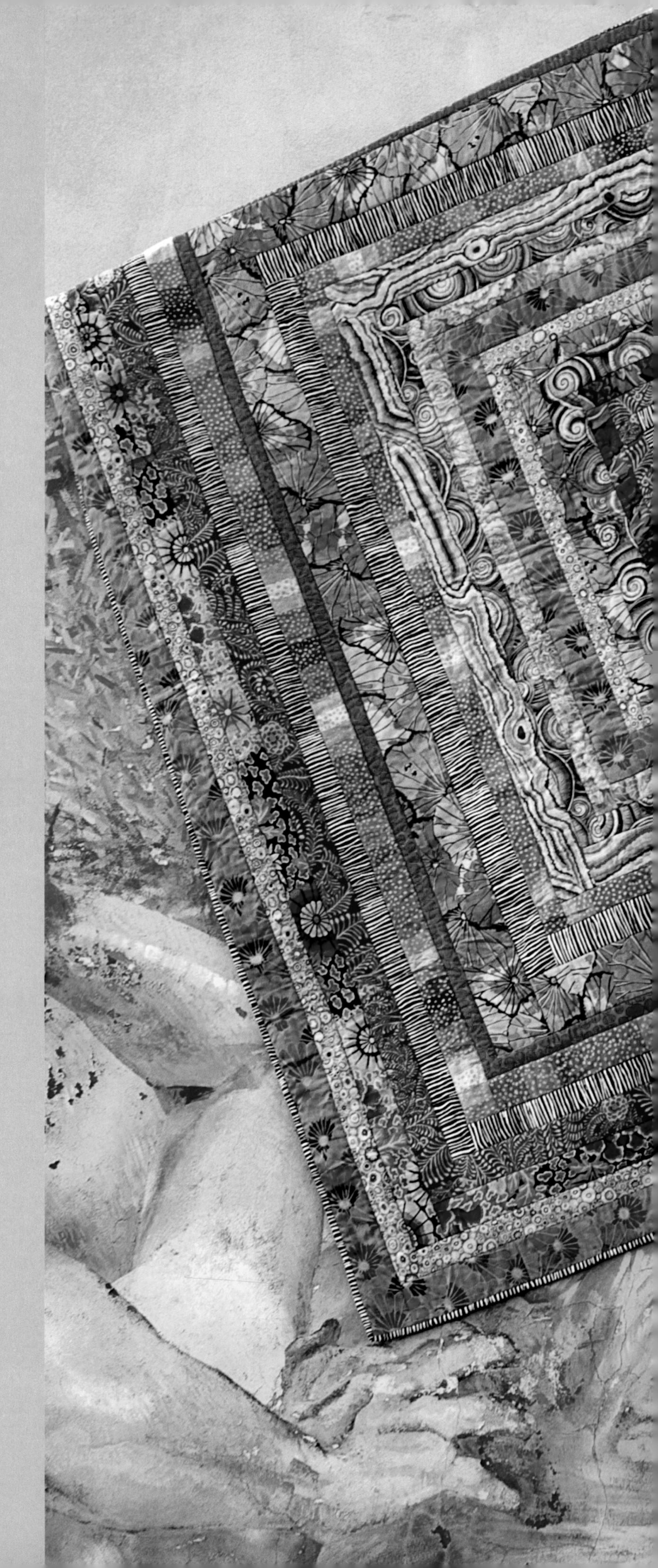

Page 1: *Desert* by Kaffe Fassett
Right: *Stone Log Cabin* by Kaffe Fassett

Contents

Introduction

In the past few years we have been giving workshops and lectures in Italy and it was suggested that I might want to photograph our yearly book there. Being me, I always want a very colorful setting and was blown away by the pictures that were sent to me of the five fishing villages, known as Cinque Terre, on Italy's West coast. Choosing it for a location was a 'no-brainer', as they say, with all those varied colourful houses built cheek by jowl up the rocky coastal hills. It was a living three-dimensional patchwork in pink, ochre, rust, sky blue and lemon-yellow! We did a recce in the Spring to see if the setting had enough possibilities to give each of our new quilts a sympathetic backdrop. It was even more amazing in reality than in the photographs. On that trip, we were there out of season so we could foresee no problems. 'It might be a bit more crowded in September when you do your shoot', they warned us, fairly casually. On arrival from England with four large bags of quilts, we were shocked to find crowds of tourists everywhere and not a room to be had in the first town, Montorosso, where we planned to do most of our shoot. Undeterred, we kept going back to hotels there to inquire if there were any cancellations and, lo and behold, two rooms suddenly became available. They more than suited us, being right on the sea front in the middle of the town – *perfetto!*

It was amazingly hot for early autumn and we had to haul camera cases and several quilts on and off the trains that took us from one town to the next. But the food was delicious, the swimming likewise and, best of all, the light was magical. Every quilt found a flattering setting and we were often helped by friendly locals. Wrought-iron gates and overgrown vines vied with old bicycles and colourful laundry to create just the mood we wanted.

Our first shoot was in Santa Margherita, 50 miles further up the coast where we were guided by our new Italian friend (Luisa Fenoglio). A few years earlier, she had decorated her daughter's wedding using the Kaffe Collective fabrics and sent me a stunning book about the glorious celebration. She found us a good hotel and walked us about her charming town. Luisa also took us to Portofino for an *al fresco* dinner beside the harbour. It was classically beautiful but I was after the humbler look of distressed paint that I knew awaited us in Cinque Terre.

The great thing about a Mediterranean location is that the love of colour in the Italian nature leads to every possible combination you could pray for. The gorgeous old carved gate that became the setting for my Lacy Log Cabin (on pages 8-9) was a brilliant way to start a shoot that went from one gorgeous colour scheme to another.

Debbie Patterson, our wonderful photographer who has such an inspired eye, picked up on so many beautiful and telling details like the beach umbrellas, boats, vegetable and fruit crates, bicycles and mosaics. Brandon not only designed one of the most richly coloured quilts in this book but also spotted many of our settings, running back and forth from location to hotel to fetch just another quilt when we found the ideal spot for it.

We were exhausted but exhilarated by the lush location and the experience of being part of Italian life with its great food (the delicious *gelato* in particular) and its wonderful, warm people.

Erdbeeren aus Südtirol
Fragole dell'Alto Adige
Brixen - Neustift - Pustertal

Rusty Squares
by Kaffe Fassett

When I was designing this quilt I was dreaming of the rusts, oranges and golds of the hill towns of Cinque Terre, Italy, but this little rustic brick and stone corner was too good a setting to pass up. The quilt is a simple idea that vibrates because of the rich tones of the fabrics.

Lacy Log Cabin
by Kaffe Fassett

This was the first shot we took for our Italian book. The exquisitely coloured arch in Santa Margherita made the best possible placement for this delicate pastel quilt. The fussy-cut flowers with dusty small print surrounds make this simple-to-make quilt seem quite complex.

Stone Log Cabin
by Kaffe Fassett

This part of the Italian coast is famous for its walking paths. The neutral palette for my quilt looks right at home in this setting. My new Dream fabric is both the centre and the backing for the quilt. Brandon's Creased fabric in black and white makes a sharp detail on the binding.

8

Blue and White
by Kaffe Fassett

The bold black and white churches in Italy had been the original inspiration for this simple striped quilt. But when we got to our location in Italy, I was delighted to find the boats and beach umbrellas in just as bold blue and white stripes – perfect!

72

Tussie Mussie
by Kaffe Fassett

The pretty spring-like palette of this quilt reminded me of the little flower and herb bouquet, known as a 'tussie mussie' that you find at the American Museum in Bath. This playful mosaic panel and green tiled wall made a delicious place to show it off.

Cool Zig Zag
by Kaffe Fassett

The turquoise Mediterranean Sea welcomes my Zig Zag quilt, created in all our newest sea-green prints. (It was a luxury to swim in these waters after a day's shoot!) My Serpentine print looks almost three-dimensional on this border.

Scaffold
by Kaffe Fassett

An old Amish quilt inspired the layout of this quilt. As I designed it in London, with the colours of Cinque Terre in mind, I was happy indeed to find this golden town with its powerful black and white features that help to make the quilt really glow. The Ombre stripe fabric in pink, orange and lime is too perfect for a backing.

Golden Strips
by Kaffe Fassett

These handsome pebbled white steps are the sort of playful detail you see so often in Italy. Doesn't it make a perfect backdrop for the shimmer of ochre, lemon, yellows and lime tones of this quilt? Philip Jacobs' Shaggy fabric is so perfect for a backing.

Chiaroscuro
by Kaffe Fassett

I conjured up all the boldest geometrics that I could find to make this melody of a quilt. I love the saturated full-blown colours in it and they sit so well with the beach furniture at Monterosso.

Contrast Weave

by Kaffe Fassett

A simple structure that we all seem to return to when making new quilts: I felt its boldness suited the exciting colours of these Italian fishing villages. Even these plastic kayaks make the quilt sing out. And that soft evening light really helps.

Desert
by Kaffe Fassett

When I was growing up in America with all its wide open spaces, I dreamed of cosy, crowded jumbles of buildings in the 'old world'. My heart sang when I came across these fishing villages on the Italian coast. This quilt, made entirely of my woven Indian striped fabrics, is right at home in these warm colours.

Red Blocks
by Kaffe Fassett

Tumbling Blocks is an old patchwork block favourite of mine. This version in hot reds, pinks, purples and blacks looks amazing on these deep terracotta coloured walls. I love the stylish black and white striped church up the street as well.

pizze al taglio
FARINATA
focacce farcite

Cassetta
by Liza Prior Lucy

Liza Lucy's striped tents in the same colours as the Cinque Terre hill towns really sparkles against the terracotta pinks of this villa in Monterosso. The grey-green Shot Cotton sets off the warm tones to perfection.

Baroque Pinwheels
by Brandon Mably

Brandon's new fabrics are shown off so glowingly in this bold quilt. The burnt intensity of the walls makes his warm browns and velvety blues really vibrate. Camouflage Stripe makes a good backing for this quilt, too.

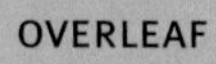

OVERLEAF

Losing My Marbles
by Julie Stockler

This corner shop with its bangles and wild sunglasses makes this playful quilt sing out. And the quilt makes great use of our range of small classic prints.

16.00

Alba
by Liza Prior Lucy

Liza has fussy cut the Corsage print and used Heraldic as a border most handsomely. You can see how at home it is with the warm colours of Italy.

Wagon Wheels
by Corienne Kramer

The cool neutral palette of this classic quilt settles onto the stones of this Italian beach as though it belongs there. My Thousand Flowers fabric in greyish colours makes just the right backing.

Cloudy Skies
by Liza Prior Lucy

These playful shapes – the unusual rounded architecture along the promenade and the rows of parasols on the beach – make just the right setting for the blue and white precision of this handsome quilt.

Whirligig
by Judy Baldwin

The bold design of this quilt deserved an equally bold setting. A huge variegated cactus made just the lively background it needed.

Embers
by Sally Davis

The warm glowing tones of this richly textured quilt with its apple green border is so at home in this Italian villa garden. The red Millefiore for the backing fabric seems the perfect choice.

rusty squares *

Kaffe Fassett

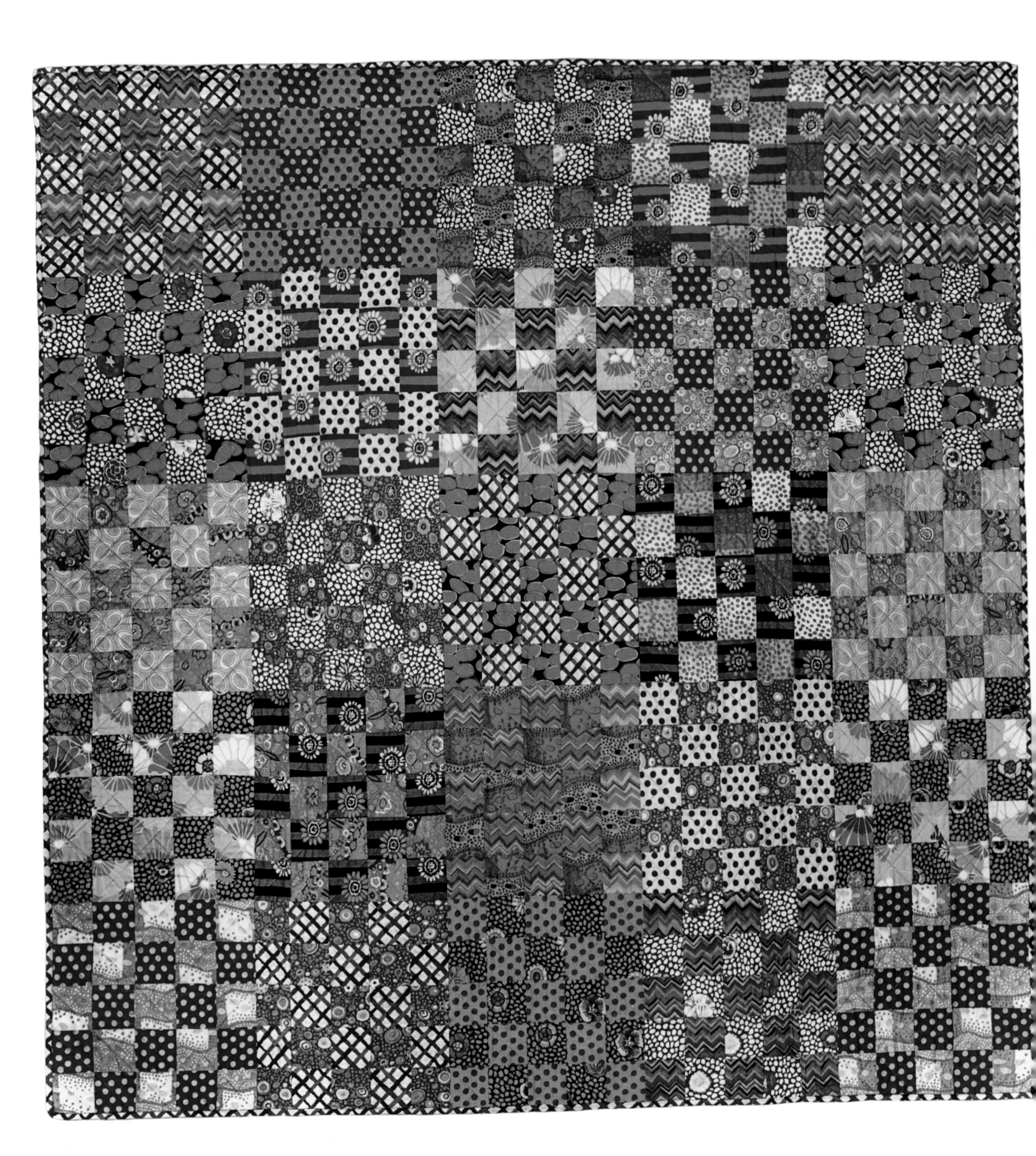

This is a scrappy style quilt; it isn't necessary to place each fabric as in the original to achieve the same effect. Just choose two fabrics, one slightly lighter than the other, for each block of 25 squares. There are 25 blocks in the whole quilt, arranged in a checkerboard effect.

SIZE OF QUILT
The finished quilt will measure approx. 62½in x 62½in (159cm x 159cm)

MATERIALS
Patchwork Fabrics

VICTORIA		
Rust	BM46RU	¼yd (25cm)
Grey	BM46GY	¼yd (25cm)
SPOT		
Magenta	GP70MG	⅜yd (35cm)
Orange	GP70OR	¼yd (25cm)
Grey	GP70GY	¼yd (25cm)
GUINEA FLOWER		
Yellow	GP59YE	⅜yd (35cm)
Brown	GP59BR	⅜yd (35cm)
ZIG ZAG		
Rare	BM43RR	¼yd (25cm)
Warm	BM43WM	¼yd (25cm)
THOUSAND FLOWERS		
Pink	GP144PK	¼yd (25cm)
MAD PLAID		
Curry	BM37CU	⅜yd (35cm)
ROMAN GLASS		
Red	GP01RD	⅜yd (35cm)
MILLEFIORE		
Tomato	GP92TM	¼yd (25cm)
REGENCY DAISY		
Brown	GP146BR	¼yd (25cm)
Red	GP146RD	¼yd (25cm)
ABORIGINAL DOT		
Lilac	GP71LI	¼yd (25cm)
OMBRE		
Brown	GP117BR	¼yd (25cm)
LABEL		
Tomato	BM45TM	¼yd (25cm)
PAPERWEIGHT		
Pink	GP20PK	⅛yd (15cm)

Backing Fabric

VICTORIA		
Rust	BM46RU	4yd (3.7m)

Binding

VICTORIA		
Rust	BM46RU	½yd (50cm)

Batting
70in x 70in (178cm x 178cm)

Quilting Thread
Machine quilting thread

CUTTING OUT
This quilt is pieced using a single 3in (7.6cm) square patch shape. The squares are pieced into simple blocks, which are then set in simple rows.
Cut 3in (7.6cm) strips across the width of each patchwork fabric and then cut into 3in (7.6cm) squares. Each strip will give you 13 squares per full width.
Cut 1 strip in GP20PK.
Cut 2 strips in GP71LI, BM46GY, BM46RU, GP70OR, GP70GY, BM43RR, BM43WM, GP144PK, GP117BR, GP146BR, GP146RD.
Cut 3 strips in GP92TM, BM45TM.
Cut 4 strips in GP70MG, GP59BR, GP59YE, GP01RD, BM37CU.
Total 625 squares.

Binding
Cut 7 strips 2½in (6.4cm) wide across the width of the fabric in BM46RU.

Backing
Cut 2 pieces 40in x 72in (102cm x 183cm) in backing fabric BM46RU.

MAKING THE QUILT
Use a ¼in (6mm) seam allowance throughout. Take 25 squares (12 of one colour and 13 of the other) to make each block, following block assembly diagrams. Make a total of 25 blocks. Join the blocks into 5 rows of 5 blocks and then join the rows to complete the quilt.

FINISHING THE QUILT
Press the quilt top. Seam the backing pieces using a ¼in (6mm) seam allowance to form a piece approx. 70in x 70in (178cm x 178cm). Layer the quilt top, batting and backing and baste together (see page 148).
Using machine quilting thread, quilt diagonal lines joining the corners of the squares to form a lattice pattern.
Trim the quilt edges and attach the binding (see page 149).

BLOCK ASSEMBLY DIAGRAM

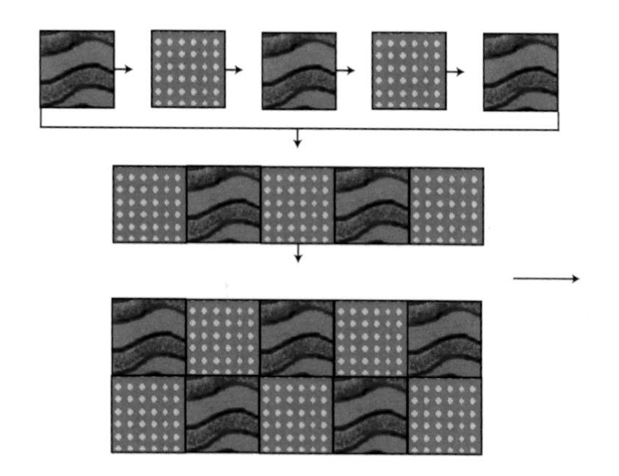

QUILT ASSEMBLY DIAGRAM

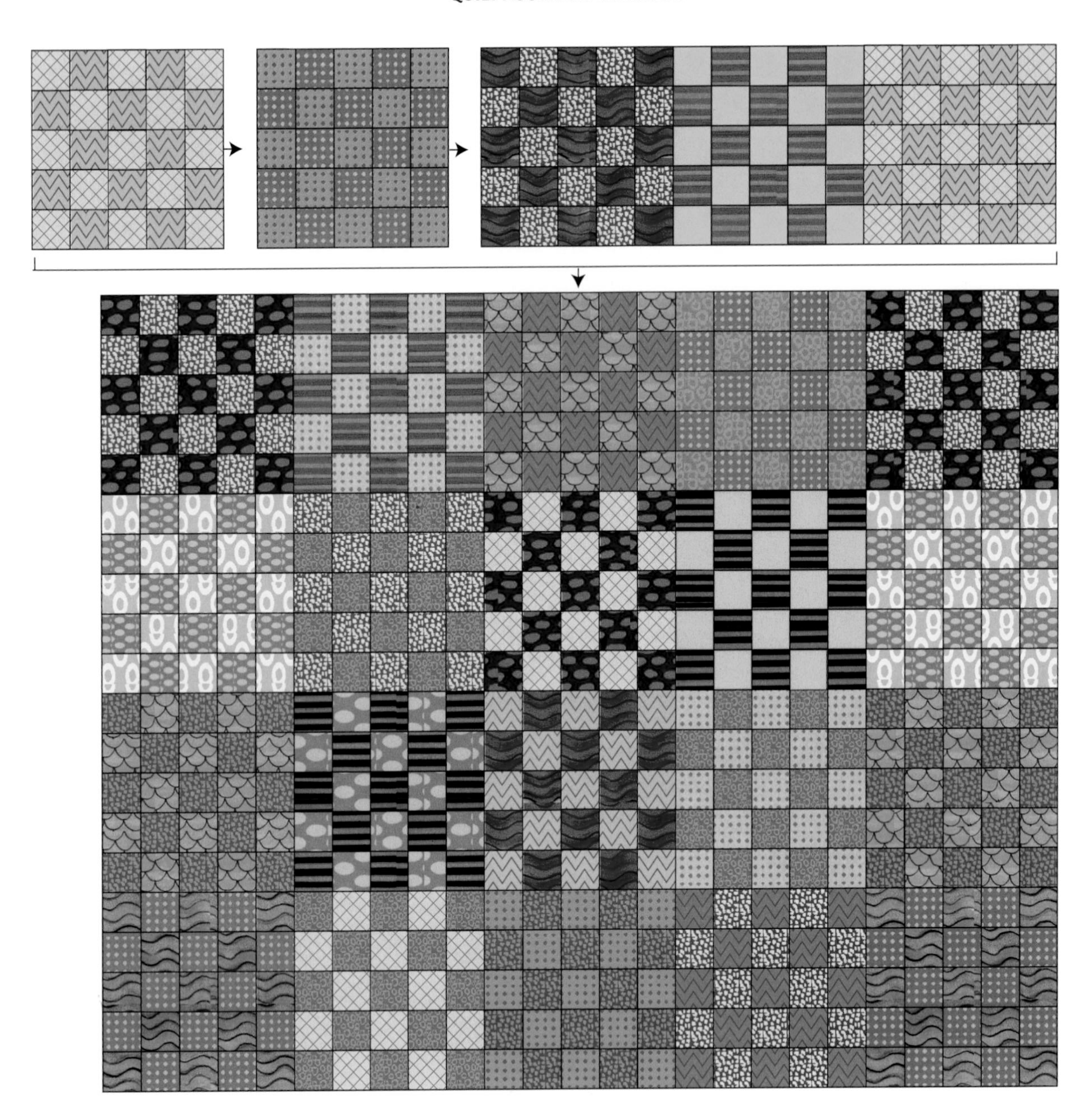

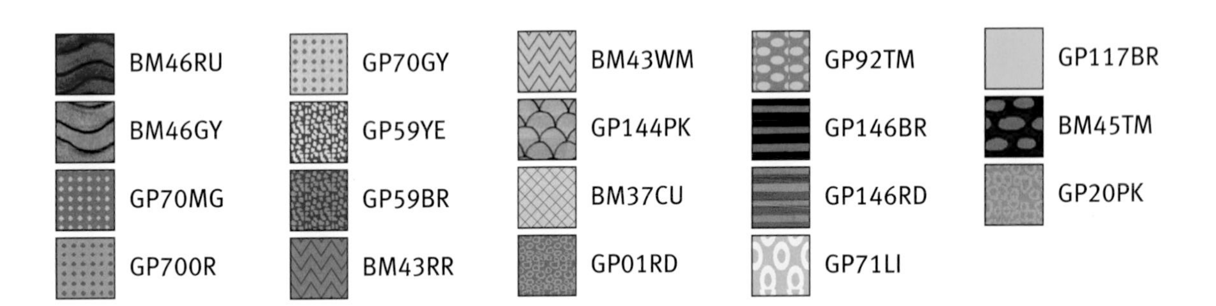

desert *

Kaffe Fassett

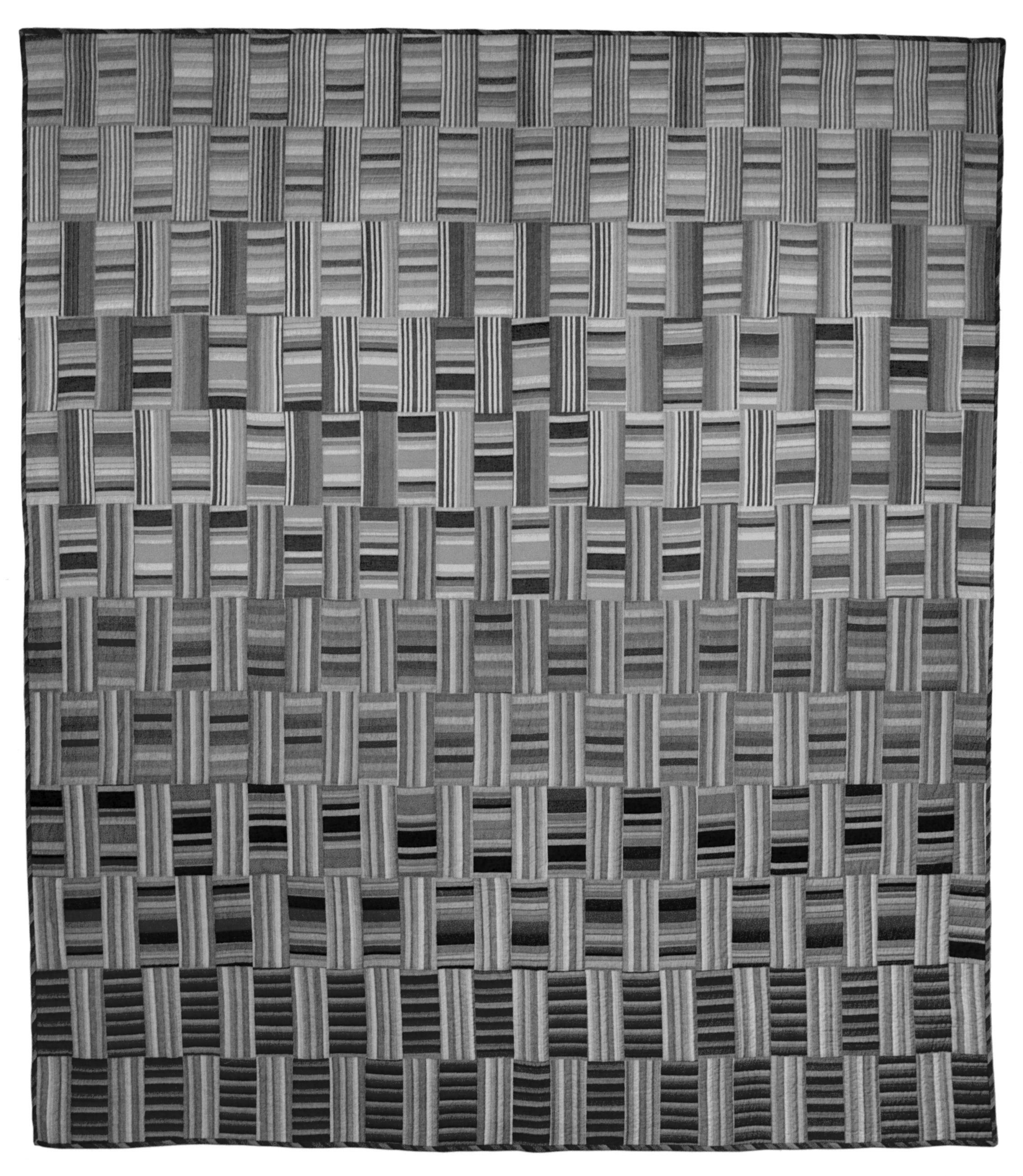

This quilt is created entirely from four different Woven Stripes fabrics in yellow, orange and red colourways. Each rectangle is cut 3½in x 7½in (8.9cm x 19cm). Lightly starching the fabric before cutting will make it simpler to cut the stripes on the grain.

SIZE OF QUILT
The finished quilt will measure approx. 78in x 84in (198cm x 213cm)

MATERIALS
Patchwork Fabrics

WOVEN CATERPILLAR STRIPE WCS		
Yellow	YE	1yd (92cm)
Sunshine	SU	¾yd (70cm)
WOVEN MULTI STRIPE WMS		
Toast	TT	1¾yd (1.6m)
Pimento	PI	¾yd (70cm)
WOVEN ROMAN STRIPE WRS		
Blood Orange	BO	¾yd (70cm)
Arizona	AR	⅞yd (80cm)
WOVEN BROAD STRIPE WBS		
Watermelon	WL	¾yd (70cm)
Bliss	BS	⅞yd (80cm)

Backing Fabric
SPOT
Lichen GP70LC 6¼yd (5.8m)

Binding
MULTI STRIPE
Pimento PI 1yd (92cm)

Batting
86in x 92in (218.5cm x 234cm)

Quilting Thread
Machine quilting thread

CUTTING OUT
Cut 7½in (19cm) strips across the width of Caterpillar Stripe YE, Caterpillar Stripe SU, and Multi Stripe TT. Each strip will give you 11 patches per full width. Cut 8 strips in Multi Stripe TT, 4 strips in Caterpillar Stripe YE and 3 strips in Caterpillar Stripe SU. Sub-cut the strips into 7½in x 3½in (19cm x 8.9cm) rectangles.
Cut 3½in (8.9cm) strips across the width of Multi Stripe PI, Roman Stripe BO, Roman Stripe AR, Broad Stripe WL, Broad Stripe BS. Each strip will give you 5 patches per full width. Cut 8 strips in Broad Stripe BS, Roman Stripe AR. Cut 6 strips in Multi Stripe PI, Roman Stripe BO, Broad Stripe WL. Sub-cut the strips into 3½in x 7½in (8.9cm x 19cm) rectangles.

Binding
The binding for this quilt is cut on the bias. Cut strips 2½in (6.4cm) wide in Multi Stripe PI and join to make a strip about 9½yd (8.7m) long.

Backing
From GP70LC, cut two pieces 95in (241.3cm) long. Cut one piece 33in (83.8cm) long. Cut the 33in (83.8cm) long piece into three strips 8½in x 33in (21.6cm x 83.8cm). Remove all selvedges.

MAKING THE QUILT
Use a ¼in (6mm) seam allowance throughout. Lay out all the pieces as in the diagram, and join together in rows.

FINISHING THE QUILT
Press the quilt top. Sew the 8½in (21.6cm) pieces end to end and trim to 95in (241.3cm). Sew one wide 95in (241.3cm) panel to the pieced strip. Sew the other wide panel to the other side of the pieced strip. The backing will measure approx. 95in x 88in (241.3cm x 223.5cm). Layer the quilt top, batting and backing and baste together (see page 148). Using machine quilting thread, quilt in the ditch and along the stripe edges within each fabric rectangle. Trim the quilt edges and attach the binding (see page 149).

QUILT ASSEMBLY DIAGRAM

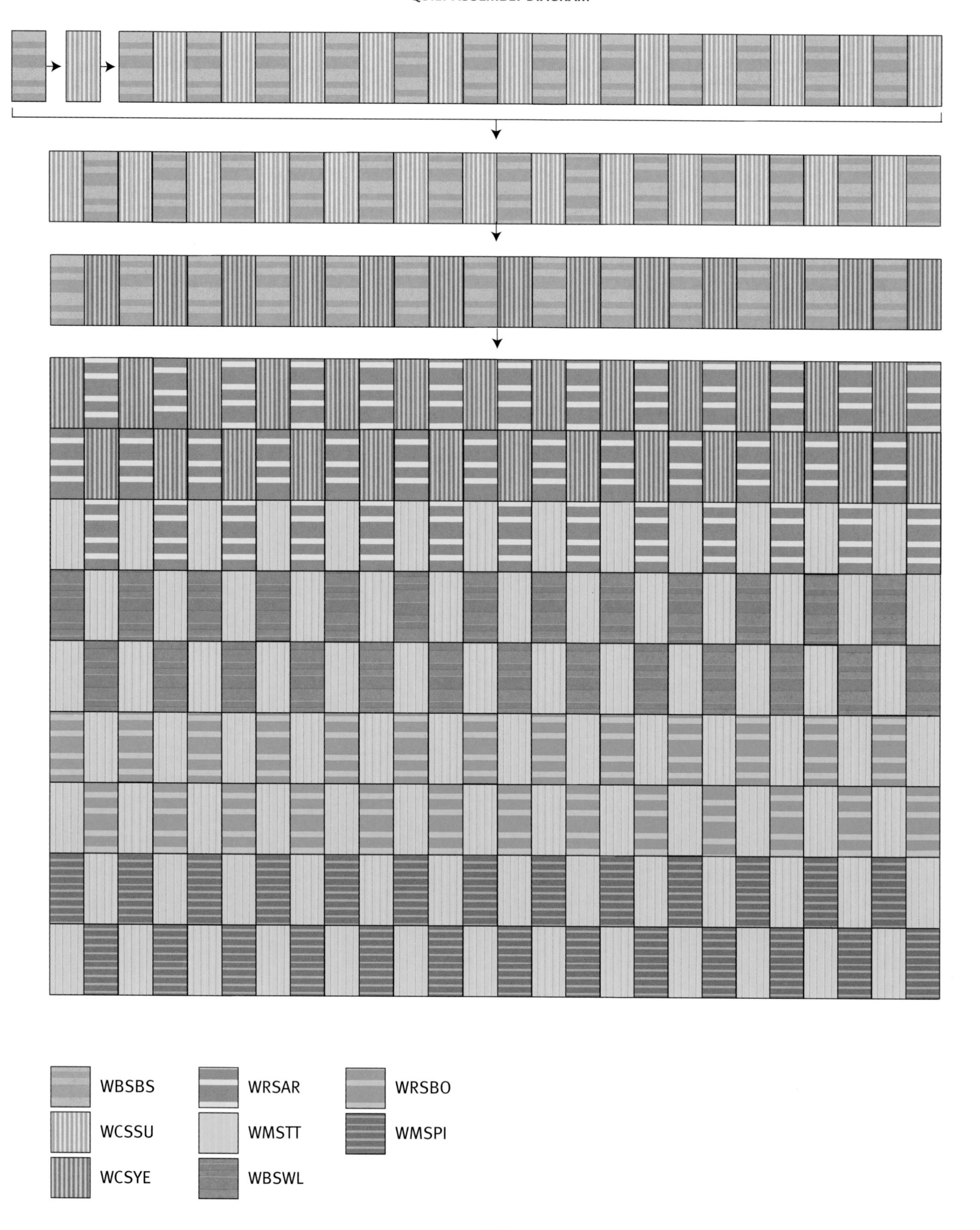

stone log cabin **

Kaffe Fassett

Creating a log cabin design on this scale requires careful attention to keep the quilt in shape: you need to start stitching a new round at the opposite end to where the previous round started. You will also need to join the strips for the 'logs' in the outer rounds.

SIZE OF QUILT
The finished quilt will measure approx. 77½in x 81½in (197cm x 207cm).

MATERIALS
Patchwork Fabrics

DREAM		
Grey	GP148GR	⅝yd (60cm)
CREASED		
Black	BM50BK	⅞yd (80cm)
FERN		
Purple	GP147PU	⅝yd (60cm)
SERPENTINE		
Dark	GP145DK	⅛yd (15cm)
SPIRAL SHELLS		
Brown	PJ73BR	⅜yd (35cm)
LOTUS LEAF		
Mauve	GP29MV	⅞yd (80cm)
PAPERWEIGHT		
Sludge	GP20SL	⅝yd (60cm)
THOUSAND FLOWERS		
Smoke	GP144SM	1yd (90cm)
BRASSICA		
Grey	PJ51GY	¼yd (25cm)
JUPITER		
Purple	GP131PU	⅜yd (35cm)
OMBRE		
Purple	GP117PU	¾yd (70cm)
JUMBLE		
Purple	BM53PU	¼yd (25cm)

Backing Fabric

DREAM		
Grey	GP148GR	6yd (5.5m)

Binding

CREASED		
Black	BM50BK	¾yd (70cm)

Batting
85½in x 89½in (217cm x 227.5cm).

Quilting Thread
Machine quilting thread

CUTTING OUT
Central Panel Fussy cut 1 rectangle 5in x 9in (12.7cm x 22.9cm) in GP148GR.

The table on page 58 shows the 'round' number, fabric code, width of each 'log' and the number of strips across the width of fabric needed for each round of logs. You will need to join some fabric strips as the quilt gets bigger with each round added. All measurements include ¼in (6mm) seam allowance. The final column shows the size that your quilt should be after adding each round of logs.

Binding Cut 9 strips, 2½in (6.4cm) wide across the width of the fabric in BM50BK.

Backing In GP148GR cut two pieces 91in (231cm) long. Cut one piece 32in (81.3cm) long. Cut the 32in (81.3cm) long piece into three strips, 7½in x 32in (19cm x 81.3cm). Remove all selvedges. Sew the 7½in (19cm) pieces end to end and trim to 91in (231cm).

MAKING THE QUILT
Use ¼in (6mm) seam allowance throughout. Take the centre panel and add 'round 1' Log A to the bottom of the centre panel, followed by Log B on the left side, Log C is added to the top and Log D to the right side to complete round 1. This is shown in Round Assembly Diagram 1. Press carefully, pressing after adding each log. Follow diagram 2 for the next and following rounds. In every 'round' the logs are added in the same sequence, but make sure that you start machine stitching at the opposite end to the one started on the previous round. This will help to keep the fabric in shape. Add all 20 'rounds' as shown in the quilt assembly diagram on page 59.

FINISHING THE QUILT
Press the quilt top. Sew one wide 91in (231cm) panel to the pieced strip. Sew the other wide panel to the other side of the pieced strip. The backing will measure approx. 91in x 87in (231cm x 221cm). Layer the quilt top, batting and backing, and baste together (see page 148). Using machine quilting thread, quilt in the ditch. Trim the quilt edges and attach the binding (see page 149).

ASSEMBLY DIAGRAM (ROUNDS)

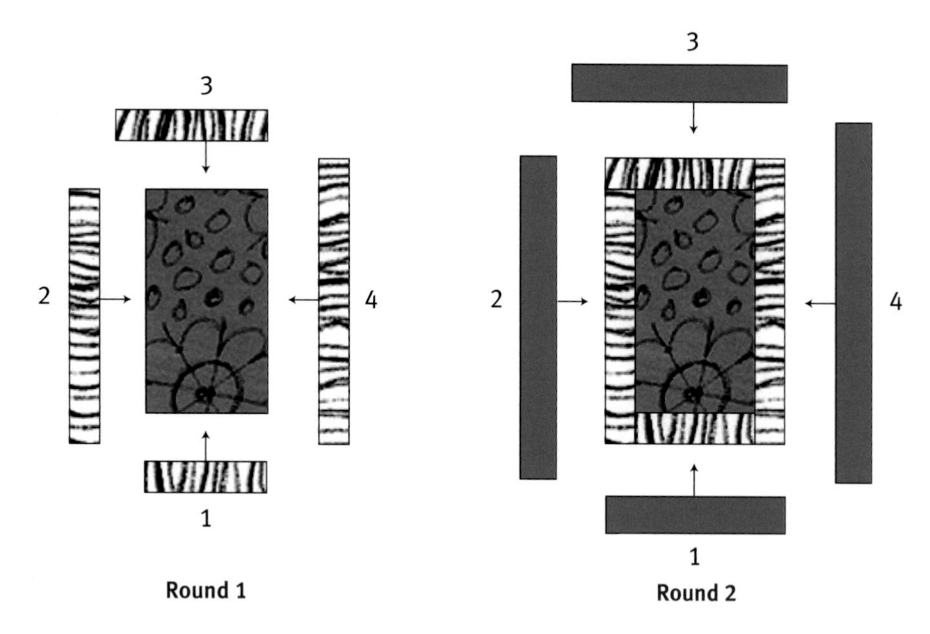

Round 1

Round 2

Round	Fabric	Log Width	Number of Strips	Log A	Log B	Log C	Log D	Size to Raw Edge
1	BM50BK	1¾in (4.5cm)	1	5in (12.7cm)	10¼in (26cm)	6¼in (15.9cm)	11½in (29.2cm)	7½in x 11½in (19cm x 29.2cm)
2	GP147PU	2in (5cm)	2	7½in (19cm)	13in (33cm)	9in (22.9cm)	14½in (36.8cm)	10½in x 14½in (26.7cm x 36.8cm)
3	GP145DK	2in (5cm)	2	10½in (26.7cm)	16in (40.6cm)	12in (30.5cm)	17½in (44.5cm)	13½in x 17½in (34.3cm x 44.5cm)
4	PJ73BR	2½in (6.4cm)	2	13½in (34.3cm)	19½in (49.5cm)	15½in (39.4cm)	21½in (54.6cm)	17½in x 21½in (44.5cm x 54.6cm)
5	GP29MV	2in (5cm)	3	17½in (44.5cm)	23in (58.5cm)	19in (48.3cm)	24½in (62.2cm)	20½in x 24½in (52cm x 62.2cm)
6	GP20SL	1¾in (4.5cm)	3	20½in (52cm)	25¾in (65.4cm)	21¾in (55.3cm)	27in (68.6cm)	23in x 27in (58.4cm x 68.6cm)
7	GP144SM	3in (7.6cm)	3	23in (58.4cm)	29½in (75cm)	25½in (64.8cm)	32in (81.3cm)	28in x 32in (71cm x 81.3cm)
8	PJ51GY	2in (5cm)	4	28in (71cm)	33½in (85cm)	29½in (75cm)	35in (89cm)	31in x 35in (78.8cm x 89cm)
9	PJ73BR	2in (5cm)	4	31in (78.8cm)	36½in (92.7cm)	32½in (82.5cm)	38in (96.5cm)	34in x 38in (86.4cm x 96.5cm)
10	GP131PU	3in (7.6cm)	4	34in (86.4cm)	40½in (102.9cm)	36½in (92.7cm)	43in (109.2cm)	39in x 43in (99cm x 109.2cm)
11	GP117PU	2in (5cm)	5	39in (99cm)	44½in (113cm)	40½in (103cm)	46in (116.8cm)	42in x 46in (106.7cm x 116.8cm)
12	BM50BK	2½in (6.4cm)	5	42in (106.7cm)	48in (122cm)	44in (111.8cm)	50in (127cm)	46in x 50in (116.8cm x 127cm)
13	GP29MV	4in (10cm)	6	46in (116.8cm)	53½in (136cm)	49½in (125.7cm)	57in (144.8cm)	53in x 57in (134.6cm x 144.8cm)
14	BM53PU	1½in (3.8cm)	6	53in (134.6cm)	58in (147.3cm)	54in (137.2cm)	59in (149.9cm)	55in x 59in (139.7cm x 149.9cm)
15	GP117PU	2½in (6.4cm)	6	55in (139.7cm)	61in (155cm)	57in (144.8cm)	63in (160cm)	59in x 63in (149.9cm x 160cm)
16	BM50BK	2in (5cm)	7	59in (149.9cm)	64½in (163.8cm)	60½in (153.7cm)	66in (167.7cm)	62in x 66in (157.5cm x 167.7cm)
17	GP147PU	2½in (6.4cm)	7	62in (157.5cm)	68in (172.7cm)	64in (162.5cm)	70in (177.8cm)	66in x 70in (167.7cm x 177.8cm)
18	GP148GR	2½in (6.4cm)	7	66in (167.7cm)	72in (183cm)	68in (172.7cm)	74in (188cm)	70in x 74in (177.8cm x 188cm)
19	GP20SL	2in (5cm)	8	70in (177.8cm)	75½in (191.8cm)	71½in (181.6cm)	77in (195.5cm)	73in x 77in (185.5cm x 195.5cm)
20	GP144SM	3in (7.6cm)	8	73in (185.5cm)	79½in (202cm)	75½in (191.8cm)	82in (208.3cm)	78in x 82in (198cm x 208.3cm)

QUILT ASSEMBLY DIAGRAM

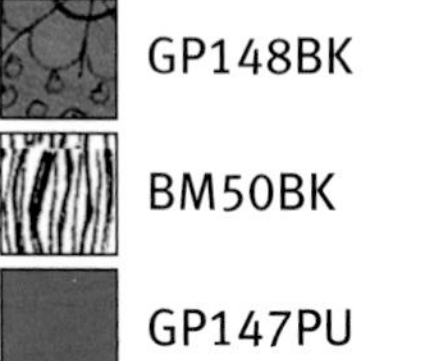

GP148BK

BM50BK

GP147PU

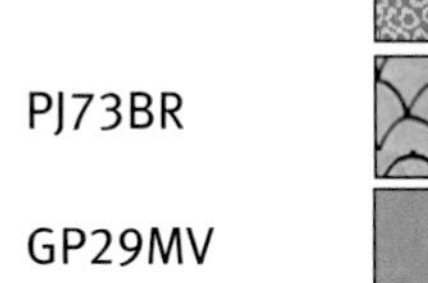

GP145DK

PJ73BR

GP29MV

GP20SL

GP144SM

PJ51GY

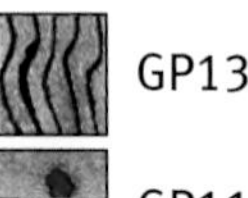

GP131PU

GP117PU

BM53PU

blue and white **

Kaffe Fassett

This strikingly graphic quilt, made from just two alternating colourways of Aboriginal Dots, produced an interesting making challenge. In order to get the strips to alternate while radiating from the centre but without having two strips of the same colour next to each other at the corners, you not only need longer templates in each round, but, by the time you get to the third and fourth rounds of the quilt, you also need to make some strip sections using a slightly larger template.

SIZE OF QUILT
The finished quilt will measure approx. 81in x 72in (206cm x 183cm)

MATERIALS
Patchwork Fabrics
ABORIGINAL DOT

Delft	GP71DF	3yd (2.75m)
Cream	GP71CM	3¼yd (3m)

Backing Fabric
MILLEFIORE

Pastel	GP92PL	5yd (4.6m)

Binding
ABORIGINAL DOT

Delft	GP71DF	⅝yd (60cm)

Batting
89in x 80in (2.26m x 2.03m)

Quilting Thread
Machine quilting thread

Templates

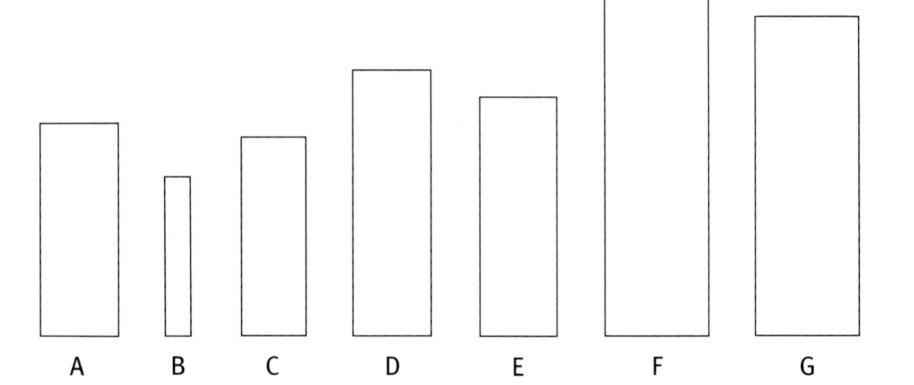

Patch Shapes
The quilt is constructed around a central rectangular panel. The rounds are constructed from strips of alternating fabrics and added to the central panel in the order shown in the diagrams on page 62. Note the order change in Rounds 3 and 4.

CUTTING OUT
Cut all rectangles as strips across the width of the fabric, placing templates horizontal to the width of the fabric. As each template shape is cut, keep the same-sized fabric shapes in separate piles, labelling them template A, B, C and so on, so you can identify them easily when assembling the quilt.

Using Template A 8½in x 3½in (21.6cm x 8.9cm) cut 1 rectangle in blue.
Using Template B 6½in x 1½in (16.5cm x 3.8cm) cut 22 rectangles in blue and 24 in cream.
Using Template C 8 x 3in (20.3cm x 7.6cm) cut 18 rectangles in blue and 22 in cream.
Using Template D 10½in x 3½in (26.7cm x 8.9cm) cut 12 rectangles in blue and 14 in cream.
Using Template E 9½in x 3½in (24.1cm x 8.9cm) cut 14 rectangles in blue and 16 in cream.
Using Template F 13½in x 4½in (34.3cm x 11.4cm) cut 14 rectangles in blue and 16 in cream.
Using Template G 12½in x 4½in (31.7cm x 11.4cm) cut 16 rectangles in blue and 18 in cream.

Binding
Cut 8 strips 2½in (6.4cm) wide across the width of the fabric in GP71DF.

Backing
Cut 2 pieces 89in x 40in (226cm x 101.5cm) in backing fabric GP92PL.

MAKING THE QUILT
Use a ¼in (6mm) seam allowance throughout. The quilt has four rounds and starts with the template A blue rectangle. Follow the quilt assembly diagrams carefully for the placement of the rounds. The use of a design wall will be useful.

Piecing round 1 Use template B shapes for this round and refer to Round 1 diagram.
Join 4 cream and 4 blue rectangles, starting with cream. Sew this unit to the right-hand side of the central rectangle.
Join 5 cream and 4 blue, starting with cream. Sew to the top of the central unit.
Join 7 cream and 7 blue, starting with blue. Sew to the left side of the central unit.
Join 5 cream and 4 blue, starting with cream. Make another unit with 3 cream and 3 blue, starting with cream. Sew these 2 units together, rotating the shorter unit so the rectangles are horizontal (see diagram). Now sew this combined unit to the bottom of the quilt.

Piecing round 2 Using template C shapes, join 4 cream and 4 blue, starting with cream. Sew to the right-hand side of the quilt.
Join 5 cream and 4 blue, starting with cream. Sew to the top of the quilt.
Join 6 cream and 5 blue, starting with cream. Sew to the left side of the quilt.
Join 5 cream and 4 blue, starting with cream. Make another unit joining 2 cream and 1 blue. Sew these 2 units together, rotating the shorter unit so rectangles are horizontal (see Round 2 diagram). Now sew this combined unit to the bottom of the quilt.

QUILT ASSEMBLY DIAGRAM ROUND 1

QUILT ASSEMBLY DIAGRAM ROUND 2

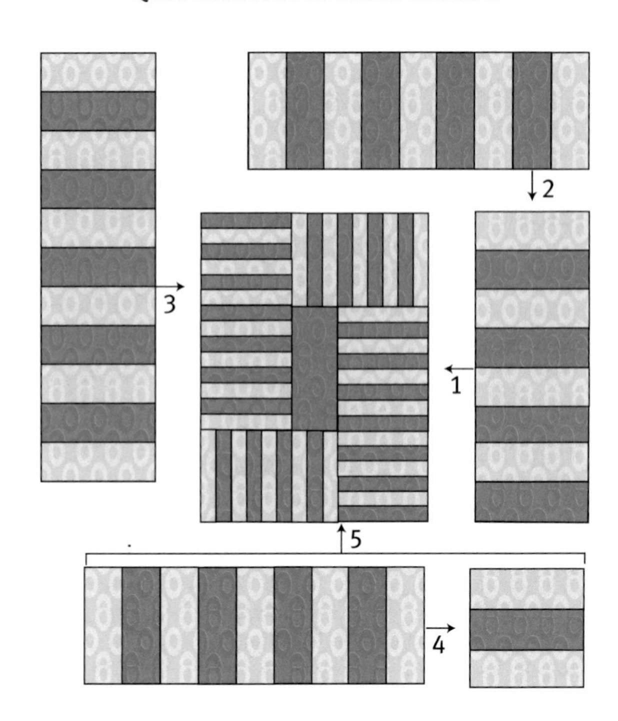

Piecing round 3 Using template D and E shapes, refer to Round 3 diagram. Note that the order of joining the units changes in this round and in round 4.
Using D shapes join 5 cream and 5 blue, starting with blue. Sew to the bottom of the quilt.
Using E shapes join 8 cream and 7 blue, starting with cream. Sew to the right-hand side of the quilt.
Using D shapes join 7 cream and 6 blue, starting with cream. Sew to the top of the quilt.
Using E shapes join 8 cream and 7 blue, starting with cream. Using D shapes make another unit joining 2 cream and 1 blue. Sew these 2 units together, rotating the shorter unit so rectangles are vertical (see diagram). Now sew this combined unit to the left side of the quilt.

Piecing round 4 Using template F and G shapes, refer to Round 4 diagram.
Using F shapes join 6 cream and 6 blue, starting with blue. Sew to the bottom of the quilt.
Using G shapes join 9 cream and 8 blue, starting with cream. Sew to the right-hand side of the quilt.
Using F shapes join 8 cream and 7 blue, starting with cream. Sew to the top of the quilt.
Using G shapes join 9 cream and 8 blue, starting with cream. Using F shapes make another unit joining 2 cream and 1 blue. Sew these 2 units together, rotating the shorter unit so the rectangles are vertical (see diagram). Now sew this combined unit to the left side of the quilt.

QUILT ASSEMBLY DIAGRAM ROUND 3

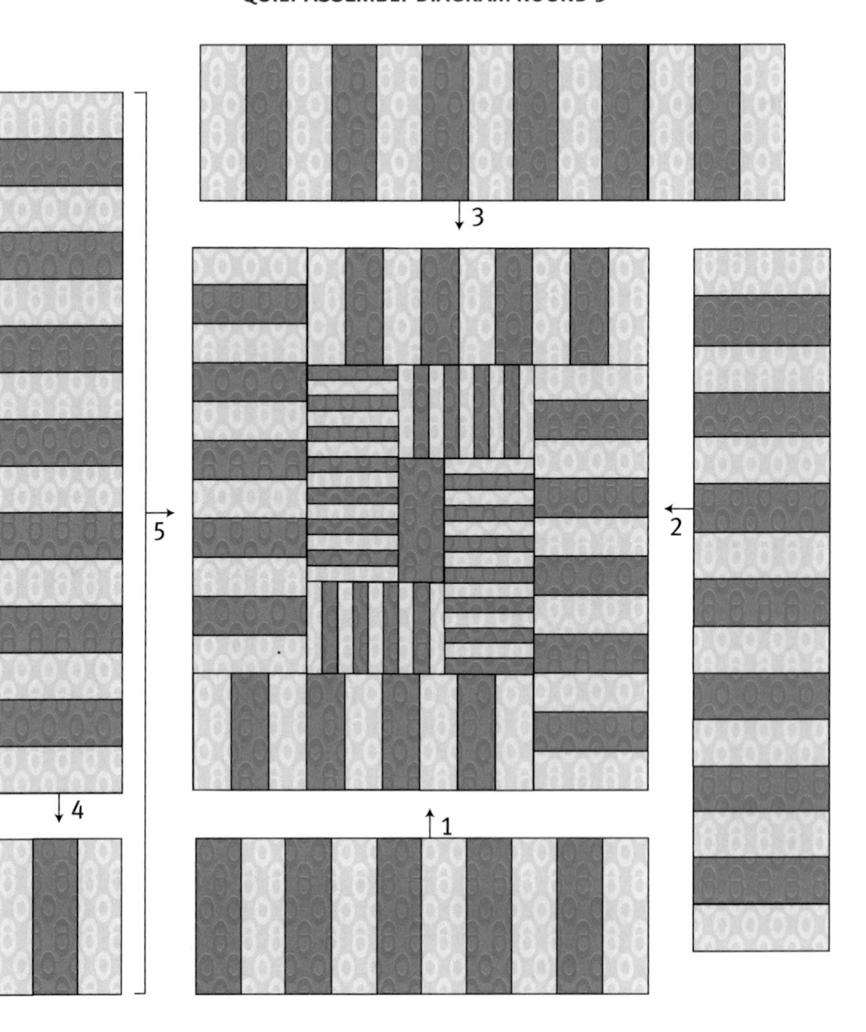

QUILT ASSEMBLY DIAGRAM ROUND 4

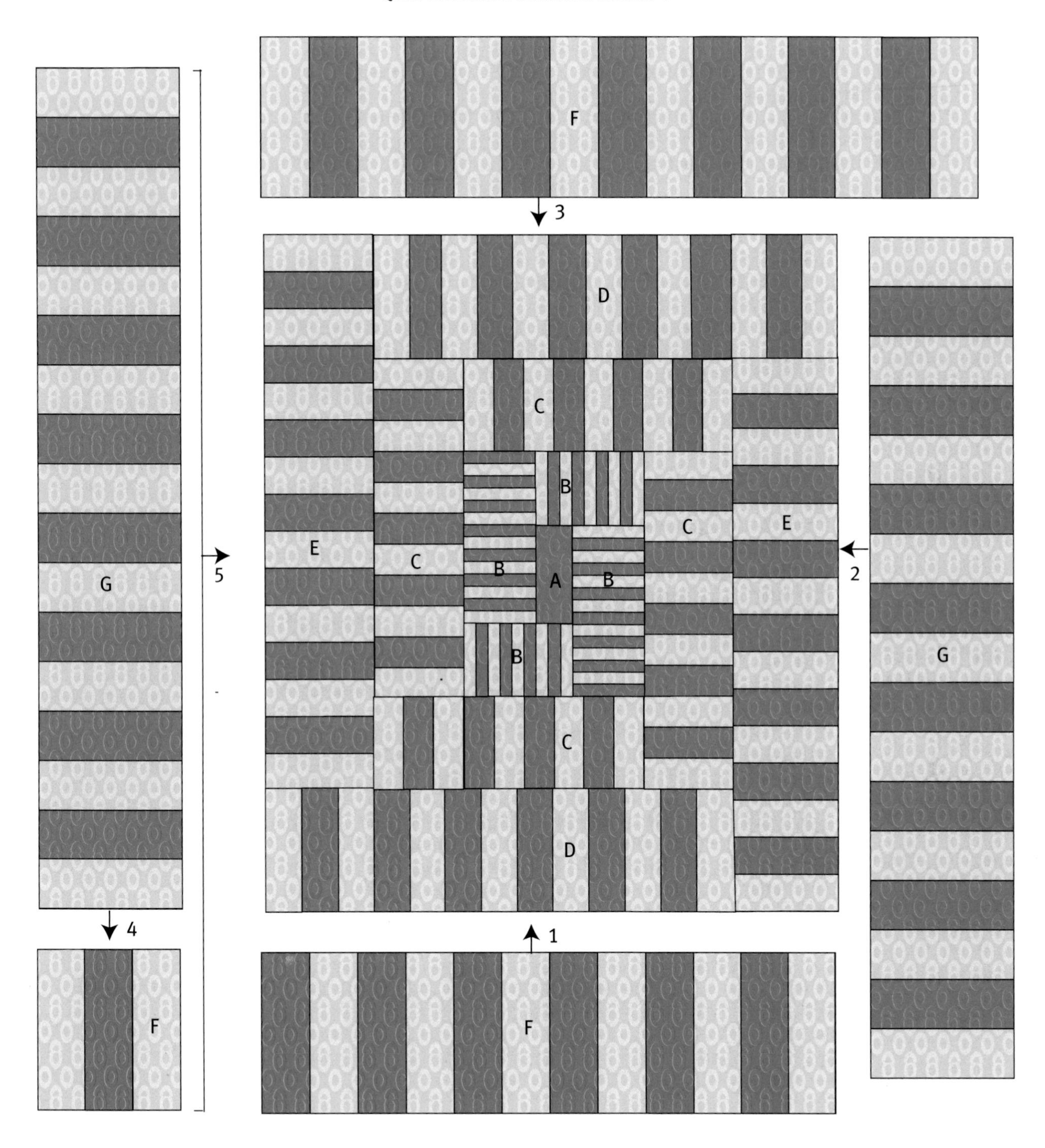

FINISHING THE QUILT

Press thoroughly. Seam the backing fabric with a ¼in (6mm) seam allowance to form a piece approximately 89in x 80in (226cm x 203cm). Layer the quilt top batting and backing (see page 148). Baste and quilt in the ditch as well as vertically down the centre of each strip. Trim the quilt edges and attach the binding (see page 149).

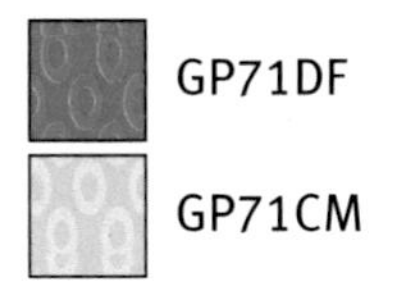

lacy log cabin *

Kaffe Fassett

The Lacy Log Cabin blocks are pieced from 'logs' cut to size around a fussy cut 3½in (8.9cm) square. The same fabric is used in each row to create a series of frames around the central square. There are four rows (or frames) to each block. They are sewn using the traditional log cabin method. The use of a design wall will help when organizing your layout of the blocks, as will a camera to take a photo of your layout before you start sewing the blocks.

SIZE OF QUILT

The finished quilt will measure approx. 72in x 72in (183cm x 183cm).

MATERIALS

Patchwork Fabrics

DREAM		
Pastel	GP148PT	3yd (2.75m)
SPOT		
Duck Egg	GP70DE	⅞yd (80cm)
Grey	GP70GY	⅝yd (60cm)
China Blue	GP70CI	⅜yd (35cm)
Taupe	GP70TA	⅜yd (35cm)
Peach	GP70PH	⅜yd (35cm)
Hydrangea	GP70HY	½yd (45cm)
Grape	GP70GP	¼yd (25cm)
Pond	GP70PO	¼yd (25cm)
Soft Blue	GP70SF	⅛yd (15cm)
FERN		
Yellow	GP147YE	⅞yd (80cm)
Turquoise	GP147TQ	½yd (45cm)
Grey	GP147GY	½yd (45cm)
MAD PLAID		
Mauve	BM37MV	⅜yd (35cm)
MILLEFIORE		
Orange	GP92OR	⅜yd (35cm)
GUINEA FLOWER		
Mauve	GP59MV	1yd (92cm)
Grey	GP59GY	¾yd (70cm)
PAPERWEIGHT		
Lime	GP20LM	¼yd (25cm)

Backing Fabric

DREAM		
Pastel	GP148PT	4½yd (4.2m)

Binding

FERN		
Grey	GP147GY	⅝yd (60cm)

Batting

80in x 80in (203cm x 203cm)

Quilting Thread

Machine quilting thread

CUTTING OUT

There are 16 different blocks that are repeated 4 times each, giving a total of 64 blocks. When sewn together, they should have a random layout in no particular order.

Cutting 3½in (8.9cm) squares, fussy cut 64 patches from GP148PT by centering a flower in each patch.

For the logs cut 1¼in (3.2cm) strips across the width of the remaining patchwork fabrics as follows: 25 strips GP59MV, 23 strips GP147YE, GP70DE, 19 strips GP59GY, 18 strips GP70GY, 14 strips GP70HY, 11 strips GP147GY, GP147TQ, 10 strips GP92OR, GP70CI, GP70TA, 8 strips GP70PH, BM37MV, 7 strips GP20LM, 5 strips GP70GP, 4 strips GP70PO, 2 strips GP70SF. Total 208 strips.

Note Some of the yellow fern fabric strips are reversed, i.e. the back of the fabric is on the right side of the block. See photograph on page 62 and fabric key on page 65 for correct placement.

Binding

Cut 8 strips 2½in (6.4cm) wide across the width of the fabric in GP147GY

Backing

From backing fabric GP148PT cut two pieces 82in (208cm) long.

BLOCK ASSEMBLY DIAGRAM 1

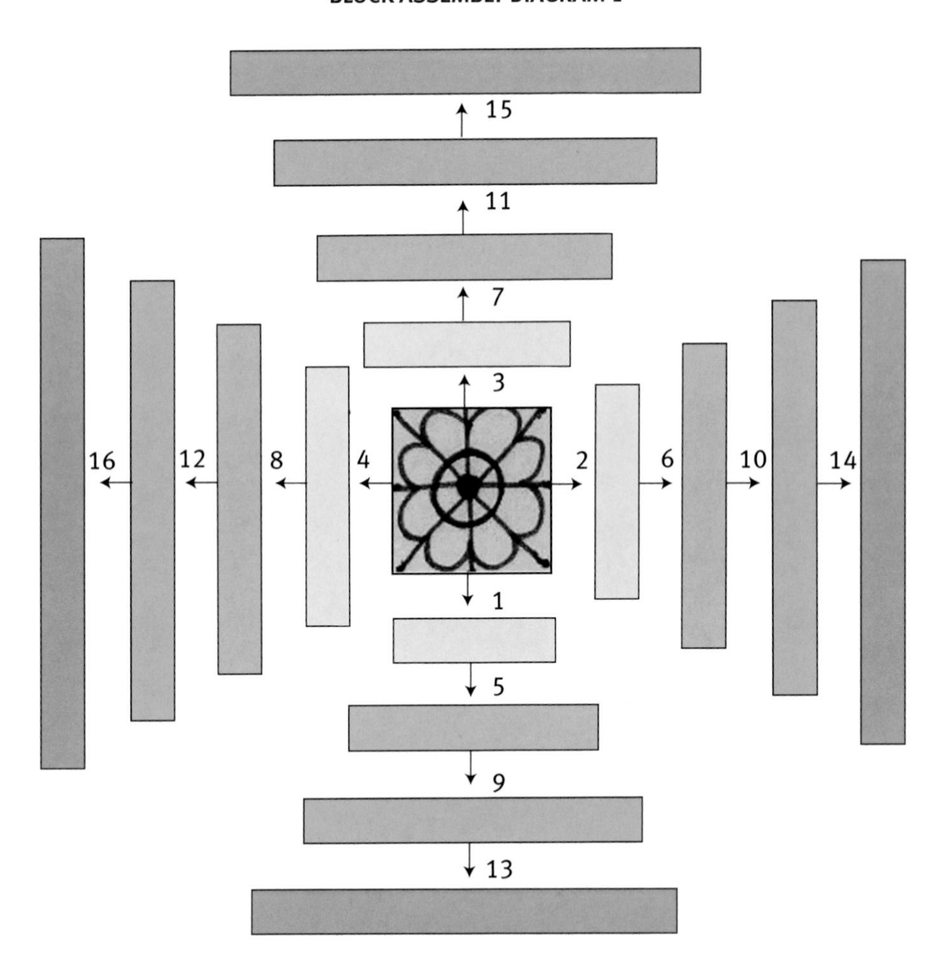

MAKING THE BLOCKS

Cut 4 of each block at the same time and label strips in order from 1–16, as shown in block assembly diagram 1. You should have 16 sets of strips numbered 1–16.

Refer to block assembly diagram 2 for fabrics to cut for each block type. For each of the 16 block types, cut:

Row 1
1: 4 strips at 3½in (8.9cm)
2 and 3: 8 strips at 4¼in (10.8cm)
4: 4 strips at 5in (12.7cm)

Row 2
5: 4 strips at 5in (12.7cm)
6 and 7: 8 strips 5¾in (14.6cm)
8: 4 strips at 6½in (16.5cm)

Row 3
9: 4 strips at 6½in (16.5cm)
10 and 11: 8 strips at 7¼in (18.4cm)
12: 4 strips at 8in (20.3cm)

Row 4
13: 4 strips at 8in (20.3cm)
14 and 15: 8 strips at 8¾in (22.2cm)
16: 4 strips at 9½in (24.1cm)

Using a ¼in (6mm) seam allowance throughout, sew strip 1 to the bottom of the central square, then continue sewing strips in the numerical order shown in block assembly diagram 1 (i.e. anticlockwise). The block should measure 9½in (24.1cm) square when all rows are completed. Keep each set of 4 blocks together.

MAKING THE QUILT

Decide your layout with 8 blocks per row. Sew each row together, then join the rows to make the quilt top.

FINISHING THE QUILT

Press the quilt top. Remove the selvedges from the backing fabric pieces and seam together to make a piece approx. 80in x 80in (203cm x 203cm). Layer the quilt top, batting and backing and baste together (see page 148).
Using machine quilting thread, quilt as desired. Trim the quilt edges and attach the binding (see page 149).

BLOCK ASSEMBLY DIAGRAM 2

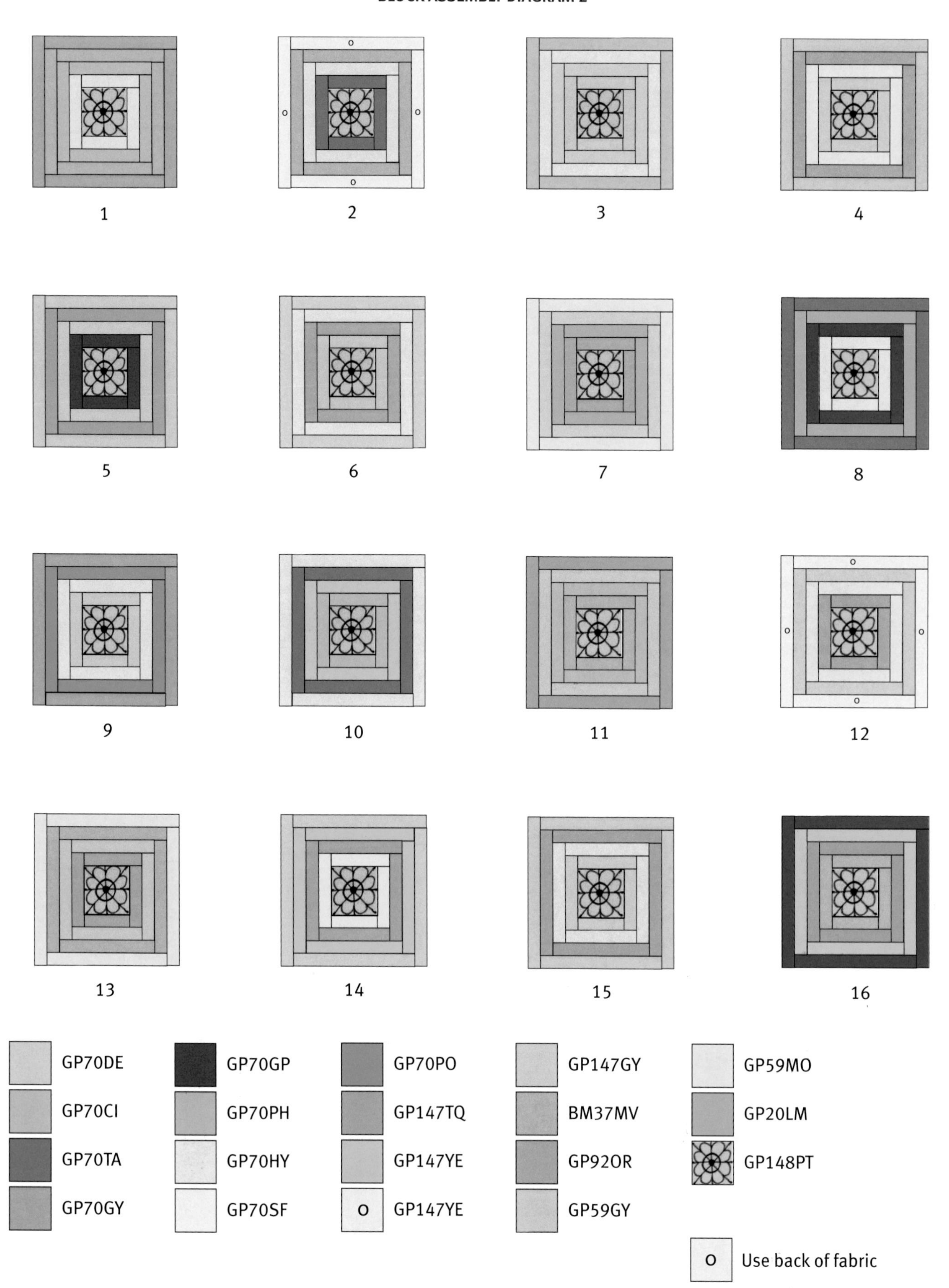

QUILT ASSEMBLY DIAGRAM

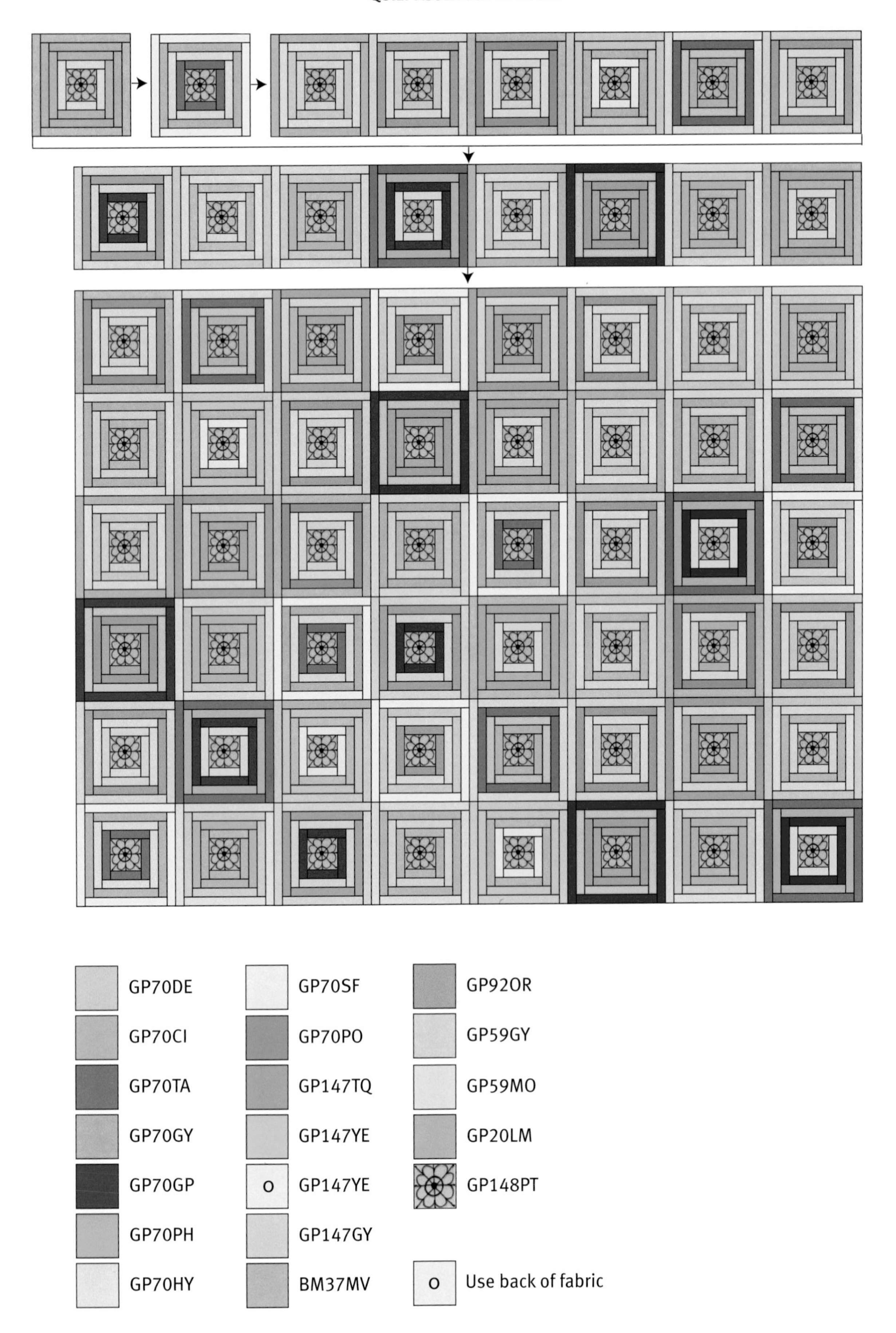

scaffold *

Kaffe Fassett

You can follow the assembly diagram on page 135 or you can treat this quilt as a scrappy quilt if you prefer. You should have plenty of spare triangles, which would allow you to vary the placement of the fabric if you want to go down the scrappy route.

SIZE OF QUILT

The finished quilt will measure approx. 63in x 70in (160cm x 178cm)

MATERIALS

Patchwork Fabrics

ABORIGINAL DOTS		
Cantaloupe	GP71CA	$\frac{3}{4}$yd (70cm)
Lime	GP71LM	$\frac{1}{4}$yd (25cm)
Lilac	GP71LI	$\frac{1}{4}$yd (25cm)
SPOT		
Taupe	GP70TA	$\frac{1}{4}$yd (25cm)
GUINEA FLOWER		
Apricot	GP59AP	$\frac{3}{4}$yd (70cm)
Gold	GP59GD	$\frac{1}{4}$yd (25cm)
FERNS		
Yellow	GP147YE	$\frac{1}{2}$yd (45cm)
ROMAN GLASS		
Gold	GP01GD	$\frac{1}{4}$yd (25cm)
SHOT COTTON		
Scarlet	SC44	$\frac{1}{2}$yd (45cm)
Watermelon	SC33	$\frac{7}{8}$yd (80cm)
Ginger	SC01	$\frac{1}{2}$yd (45cm)
Pink	SC83	$\frac{1}{2}$yd (45cm)
Apricot	SC79	$\frac{1}{2}$yd (45cm)
Pudding	SC68	$\frac{1}{4}$yd (25cm)
Aqua	SC77	$\frac{1}{2}$yd (45cm)
Sky	SC62	$\frac{1}{2}$yd (45cm)
Lemon	SC34	$\frac{1}{2}$yd (45cm)
Squash	SC100	$\frac{1}{2}$yd (45cm)
Sprout	SC94	$\frac{1}{4}$yd (25cm)

Backing Fabric

OMBRE		
Pink	GP117PK	4yd (3.75m)

Binding

ABORIGINAL DOT		
Lime	GP71	$\frac{5}{8}$yd (60cm)

Batting

71in x 78in (180cm x 198cm)

Quilting Thread

Machine quilting thread

Templates

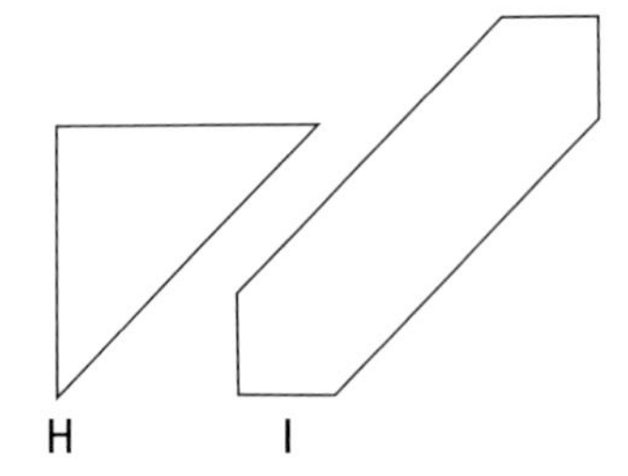

Patch Shapes

The quilt has 90 blocks made by sewing 2 triangle patch shapes (Template H) to a polygon patch shape (Template I).

CUTTING OUT

Template H Cut 6in (15.2cm) strips across the width of the fabric. Each strip will give you 12 patches per full width, if the shape is rotated alternately along the strip.
Cut 1 strip in GP71LM, GP71LI, GP70TA, GP59AP, GP59GD, GP01GD, SC44, SC33, SC68, SC77, SC62, SC34, SC100, and SC94. Cut 2 strips in GP71CA, GP147YE, SC83, and SC79. (Total number of triangle patches required is 180.)
Template I Cut $7\frac{1}{2}$in (19cm) strips across the width of the fabric. Each strip will give you 8 patches per full width. Have the fabric grain and the template grain line arrow running horizontally.
Cut 1 strip in GP71CA, SC01, SC77, SC62, SC34, and SC100. Cut 2 strips in SC44 and GP59AP. Cut 3 strips in SC33. (Total number of patches required is 90.)

Binding

Cut 7 strips $2\frac{1}{2}$in (6.4cm) wide across the width of the fabric in GP71LM.

Backing

Cut 2 pieces 72in x 40in (183cm x 101.5cm) in GP117PK.

MAKING THE QUILT

Use a $\frac{1}{4}$in (6mm) seam allowance throughout.
Using the quilt assembly diagram as a guide for fabric placement, make 90 blocks as shown in the block assembly diagram. Piece the blocks into 10 rows of 9 units, and then join the rows to form the quilt.

FINISHING THE QUILT

Press the quilt top. Remove the selvedges from the backing pieces and sew together using a $\frac{1}{4}$in (6mm) seam allowance to form a piece approx. 72in x 80in (183cm x 203cm). Layer the quilt top, batting and backing and baste together (see page 148).
Using machine quilting thread, quilt in the ditch of the diagonal seams and between blocks, as well as diagonally along the centre of each block. Trim the quilt edges and attach the binding (see page 149).

BLOCK ASSEMBLY DIAGRAM

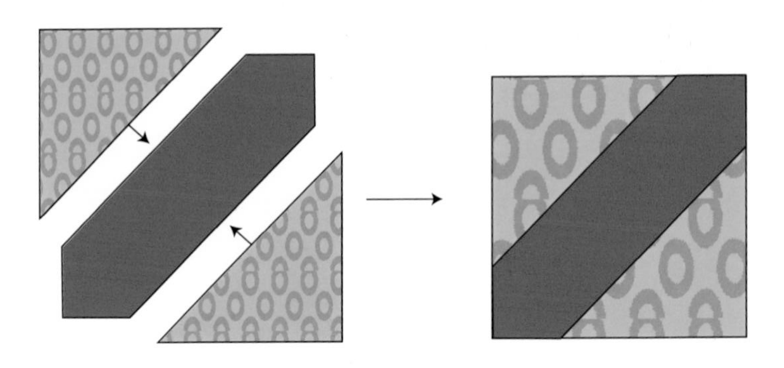

QUILT ASSEMBLY DIAGRAM

tussie mussie *

Kaffe Fassett

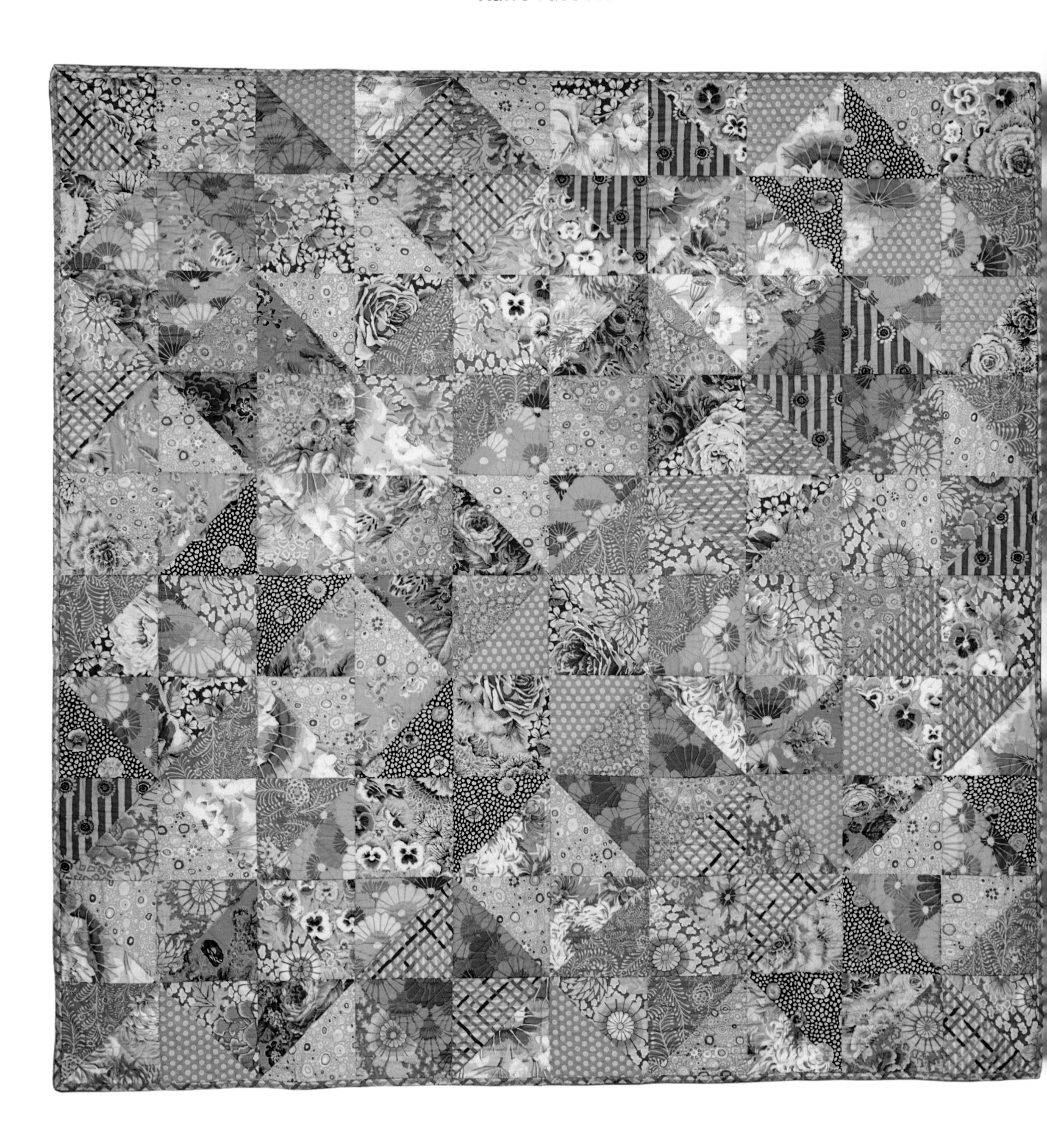

This is an ideal quilt for a beginner as it is composed of just one large triangle shape, created from a half-square. Although the exact number of patches in each fabric is given, you could easily make more in one fabric and fewer in another.

SIZE OF QUILT
The finished quilt will measure approx. 80in x 80in (203cm x 203cm)

MATERIALS
Patchwork Fabrics

THOUSAND FLOWERS		
Pink	GP144PK	½yd (45cm)
Vibrant	GP144VB	¼yd (25cm)
ROSE BLOOM		
Grey	PJ77GY	½yd (45cm)
LAKE BLOSSOMS		
Green	GP93GN	¼yd (25cm)
Pink	GP93PK	¼yd (25cm)
DREAM		
Moss	GP148MS	¾yd (70cm)
Dusty	GP148DY	½yd (45cm)
BRASSICA		
Moss	PJ51MS	¼yd (25cm)
SHAGGY		
Grey	PJ72GY	¼yd (25cm)
MAD PLAID		
Mauve	BM37MV	½yd (45cm)
Candy	BM37CD	¼yd (25cm)
FERNS		
Turquoise	GP147TQ	½yd (45cm)
PANSIES		
Grey	PJ76GY	¼yd (25cm)
ROMAN GLASS		
Pink	GP01PK	¾yd (70cm)
MILLEFIORE		
Green	GP92GN	½yd (45cm)
REGENCY DAISY		
Green	GP146GN	¼yd (25cm)
GUINEA FLOWER		
Green	GP59GN	½yd (45cm)
SPOT		
Lavender	GP70LV	½yd (45cm)
FLORAL DELIGHT		
Lavender	PJ75LV	½yd (45cm)
Green	PJ75GN	½yd (45cm)

Backing Fabric

ROSE BLOOM		
Grey	PJ77GY	6yd (5.5m)

Binding

MAD PLAID		
Mauve	BM37MV	¾yd (70cm)

Batting
88in x 88in (223.5cm x 223.5cm)

Quilting Thread
Machine quilting thread

Template

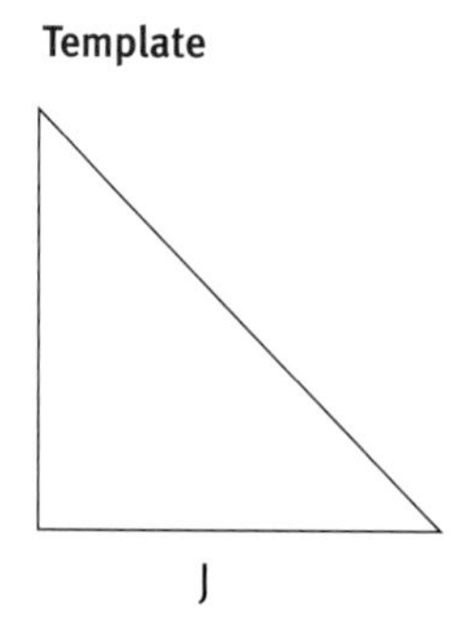

BLOCK ASSEMBLY DIAGRAMS

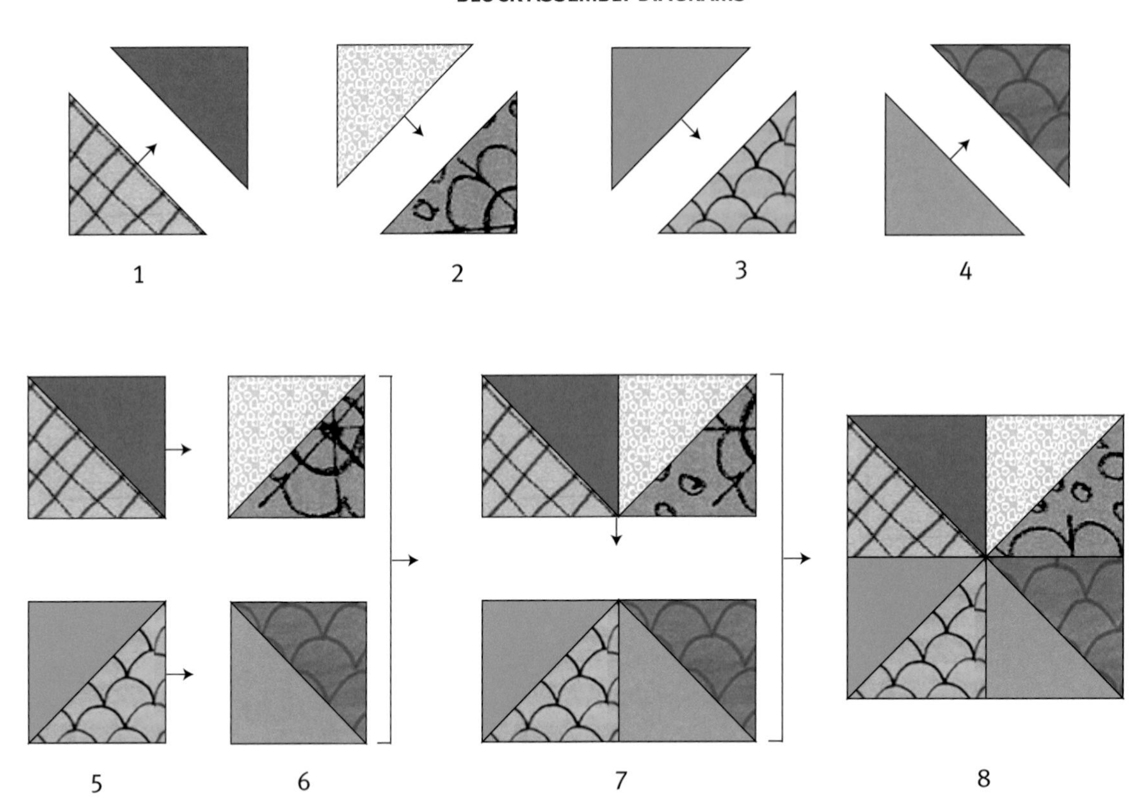

Tip

The finished size of each square block (made of 2 right-angle triangles pieced on the diagonal) is 8in (20.3cm). Instead of cutting the fabric using template J, you can cut 8⅞in (22.5cm) strips across the width of the fabric. Cut 8⅞in (22.5cm) squares from those strips and then cut each square in half on the diagonal. You will obtain the same size right-angle triangle as per template J. The formula to cut half square triangles from squares is to add ⅞in (2.2cm) for seam allowances to the finished size of the square block.

CUTTING OUT

This quilt is pieced using a single right-angle triangle patch shape (template J). Follow the block assembly diagrams to piece each block. The blocks are then pieced into straight set rows.

Template J Cut 8⅞in (22.5cm) strips across the width of the fabric. Each strip will give you 8 patches per full width, if the shape is rotated alternately along the strip. Cut 1 in GP144VB, GP93GN, GP93PK, PJ51MS, PJ72GY, BM37CD, PJ76GY, GP146GN. Cut 2 in GP144PK, PJ77GY , GP148DY, BM37MV, GP147TQ, GP92GN, GP59GN, GP70LV, PJ075LV, PJ75GN. Cut 3 in GP01PK, GP148MS. Total 272 triangles; only 200 are required in the quilt.

Binding

Cut 9 strips 2½in (6.4cm) wide across the width of the fabric in BM37MV.

Backing

For the backing pieces, cut two pieces in PJ77GY 90in (228.6cm) long. Cut one piece 31in (78.7cm) long. Cut the 31in (78.7cm) long piece into 3 strips 10½in x 31in (26.7cm x 78.7cm). Remove all selvedges.

MAKING THE QUILT

Use a ¼in (6mm) seam allowance throughout. Take 8 triangles to make each block, following the block assembly diagrams. Make a total of 25 blocks. Arrange the blocks following the quilt assembly diagram. Join the blocks into 5 rows of 5 blocks each and then join the rows to complete the quilt.

FINISHING THE QUILT

Press the quilt top. Sew the 10½in (26.7cm) pieces end to end and trim to 90in (228.6cm). Sew a 90in (228.6cm) panel to each side of the pieced strip. The backing will measure approx 90in (228.6cm) squre. Layer the quilt top, batting and backing and baste together (see page 148).

Quilt in the ditch between blocks and diagonally from corner to corner in both directions. Trim the quilt edges and attach the binding (see page 149).

QUILT ASSEMBLY DIAGRAM

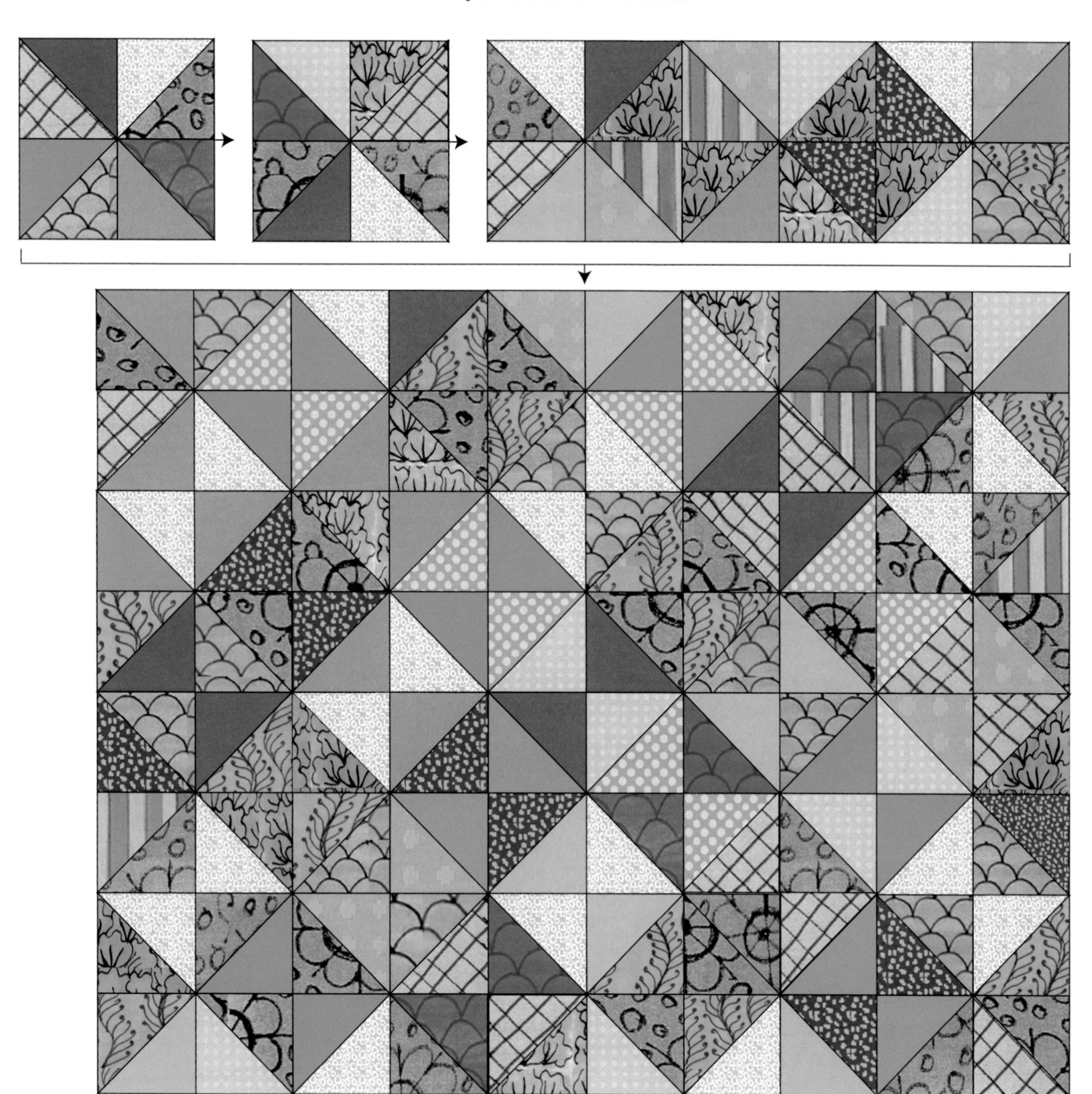

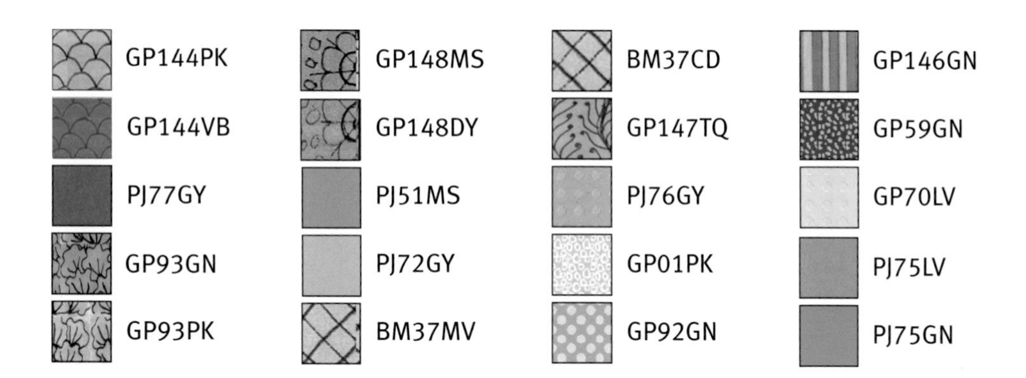

contrast weave *

Kaffe Fassett

This quilt is has a three-bar 'rail fence' block for the central panel of the quilt, and pieced rectangles for the borders with a courthouse steps variation of the traditional log cabin block at each corner. The impact of the quilt springs from the use of contrasting light and dark fabrics in each block.

SIZE OF QUILT
The finished quilt will measure approx. 67½in x 82½in (171.5cm x 209.5cm)

MATERIALS

Patchwork Fabrics

ABORIGINAL DOT		
Charcoal	GP71CC	¼yd (25cm)
Ochre	GP71OC	¼yd (25cm)
Gold	GP71GD	1yd (90cm)
SPOT		
Peacock	GP70PC	¼yd (25cm)
Black	GP70BK	¼yd (25cm)
Ochre	GP70OC	½yd (45cm)
ROLLER COASTER		
Charcoal	BM49CC	¼yd (25cm)
PANSIES		
Purple	PJ76PU	1yd (90cm)
OMBRE		
Red	GP117RD	¼yd (25cm)
Pink	GP117PK	¼yd (25cm)
CAMOUFLAGE STRIPE		
Dark	BM52DK	¼yd (25cm)
CREASED		
Orange	BM50OR	¼yd (25cm)
JUMBLE		
Pink	BM53PK	¼yd (25cm)
Orange	BM53OR	¼yd (25cm)
SERPENTINE		
Dark	GP145DK	¼yd (25cm)
GUINEA FLOWER		
Apricot	GP59AP	¼yd (25cm)
FERNS		
Black	GP147BK	½yd (45cm)
ROMAN GLASS		
Gold	GP01GD	½yd (45cm)

Backing Fabric

ROSE BLOOM		
Cobalt	PJ77CB	5¼yd (4.8m)

Binding

JUMBLE		
Orange	BM53OR	⅝yd (60cm)

Batting
75½in x 90½in (192cm x 230cm)

Quilting Thread
Machine quilting thread

Templates

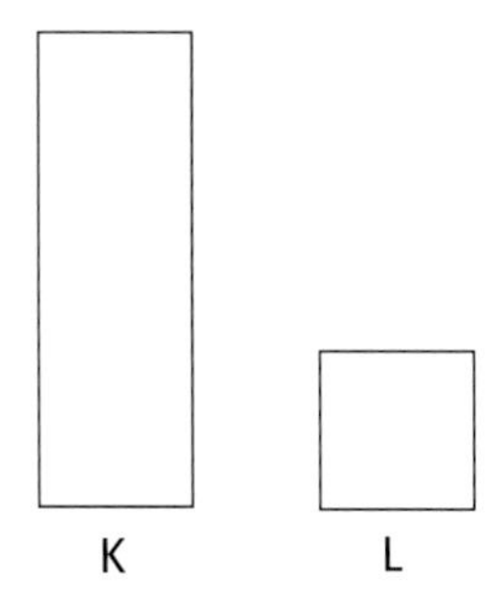

Patch Shapes
This quilt is composed of a central panel and a pieced border with corner blocks. The central panel consists of 63 square blocks. Each block is made up of 3 rectangular patch shapes (Template K). The three-bar unit that forms the rail fence block is a combination of either dark-light-dark or light-dark-light fabric rectangles.

The central panel is surrounded by a pieced border made up of 4 pieced strips and 4 corner squares. The border strips consist of rectangular patch shapes (Template K) pieced together. The corner squares follow the courthouse steps variation of the log cabin block, where the central log is made up of 3 squares (Template L) with 2 logs (Template K added to opposite sides.

Tip
Straight and accurately cut strips are essential when stitching the rail fence block. Cut all fabric strips across the fabric width, unless instructed otherwise.

BLOCK ASSEMBLY DIAGRAM 1

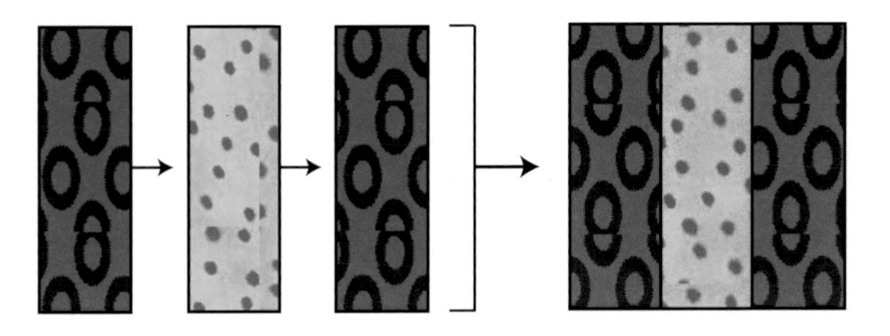

BLOCK ASSEMBLY DIAGRAM 2

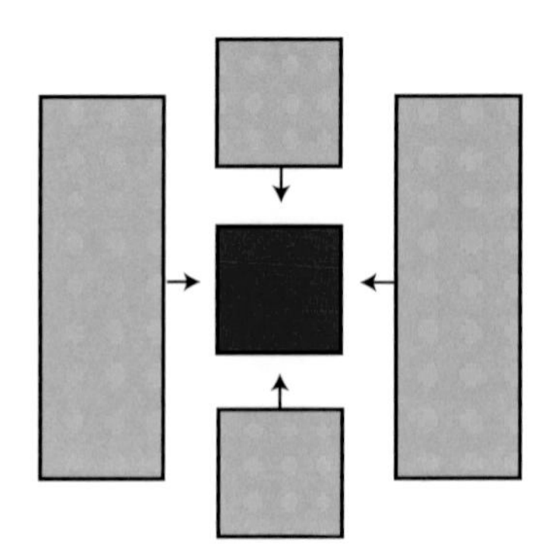

CUTTING OUT

Block Rectangles

All rectangular patch shapes that make up the rail fence blocks measure 8in x 3in (20.3cm x 7.6cm).

Template K Cut 3in (7.6cm) strips across the width of the fabric. Each strip will give you 5 rectangles per full width.

Cut 1 strip in GP71GD, PJ76PU.

Cut 2 strips in GP71OC, GP70OC, BM49CC, BM52DK, BM50OR, BM53OR and GP59AP.

Cut 3 strips in GP71CC, GP70PC, GP70BK, GP117RD, GP117PK, BM53PK and GP145DK.

Cut 4 strips in GP147BK and GP01GD. (The total number of rectangles needed is 189, so you will have some to spare.)

Pieced Border

All rectangular patch shapes that make up the pieced border measure 8in x 3in (20.3cm x 7.6cm).

Template K Cut 3in (7.6cm) strips across the width of the fabric.

Cut 10 strips in GP71GD (46 rectangles needed) and PJ76PU (50 rectangles needed).

4 Corner Squares

Template K Cut 3in (7.6cm) strips across the width of the fabric.

Cut 2 strips in GP70OC (8 rectangles needed).

Template L Cut 3in (7.6cm) strips across the width of the fabric. Each strip will give you 13 square patches per full width.

Cut 1 strip in GP70OC (8 squares needed) and PJ76PU (4 squares needed).

Binding

Cut 8 strips 2½in (6.4cm) wide across the width of the fabric in BM53OR.

Backing

Cut 2 pieces 93in (236.2cm) long in PJ77CB. Remove the selvedges.

MAKING THE QUILT

Use a ¼in (6mm) seam allowance throughout.

To make the central piece, follow block assembly diagram 1 to sew three rectangles together. Make a total of 63 blocks, using the quilt assembly diagram as a guide for fabric placement and for the layout.

Piece the blocks in rows of 7 units, and then join the rows to form the quilt.

To make the pieced border strips follow the quilt assembly diagram (opposite). For the top and bottom strips, stitch together 21 rectangles starting with PJ76PU (11 units) and alternating it with GP71GD (10 units).

For the left and right strips, stitch together 27 rectangles starting with PJ76PU (14 units) and alternating it with GP71GD (13 units).

To make the corner square blocks follow block assembly diagram 2.

Stitch a square piece to the top and bottom of the centre square, and then add a rectangle unit to each side.

Stitch a corner block to each end of the top pieced strip. Repeat for the bottom pieced strip.

You are now ready to attach the left and right border strips (consisting of 27 rectangles) to each side of the 63-block central piece. Then sew the top and bottom border strips to the main piece.

FINISHING THE QUILT

Press the quilt top. Sew the backing pieces together using a ¼in (6mm) seam allowance to form a piece approx. 80in x 93in (203cm x 236cm). Layer the quilt top, batting and backing and baste together (see page 148).

Using machine quilting thread, quilt in the ditch between each rectangle. Trim the quilt edges and attach the binding (see page 149).

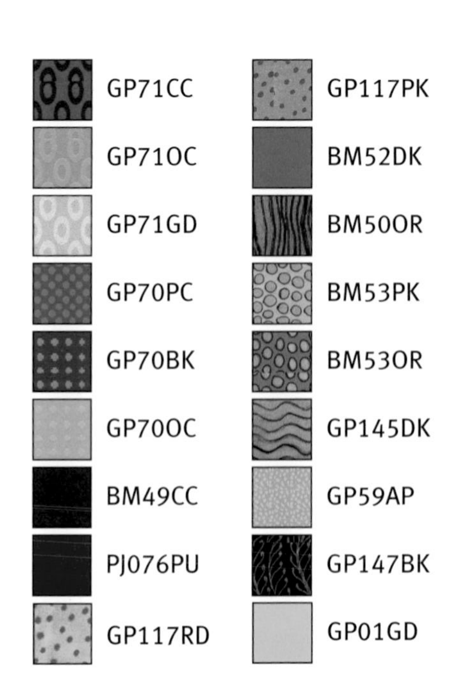

QUILT ASSEMBLY DIAGRAM

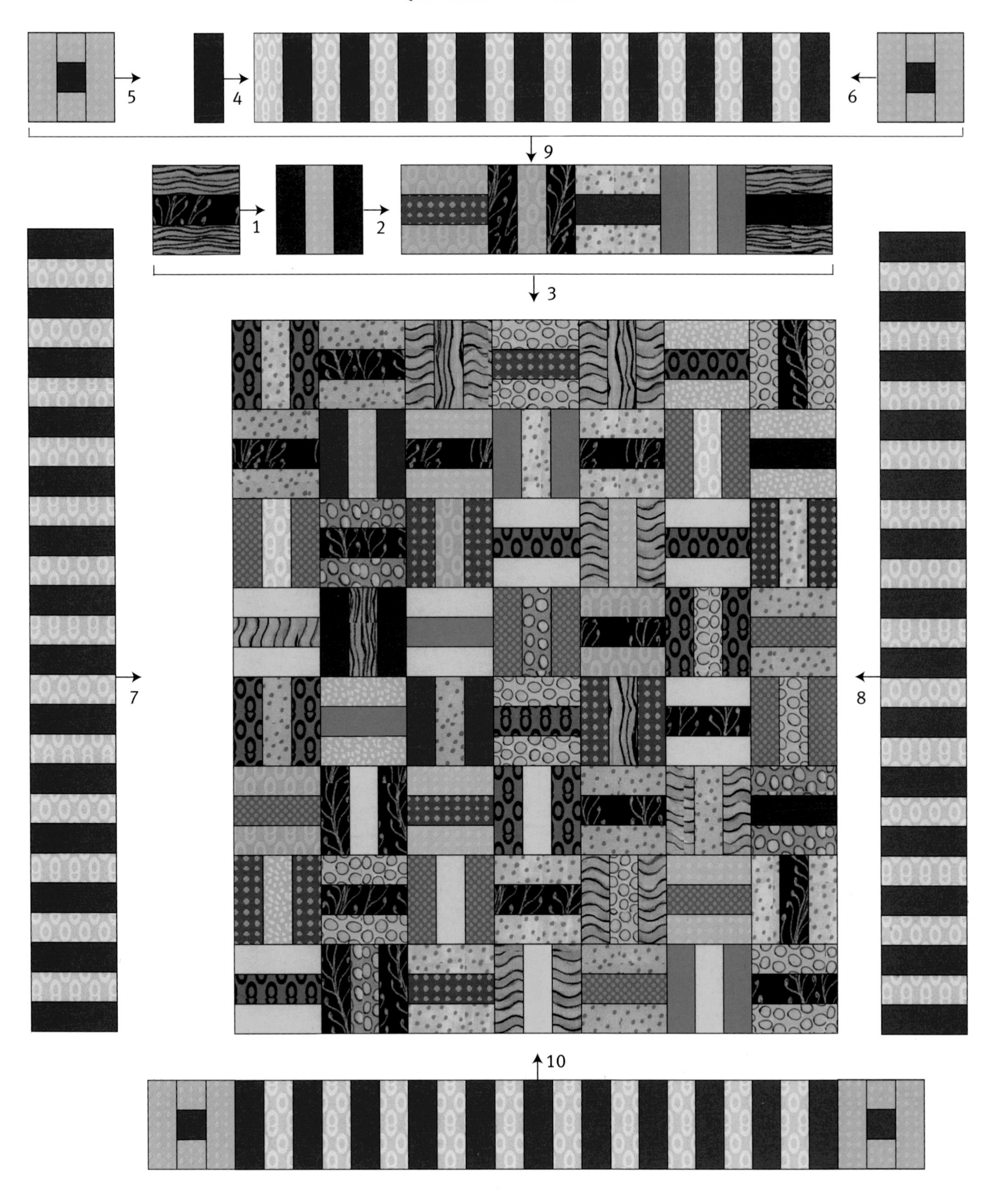

red blocks * *

Kaffe Fassett

This classic tumbling blocks pattern is made the easy way by splitting the top of each tumbling block into 2 triangles, then piecing the quilt in vertical rows. It is made using 1 diamond patch (Template M), 1 equilateral triangle (Template N) and 1 right angle triangle to fill the column ends (Template O and Reverse O). The quilt is surrounded with a border, which is fussy cut to showcase the design of the fabric.

SIZE OF QUILT
The finished quilt will measure approx.
64in x 82in (162.5cm x 208cm)

MATERIALS

Patchwork Fabrics

CAMOUFLAGE STRIPE		
Summer	BM52SU	3/8yd (35cm)
BRASSICA		
Red	PJ51RD	3/8yd (35cm)
DREAM		
Red	GP148RD	3/8yd (35cm)
SPIRAL SHELLS		
Red	PJ73RD	3/8yd (35cm)
BRANDON'S BROCADE		
Red	BM48RD	3/8yd (35cm)
JUMBLE		
Pink	BM53PK	3/8yd (35cm)
Orange	BM53OR	3/8yd (35cm)
CREASED		
Orange	BM50OR	1/4yd (25cm)
SHAGGY		
Red	PJ72RD	3/8yd (35cm)
FLORAL DELIGHT		
Orange	PJ75OR	3/8yd (35cm)
ROLLER COASTER		
Orange	BM49OR	1/4yd (25cm)
FERNS		
Red	GP147RD	1/4yd (25cm)
SHOAL		
Tomato	BM51TM	3/8yd (35cm)
ANNE MARIE		
Purple	PJ74PU	3/4yd (70cm)
Black	PJ74BK	3/4yd (70cm)
ROSE BLOOM		
Red	PJ77RD	1/4yd (25cm)

Border Fabric

THOUSAND FLOWERS		
Dark	GP144DK	3yd (2.75m)

Backing Fabric

ROSE BLOOM		
Red	PJ77RD	5yd (4.6m)

Binding

JUMBLE		
Orange	BM053OR	5/8yd (60cm)

Batting
74in x 90in (188cm x 229cm)

Quilting thread
Hand or machine quilting thread

Templates

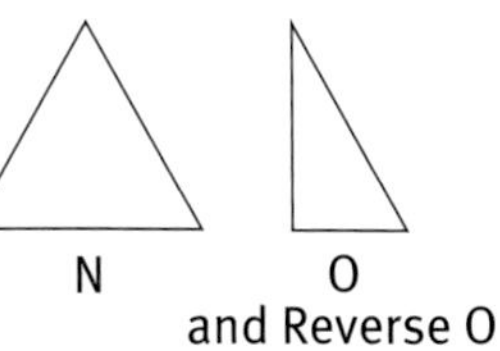

LEFT HAND ROW ASSEMBLY DIAGRAM

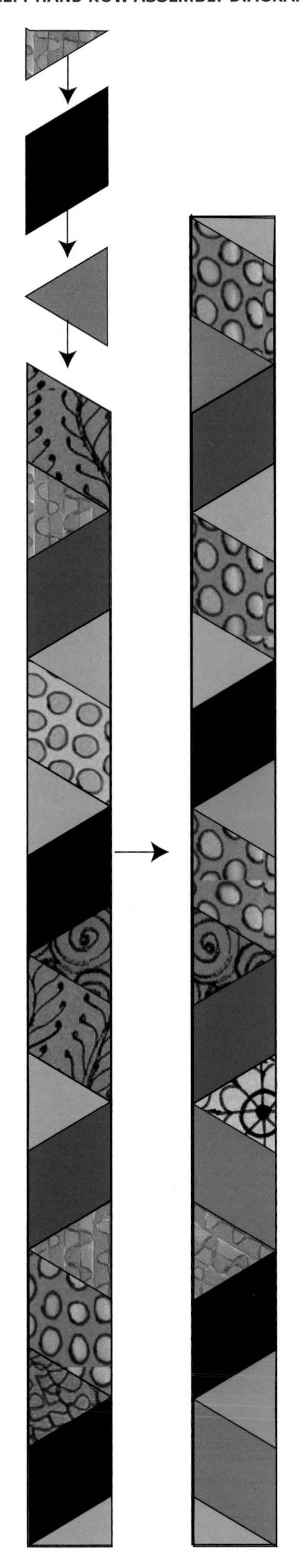

CUTTING OUT

Border

This fabric has a large pattern repeat, so allow some time to plan where you want the pattern to appear in the border.

In fabric GP144DK cut two matching strips down the length parallel with the selvedge 73in x 5½in (185.5cm x 14cm).

Cut two sets of two strips 5½in (14cm) across the width of the fabric for the top and bottom borders. Fussy cut to pattern match, and join the fabric to make two borders top and bottom, each measuring 67½in x 5½in (171.5cm x 14cm). These are slightly oversized but will be trimmed down later.

Template M Cut 5in (12.7cm) strips across the width of the fabrics. Each strip will give you 6 diamonds. Cut 27 diamonds in PJ74PU, PJ74BK, 12 in BM48RD, BM53OR, 6 in BM53PK, BM50OR, BM49OR, GP147RD, PJ77RD. Total 108 diamonds.

Template N Cut 5¼in (13.3cm) strips across the width of the fabric. Each strip will give you 12 triangles across the full width if you rotate the template 180 degrees alternately. Cut 21 triangles in PJ75OR, 17 in BM51TM, 8 in PJ73RD, 15 in BM52SU, 13 in PJ51RD, 12 in GP148RD, 10 in PJ72RD. Total 96 triangles.

Template O and reverse O Using leftover fabric from the N triangles, cut 8 in BM51TM (4 O and 4 O reversed), 7 in PJ51RD (3 O and 4 O reversed), 4 in PJ75OR, 4 in PJ72RD (2 O and 2 O reversed), 1 in BM52SU (1 O).

Total 24 triangles (12 plus 12 reversed).

Binding

Cut 8 strips 2½in (6.4cm) wide across the width of the fabric in BM053OR.

Backing

From PJ77RD cut 2 pieces 90in x 40in (229cm x 101.5cm).

MAKING THE QUILT

Use a ¼in (6mm) seam allowance throughout. Using the quilt assembly diagram as a guide for fabric placement, lay out the whole quilt. We suggest using a design wall for this. Make sure the N triangles come together in the same fabric, as they form the diamonds at the top of the tumbling blocks. Separate the patches into 12 vertical rows and begin piecing each in order (see Row Assembly Diagram).

Note Rows will only have straight edges once sewn if seams are offset.

Join the rows to complete the quilt centre. Add the side borders, trimming to fit exactly, then add the top and bottom borders, again trimming to fit to complete the quilt.

FINISHING THE QUILT

Press the quilt top. Seam the backing pieces using a ¼in (6mm) seam allowance to form a piece approx. 80in x 90in (203cm x 228.5cm). Layer the quilt top, batting and backing and baste together (see page 148).

Using machine quilting thread, quilt as desired. Trim the quilt edges and attach the binding (see page 149).

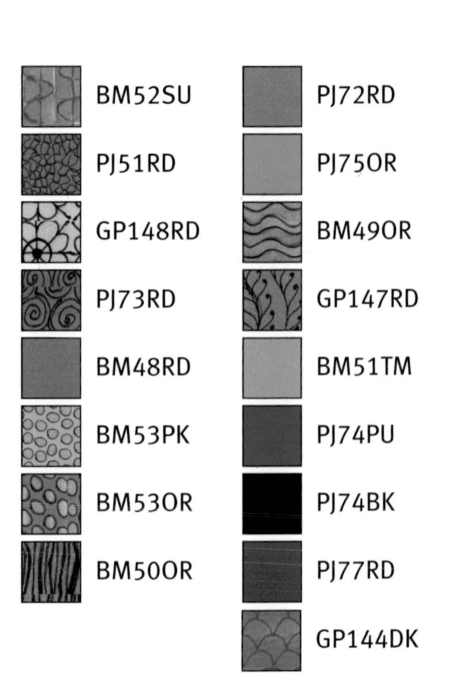

QUILT ASSEMBLY DIAGRAM

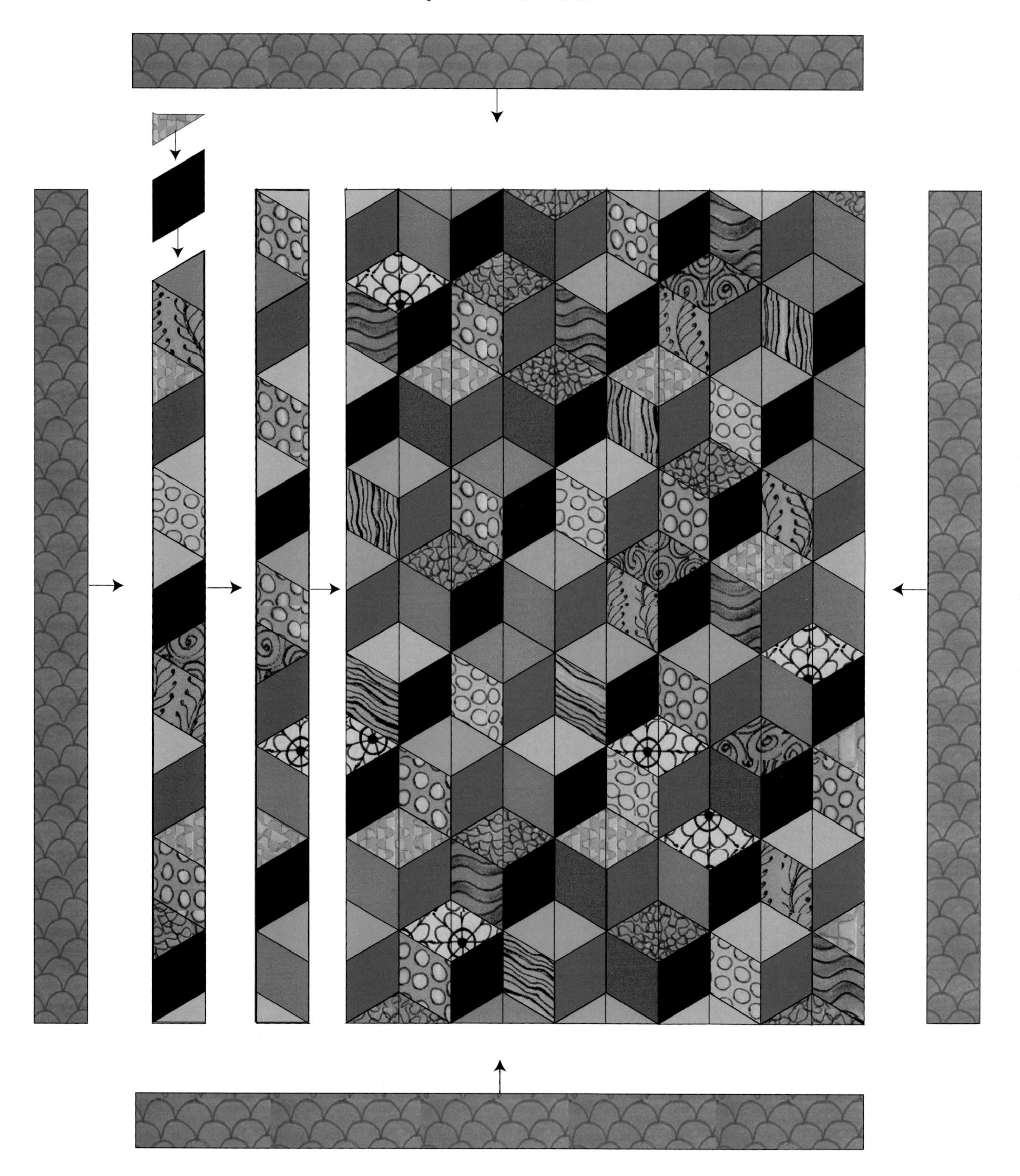

chiaroscuro ***

Kaffe Fassett

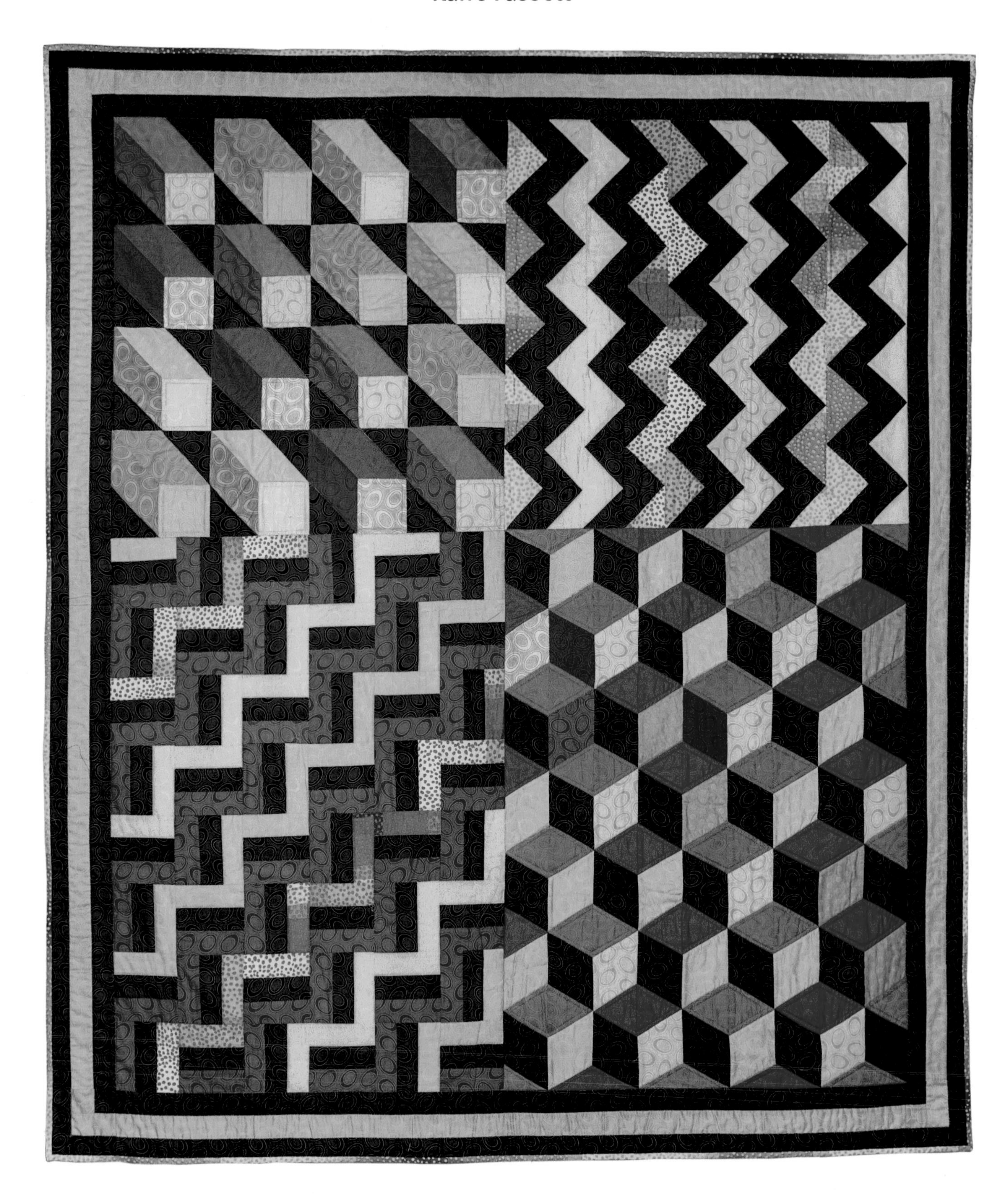

This challenging quilt is made up of four panels of different designs: Roman blocks, rail fence, zig zag and tumbling blocks. The clever choice of the fabrics in the panels brings the whole quilt together to produce a geometric design bordered with straight lines.

Important Check the grain lines marked on the templates and align with the grain of the fabric. The use of spray starch will help stabilize the patches before sewing. The use of a design wall will help with placement of the designs. Unless otherwise stated cut along the width of the fabric and use a ¼in (6mm) seam allowance.

SIZE OF QUILT
The finished quilt will measure approx. 63in x 72in (161cm x 184cm)

MATERIALS
Patchwork and Border fabrics
ABORIGINAL DOT

Lilac	GP71LI	¼yd (25cm)
Lime	GP71LM	¼yd (25cm)
Pumpkin	GP71PN	⅝yd (60cm)
Plum	GP71PL	¼yd (25cm)
Ochre	GP71OC	1⅛yd (1m)
Chocolate	GP71CL	2½yd (2.3m)
Gold	GP71GD	⅝yd (60cm)
Cantaloupe	GP71CA	⅝yd (60cm)
Olive	GP71OV	¼yd (25cm)
Red	GP71RD	½yd (45cm)
Orange	GP71OR	½yd (45cm)
Forest	GP71FO	¼yd (25cm)
Leaf	GP71LF	¼yd (25cm)
SPOT		
Taupe	GP70TA	¼yd (25cm)
OMBRE		
Brown	GP117BR	½yd (45cm)
Pink	GP117PK	¼yd (25cm)

Backing Fabric
DREAM

Brown	GP148BR	4yd (3.7m)

Batting
71in x 80in (180cm x 203cm)

Binding
OMBRE

Pink	GP117PK	⅝yd (60cm)

Quilting Thread
Machine/hand quilting thread

CUTTING OUT
Border sides
In GP71CL cut 4 x 2in (5cm) strips down the length of the fabric, 63½in (161.3cm) long.
Cut 4 x 2in (5cm) strips down the length of the fabric, 54½in (138.4cm) long.
This will give you an approx. width of 24in (61.5cm) remaining so there should be plenty of fabric for cutting out the shapes used in the panels.
In GP71OC cut 8 x 2in (5cm) strips across the width of the fabric. Join strips in pairs to make the 4 strips for the centre of the border. Cut 2 at 63½in (161.3cm) long and 2 at 54½in (138.4cm) long.

Border corners
From GP71CL cut 4 rectangles 2in x 5in (5cm x 12.7cm), 4 rectangles 3in x 2in (7.6cm x 5cm), 4 2in (5cm) squares.
From GP71OC cut 4 rectangles 3in x 2in (7.6cm x 5cm) and 4 2in (5cm) squares.

Binding
Cut 7 strips 2½in (6.4cm) wide across the width of the fabric in GP117BL.

Backing
Cut two pieces 72in (183cm) long in GP148BR.

roman blocks panel

Fabrics

ABORIGINAL DOT

Lilac	GP71LI
Lime	GP71LM
Pumpkin	GP71PN
Plum	GP71PL
Ochre	GP71OC
Chocolate	GP71CL
Gold	GP71GD
Cantaloupe	GP71CA
Olive	GP71OV
Red	GP71RD
Orange	GP71OR
Forest	GP71FO
Leaf	GP71LF
SPOT	
Taupe	GP70TA

Templates

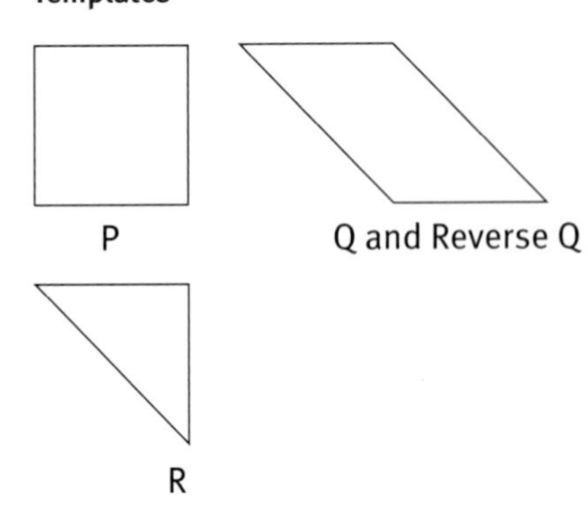

The patchwork 'cubes' are made from three patch shapes – a square (template P) and two mirror-image parallelograms (templates Q and reverse Q. The patchwork background between the cube is made from 2 single right-angle triangles (template R). Set in seams will be needed.

CUTTING OUT

Using Template P Cut 4 squares of GP71LI, GP71LM, GP71GD, GP71CA.
Using Template Q Cut 4 in GP71OR, GP71RD, GP71OC, GP71LF.
Using Template Q Reverse Cut 4 in GP71PN, GP71PL, GP71FO. Cut 3 in GP71OV, and 1 in GP70TA.
Using Template R Cut 32 triangles in GP071CL.

MAKING THE BLOCKS

Using the Roman block assembly diagram and ¼in (6mm) seam allowance, make each block as follows. Sew the two parallelograms together, stopping ¼in (6mm) from the end as in diagram 1. Sew the square to the edge of one parellogram, stopping ¼in (6mm) from the end of the seam (diagram 2). Adjust the position of the square to sew the remaining seam (diagram 3). Take one of the triangle pieces and sew it to one side of the parallelogram (diagram 4). Repeat on the other side (diagram 5).

Note The block should be 7¼in (18.4cm) square.

Make 16 blocks.

Sew the blocks in rows of 4, then join the rows to make a 4 x 4 block panel. The panel should be 27½in (69.8cm) square.

ROMAN BLOCKS BLOCK ASSEMBLY DIAGRAM **ROMAN BLOCKS PANEL ASSEMBLY DIAGRAM**

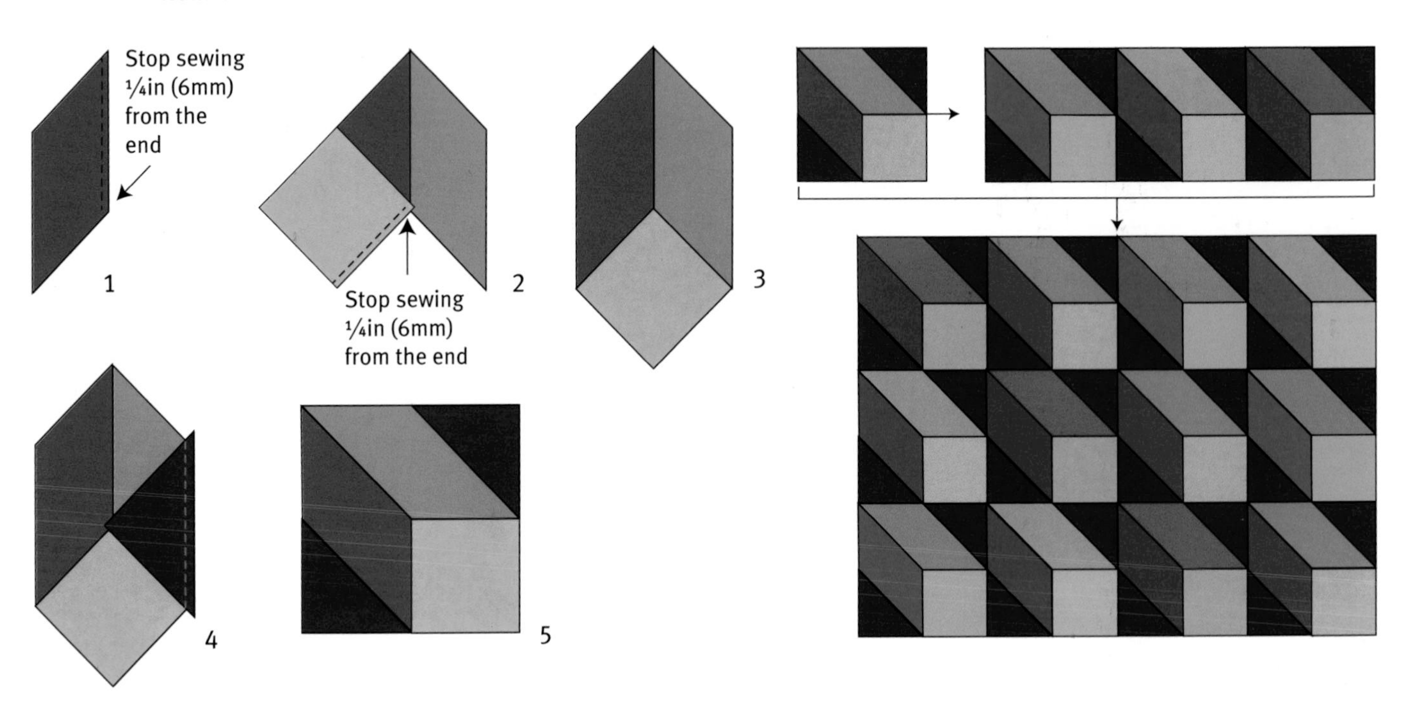

rail fence panel

Fabrics
ABORIGINAL DOT
Pumpkin G71PN
Ochre GP71OC
Chocolate GP71CL
Gold GP71GD
OMBRE
Brown GP117BR

Template

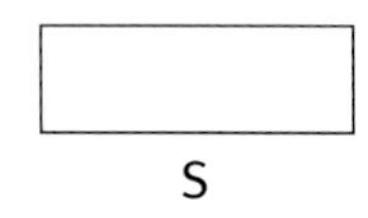

CUTTING
Using Template S Cut 16 in GP71GD, GP71OC, GP117BR, 48 in GP71CL, GP71PN. Total 144 rectangles.

MAKING THE BLOCKS
Using the rail fence block assembly diagram and ¼in (6mm) seam allowance, make the blocks by sewing three strips in the order of the design, to make5in (12.7cm) squares.

Following the diagram, join to form rows of 6 blocks, then join the rows to make a 6 x 8 block panel. This panel should be 27½in x 36½in (69.8cm x 92.7cm) at this stage.

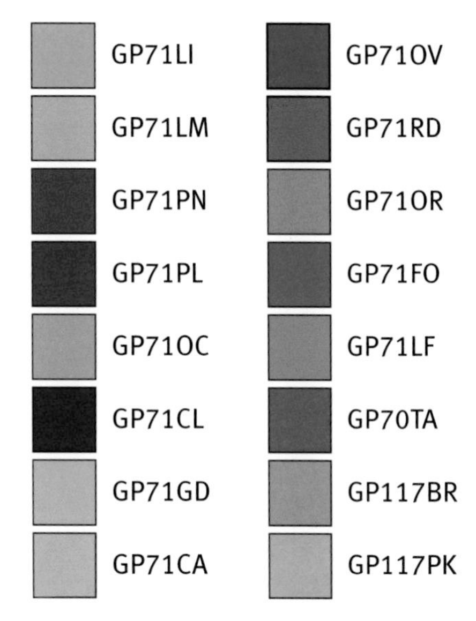

RAIL FENCE BLOCK ASSEMBLY DIAGRAM

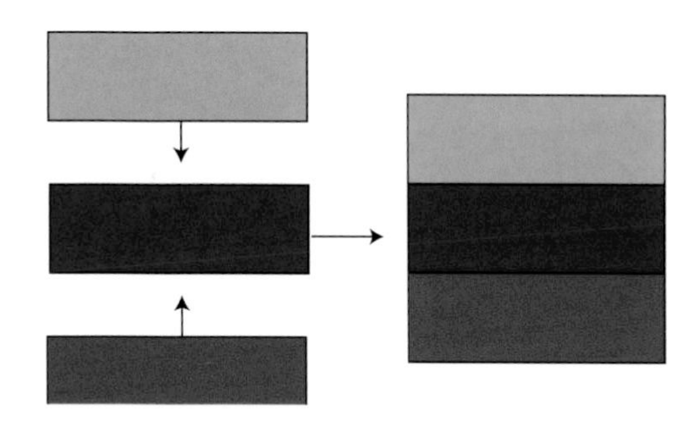

RAIL FENCE PANEL ASSEMBLY DIAGRAM

zig zag panel

Fabrics

ABORIGINAL DOT

Chocolate	GP71CL
Gold	GP71GD
Cantaloupe	GP71CA

OMBRE

Brown	GP117BR
Pink	GP117PK

Templates

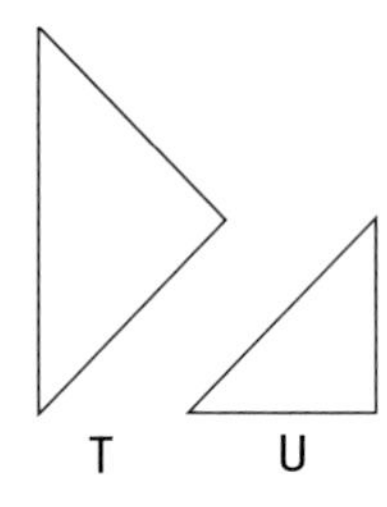

CUTTING OUT

Using Template T Cut 45 triangles in GP71CL, 14 in GP117PK, 9 in GP117BR, 13 in GP71GD, 9 in GP71CA.

Using Template U Cut 10 triangles in GP71CL, 4 in GP71GD, 2 in GP71CA, GP117PK, GP117BR.

MAKING THE BLOCKS

Using the zig zag strip assembly diagram, lay out the triangles in the order of sewing. The use of the design wall will help. Using a ¼in (6mm) seam allowance, and following the zig zag panel assembly diagram, sew each row in order. Join the rows to form the panel, taking care to piece the triangles so they create straight sides. This panel should be 27½in (69.8cm) square at this stage.

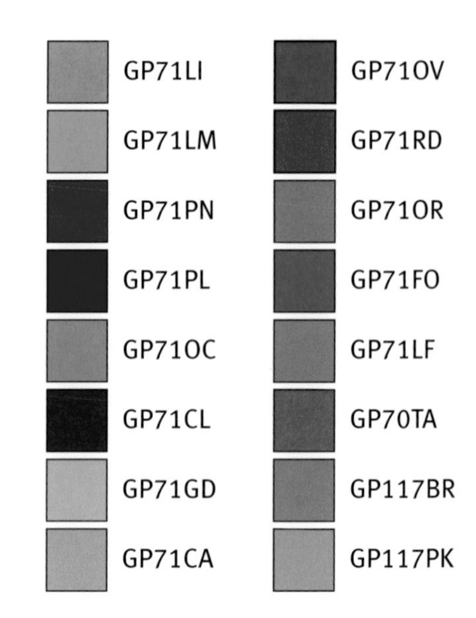

ZIG ZAG STRIP ASSEMBLY DIAGRAM

ZIG ZAG PANEL ASSEMBLY DIAGRAM

tumbling blocks panel

Fabrics
ABORIGINAL DOT

Lilac	GP71LI
Lime	GP71LM
Pumpkin	GP71PN
Plum	GP71PL
Orange	GP71OR
Chocolate	GP71CL
Cantaloupe	GP71CA
Olive	GP71OV
Red	GP71RD

SPOT

Taupe	GP70TA

Templates

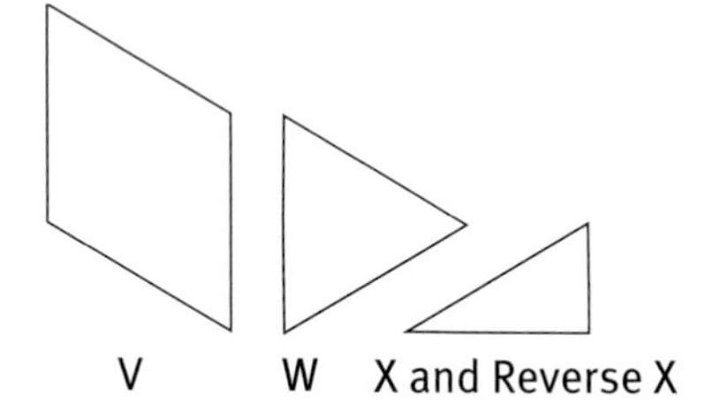

CUTTING OUT

Using template V Cut 30 diamonds in GP71CL, 13 GP71OC, 9 GP71CA, 6 GP70TA, 2 GP71PL, 1 GP71LI, GP71LM, GP71PN. Total 63 diamonds.
Using Template W Cut 27 triangles in GP71RD, GP71OR. Total 54 triangles.
Using Template X Cut 5 triangles in GP71RD, GP71OR. Total 10 triangles.
Using Template X reverse Cut 4 triangles in GP71RD, GP71OR. Total 8 triangles.

MAKING THE BLOCKS

Lay out the pieces of the panel in order, following the tumbling blocks panel assembly diagram. The use of a design wall will help. Using a ¼in (6mm) seam allowance sew each piece in order in vertical rows as in the tumbling blocks strip assembly diagram, taking care to keep straight side edges. Join the rows to complete the panel. This panel should be 27½in x 36½in (69.8cm x 92.7cm) at this stage.

TUMBLING BLOCKS STRIP ASSEMBLY DIAGRAM

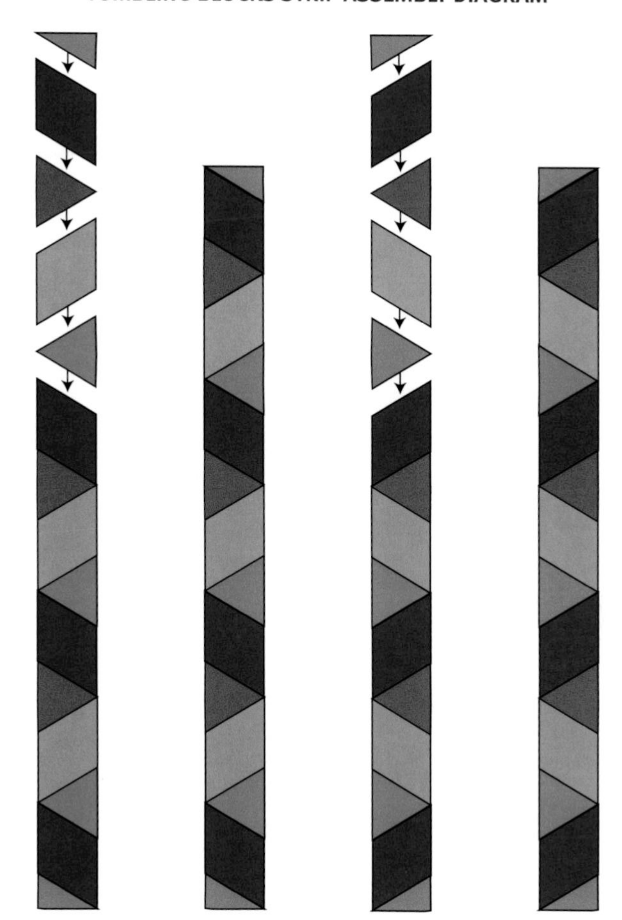

TUMBLING BLOCKS PANEL ASSEMBLY DIAGRAM

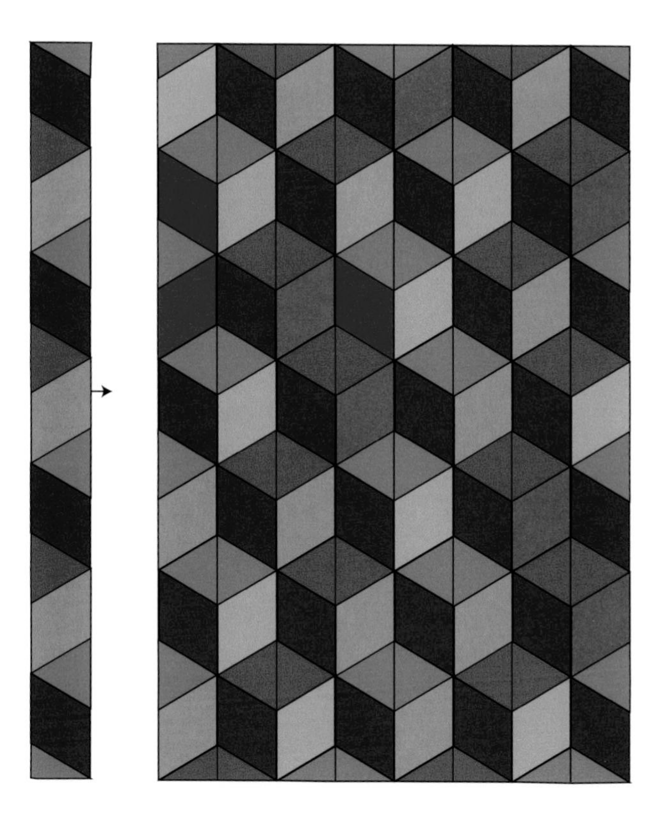

MAKING THE QUILT

Join the four completed panels as in the quilt assembly diagram, pinning well and easing to fit as necessary.

MAKING THE BORDERS

Join the dark and light 2in (5cm) border strips together as in quilt assembly diagram. When sewing the strips sew each seam in a different direction to eliminate bowing in the seam.

CORNER BLOCKS

Join together the pieces cut earlier to make 4 corner blocks, as shown in the corner block assembly diagram. Now join to each end of the top and bottom borders.

Join the two side borders to the main part of the quilt top and trim to fit if necessary. Add the top and bottom borders, making sure the seams match.

FINISHING THE QUILT

Press the quilt top. Join the backing fabric GP148BR using a ¼in (6mm) seam allowance to form a piece approx. 80in x 72in (203cm x 183cm).

Layer the quilt top, batting and backing and baste together (see page 148).

Quilt as desired using quilting thread. Trim the edges and attach the binding (see page 149).

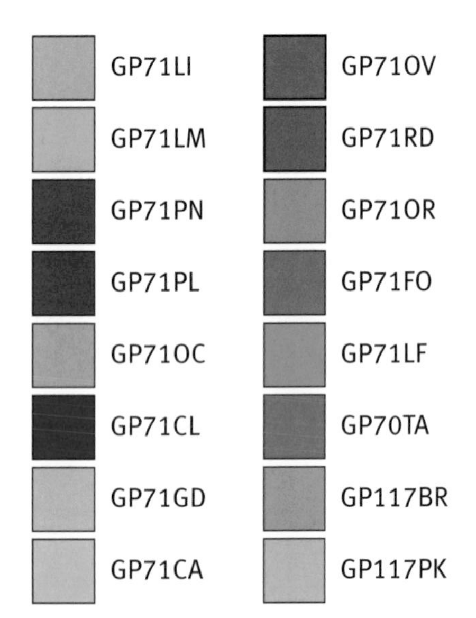

CORNER BLOCK ASSEMBLY DIAGRAM

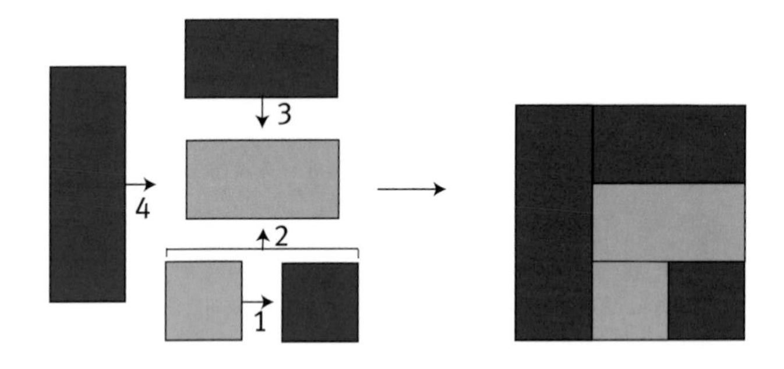

QUILT ASSEMBLY DIAGRAM

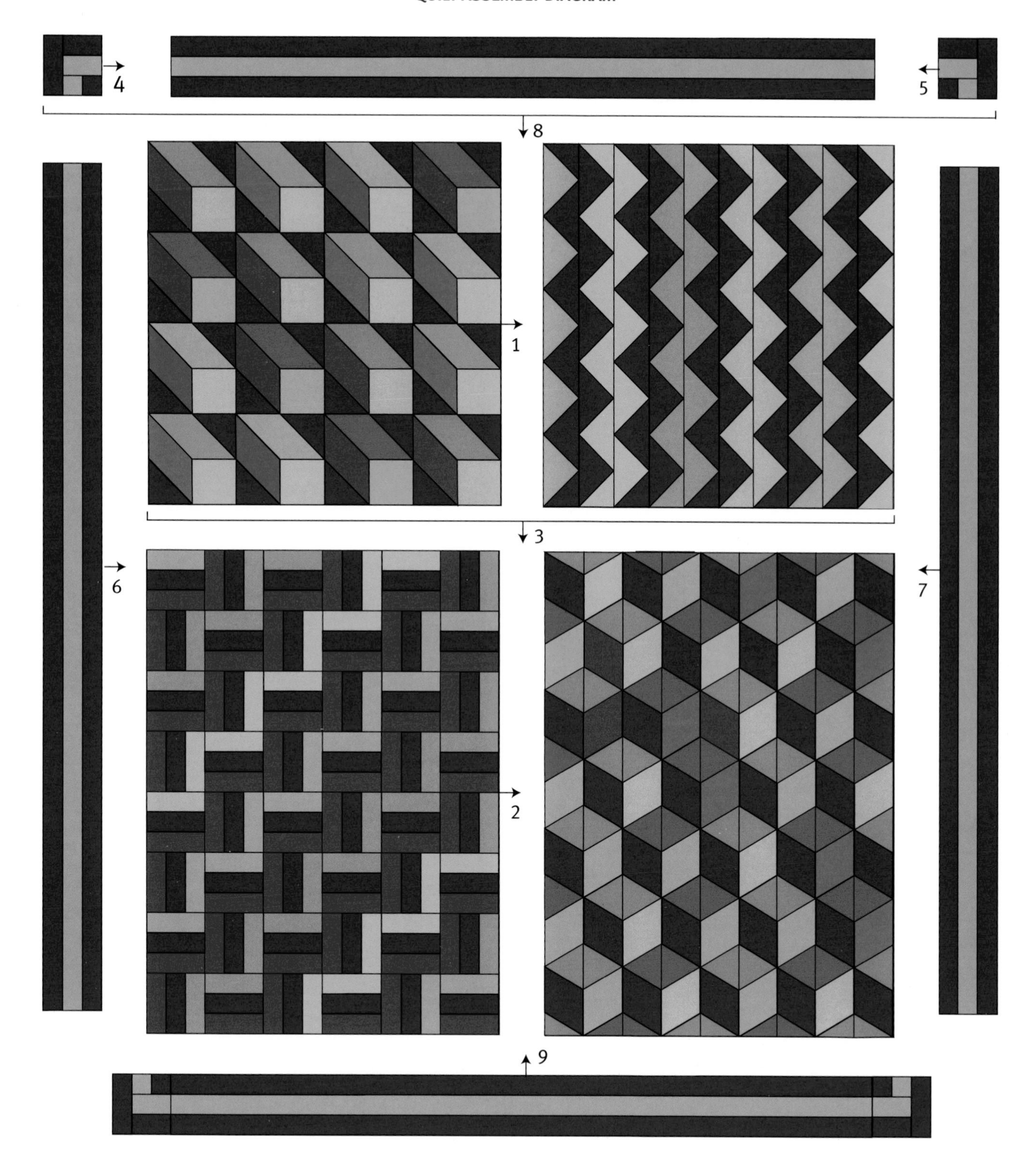

cool zig zag **

Kaffe Fassett

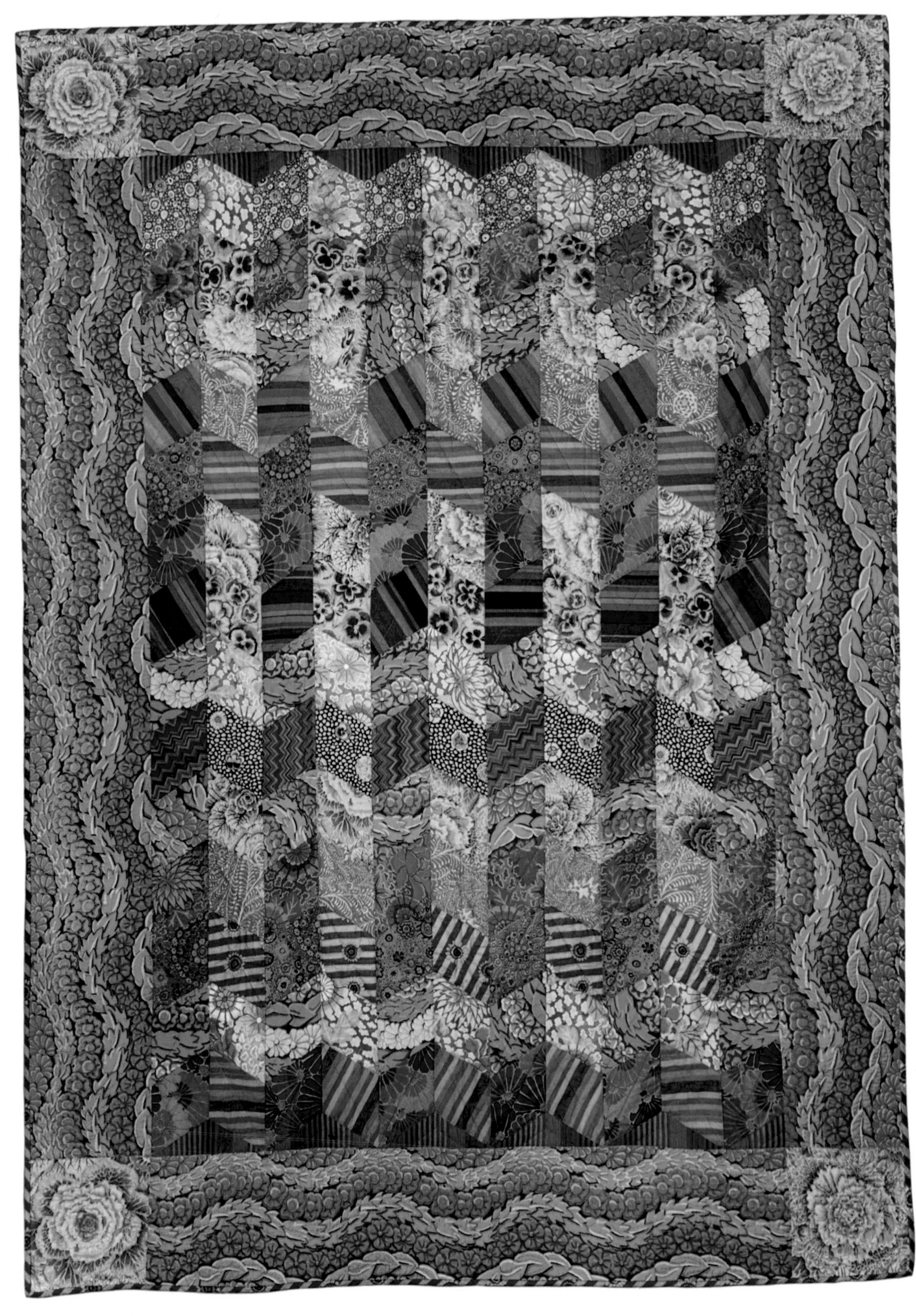

This quilt is assembled in vertical columns, which are then stitched together. The flowers for the squares at each corner of the border pieces are fussy cut (see page 146). The zig zag effect is enhanced by alternating dark and light diamonds across each horizontal row, creating a 3D effect in much the same way as in a traditional Tumbling Blocks pattern.

SIZE OF QUILT

The finished quilt will measure approx. 67in x 92in (170cm x 234cm).

MATERIALS

Patchwork fabrics

SERPENTINE		
Blue	GP145BL	¼yd (25cm)
Green	GP145GN	½yd (45cm)
BRASSICA		
Moss	PJ51MS	⅜yd (35cm)
Green	PJ51GN	¼yd (25cm)
GUINEA FLOWER		
Green	GP59GN	¼yd (25cm)
REGENCY DAISY		
Green	GP146GN	¼yd (25cm)
ROMAN GLASS		
Leafy	GP01LF	¼yd (25cm)
WOVEN BROAD STRIPES		
Subterranean	WBSSA	¼yd (25cm)
WOVEN ROMAN STRIPES		
Dusk	WRSDU	⅜yd (35cm)
ZIG ZAG		
Cool	BM43CL	¼yd (25cm)
WOVEN NARROW STRIPES		
Spring	WNSSP	¼yd (25cm)
FERNS		
Turquoise	GP147TQ	⅜yd (35cm)
PANSIES		
Green	PJ76GN	⅜yd (35cm)
DREAM		
Blue	GP148BL	⅜yd (35cm)
Moss	GP148MS	½yd (45cm)
MILLEFIORE		
Jade	GP92JA	⅜yd (35cm)
THOUSAND FLOWERS		
Blue	GP144BL	⅜yd (35cm)
WOVEN CATERPILLAR STRIPE		
Aqua	WCSAQ	⅜yd (35cm)

Border

SERPENTINE		
Blue	GP145BL	2¼yd (2m)
BRASSICA		
Green	PJ51GN	½yd (45cm)

for fussy-cut corner squares

Backing fabric

LOTUS LEAF		
Purple	GP29PU	5⅝yd (5.1m)

Binding

REGENCY DAISY		
Green	GP146GN	¾yd (70cm)

Batting

75in x 100in (190cm x 254cm)

Quilting thread

Machine quilting thread

Templates

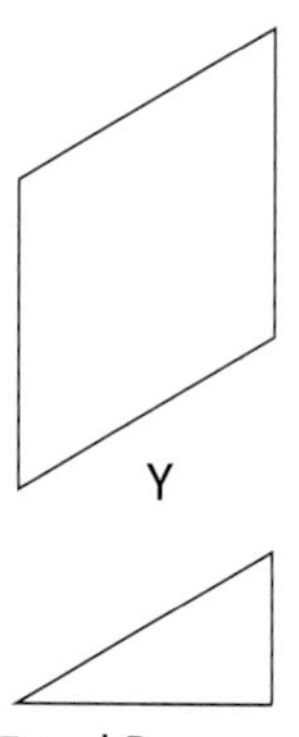

Y

Z and Reverse Z

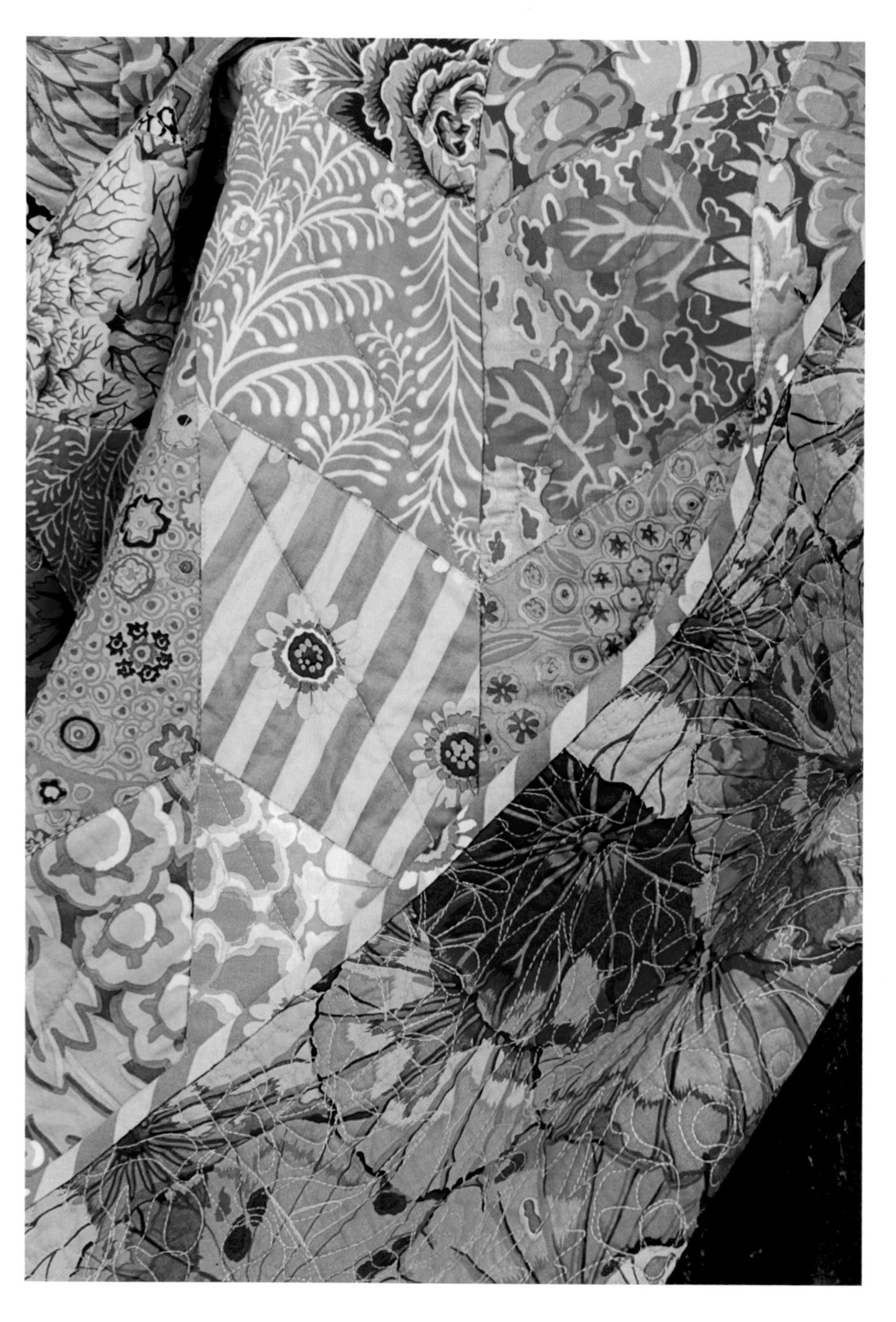

CUTTING OUT
When cutting the diamonds, cut the printed fabrics into strips 5in (12.7cm) wide. Place template Y on the strip and cut out the required number of shapes. For the striped fabrics, don't cut strips but place the template on the stripes at different angles to get a random effect.
Template Y Cut 5 diamonds in GP59GN, PJ51GN and GP146GN; 6 in GP01LF, WBSSA, WNSSP, BM043CL and GP145BL; 10 in PJ51GN, WRSDU, GP147TQ and PJ76GN; 12 in GP148BL, GP92JA and GP144BL; 15 in GP148MS; and 18 in GP145GN. A total of 154 diamonds.
Note Take care to cut the 6 GP145BL diamonds from the 1/4yd (25cm) fabric piece, not from the border yardage.
Template Z Cut 22 triangles (12 Z and 10 Reverse Z) in WCSAQ.

Borders
Cut 4 borders 10in (25cm) wide down the entire length of the fabric in GP145BL. (They will be cut to size later.) Fussy cut (see page 146) 4 corner squares measuring 10in (25.4cm) in PJ51MS, centering a large flower in each.

Binding
Cut strips 2 1/2in (6.4cm) wide in the bias direction in GP148GN and seam together to create a total length of at least 330in (840cm).

Backing
Cut 2 pieces 38in x 100in (96.5cm x 254cm) in GP29PU.

MAKING THE QUILT
Use a 6mm (1/4in) seam allowance throughout.
Referring to the photo on page 90 and the quilt assembly diagram opposite for the fabric placement and the orientation of the diamonds, lay out the diamonds and triangles in 11 vertical rows of 14 diamonds and 2 triangles each. Assemble each vertical column shown in the quilt assembly diagram first. Then sew the 11 columns together.

ADDING THE BORDERS
Measure the height of the quilt down the middle. From the strips cut for the borders, cut 2 matching borders to this length. Sew a border strip to each side. Measure the width of the quilt. Cut 2 matching borders to this size plus 1/2in (1.2cm) for seam allowances, add a 10in (25.4cm) PJ51GN square to each end of each strip, and attach to the top and bottom of the quilt, matching the seams neatly.

FINISHING THE QUILT
Press the quilt top. Using a 1/4in (6mm) seam allowance, seam the backing pieces to form a piece approx. 75in x 100in (190cm x 254cm). Layer the quilt top, batting and backing and baste together (see page 148). Using machine quilting thread, quilt as desired. Trim the quilt edges and attach the binding (see page 149).

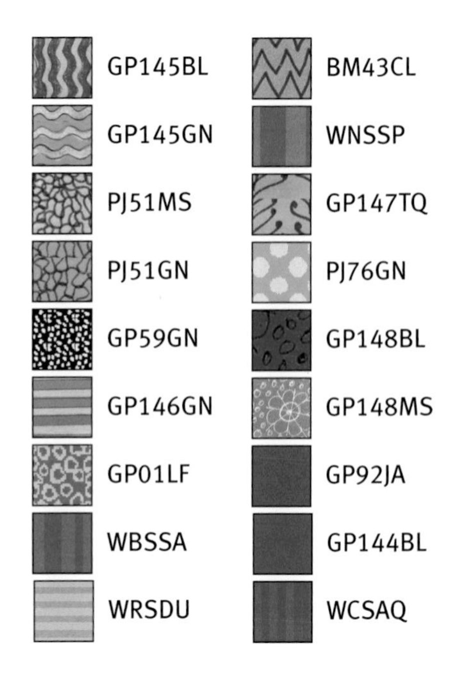

QUILT ASSEMBLY DIAGRAM

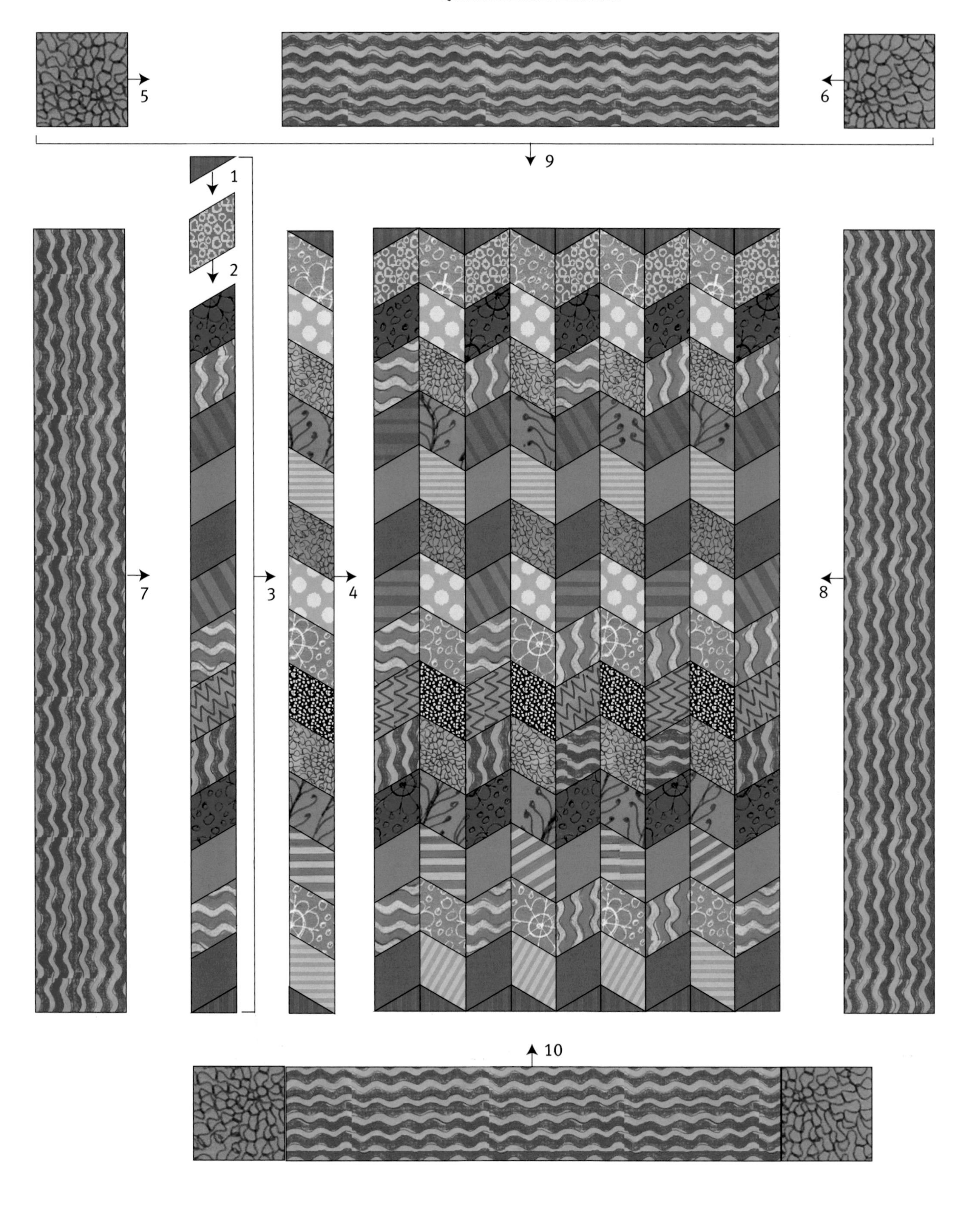

golden strips *

Kaffe Fassett

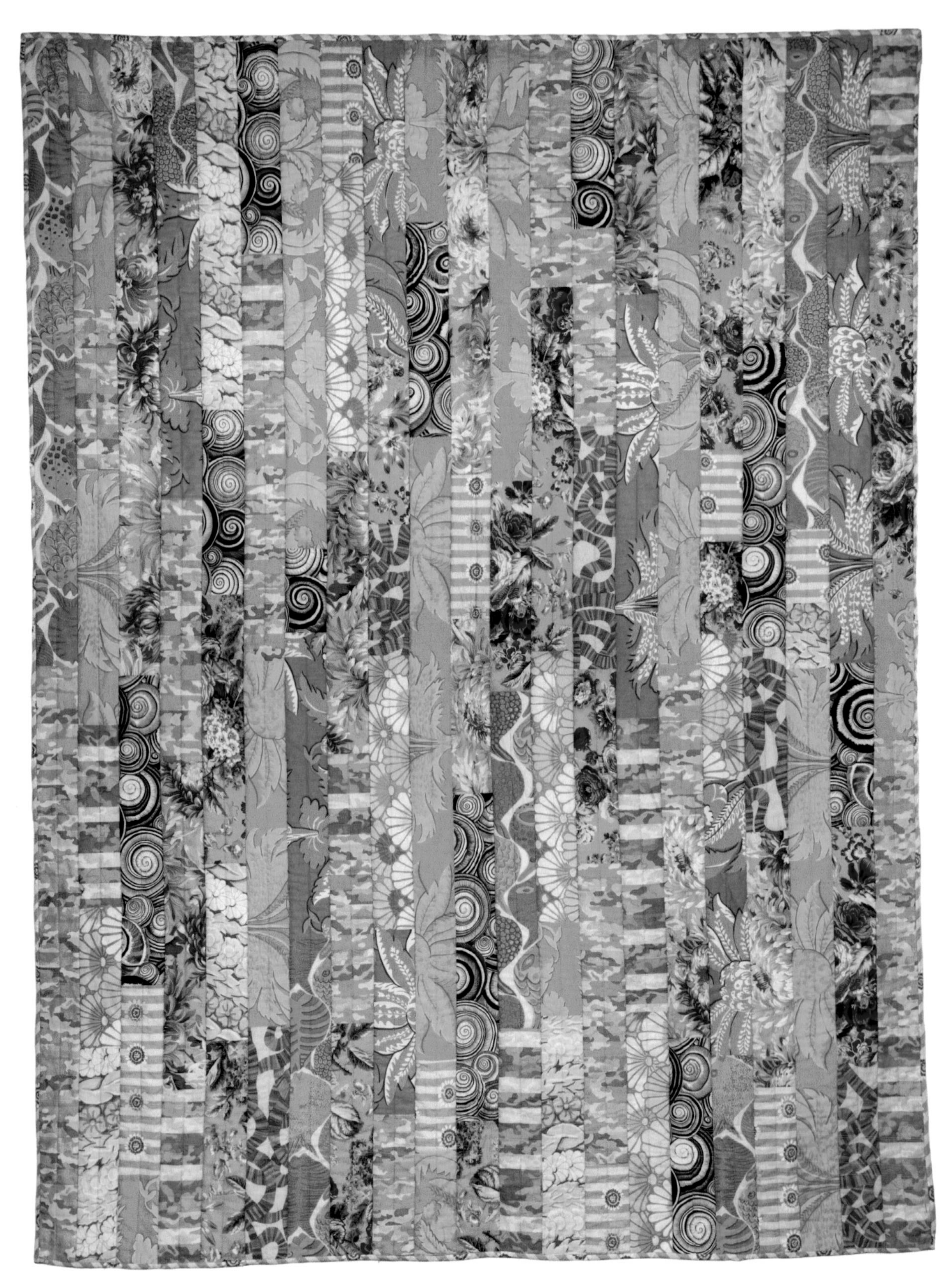

This is an easy quilt if you treat it as a strippy quilt. If you want to copy it exactly, you will need to mark the measurements on each cut piece to enable you to compose the columns as shown. Each pieced column has a fixed width of 3½in (8.9cm). Each pieced and stiched column is trimmed to 80½in (204.5cm). In all, it has 21 pieced columns.

SIZE OF QUILT
The finished quilt will measure approx. 63in x 80in (160cm x 203.2cm).

MATERIALS

Patchwork Fabrics

SHOAL		
Yellow	BM51YE	½yd (45cm)
STRIPE CAMOUFLAGE		
Spring	BM52SP	½yd (45cm)
Mauve	BM52MV	⅜yd (35cm)
BRANDON'S BROCADE		
Pastel	BM48PT	⅞yd (80cm)
Grey	BM48GY	½yd (45cm)
THOUSAND FLOWERS		
Yellow	GP144YE	⅜yd (35cm)
SERPENTINE		
Yellow	GP145YE	¼yd (25cm)
SHAGGY		
Yellow	PJ72YE	½yd (45cm)
SPIRAL SHELLS		
Multi	PJ73MU	½yd (45cm)
REGENCY DAISY		
Yellow	GP146YE	¼yd (25cm)
FLORAL DELIGHT		
Yellow	PJ75YE	⅝yd (60cm)
ROLLER COASTER		
Yellow	BM49YE	¼yd (25cm)

Backing Fabric

SHAGGY		
Yellow	PJ72YE	5yd (4.75m)

Binding

REGENCY DAISY		
Yellow	GP146YE	¾yd (70cm)

Batting
71½in x 88½in (182cm x 225cm)

Quilting Thread
Machine quilting thread

CUTTING OUT
Cut 3½in (8.9cm) wide strips across the width of each fabric as follows:
Cut 8 in BM48PT, 6 in PJ75YE, 5 in BM52SP, BM48GY ,PJ72YE, 4 in PJ73MU, BM51YE, 3 in BM52MV, GP144YE, 2 in GP145YE, GP146YE, BM49YE.

Backing Fabric
Cut 2 pieces 88in (223.5cm) long in PJ72YE.

Binding
Cut strips in the bias direction 2½in (6.4cm) wide using GP146YE. Seam together to make a total length of at least 308in (782cm).

MAKING THE QUILT

Lay out the strips of fabric in 12 piles, keeping the same fabric together.

It is best to cut and sew together the pieces for each column one column at a time. Begin with Column 1 and work through each column in turn, cutting the strips into the lengths given for each column (below). The fabric sizes are given in order, from the top of the quilt to the bottom). Follow the quilt layout diagram opposite to check you are using the correct fabrics for each column.

Sew the pieces for each column together using a ¼in (6mm) seam. When each column is sewn, trim it to 80½in (204.5cm) long. When a column is sewn and trimmed, make a note of the number (or place it on a design wall or floor) so that you have the columns in the correct order when they are sewn together later.

Column 1 BM51YE 40½in (103cm) and BM52SP 40½in (103cm).

Column 2 BM48PT 2 strips each 24¼in (61.6.cm) joined together in a strip 48in (122cm), BM52MV 12¾in (32.4cm), GP144YE 11in (27.9cm) and GP145YE 14¼in (36.2cm).

Column 3 PJ72YE 40½in (103cm), PJ73MU 21½in (54.6cm), GP146YE 14in (35.6cm) and BM48PT 7in (17.8cm).

Column 4 BM48GY 31½in (55.9cm), BM52SP 18½in (47cm), PJ072YE 23in (58.7cm) and BM52MV 13in (33cm).

Column 5 GP145YE 25in (63.5cm), PJ73MU 13in (33cm), PJ075YE 19in (48.3cm), GP145YE 12½in (31.7cm) and PJ075YE 17in (43.2cm).

Column 6 PJ73MU 16in (40.6cm), BM52MV 8½in (21.6cm), BM52SP 20½in (52.1cm), BM48PT 25½in (64.8cm) and BM49YE 16in (40.6cm).

Column 7 BM48PT 35in (88.9cm), PJ73MU 6in (15.2cm), BM48GY 20in (50.8cm) and BM51YE 25in (63.5cm).

Column 8 GP146YE 8½in (21.6cm), GP144YE 20in (50.8cm), PJ72YE 21½in (54.6cm), BM52SP 14in (35.6cm), BM52MV 6in (15.2cm) and PJ75YE 17in (43.2cm).

Column 9 BM48GY 21½in (54.6cm), PJ75YE 12in (30.5cm), BM49YE 9½in (24.1cm), GP144YE 19½in (49.5cm), BM48GY 13in (33cm) and BM52SP 11½in (29.2cm).

Column 10 BM48PT 12½in (31.7cm), PJ73MU 15½in (39.4cm), BJM48PT 40½in (103cm), GP146YE 6½in (16.5cm) and BM48PT 8½in (21.6cm).

Column 11 PJ72YE 30in (76.2cm), GP146YE 10½in (26.7cm), PJ72YE 12½in (31.7cm), PJ73MU 22½in (57.2cm) and PJ75YE 11in (27.9cm).

Column 12 BM48PT 30in (76.2cm), PJ075YE 20in (50.8cm), BM51YE 21in (53.3cm) and BM52MV 15in (38.1cm).

Column 13 BM52SP 17in (43.2cm), PJ075YE 25½in (64.8cm), GP144YE 20in (50.8cm), BM48PT 6in (15.2cm), and GP145YE 18in (45.7cm).

Column 14 PJ73MU 13in (33cm), BM052SP 14in (35.6cm), BM49YE 21in (53.3cm), PJ75YE 13¾in (34.9cm), BM52SP 18¾in (47.6cm) and GP146YE 6½in (15.2cm).

Column 15 PJ72YE 17½in (75.6cm), BM48GY 30½in (77.5cm), BM52MV 20½in (52.1cm) and GP144YE 17½in (44.4cm).

Column 16 BM48PT 40½in (103cm), BM052SP 11in (27.9cm), PJ72YE 16in (40.6cm) and PJ73MU 16in (40.6cm).

Column 17 PJ75YE 28in (71.1cm), GP146YE 6in (15.2cm), PJ75YE 6in (15.2cm), GP144YE 10in (25.4cm), BM48GY 22½in (57.1cm) and BM51YE 14½in (36.8cm).

Column 18 PJ72YE 21in (53.3cm), PJ73MU 21in (53.3cm), BM49YE 13in (33cm), PJ72YE 17½in (44.5cm) and GP146YE 14in (35.6cm).

Column 19 BM51YE 32½in (82.6cm), GP146YE 5½in (14cm), GP145YE 5in (12.7cm) and BM48PT 40½in (103cm).

Column 20 BM48GY 40½in (103cm), PJ73MU 12in (30.5cm), PJ75YE 17in (43.2cm) and BM49YE 14in (35.6cm).

Column 21 BM52MV 9in (22.9cm), PJ75YE 30in (76.2cm), BM48PT 10in (25.4cm), BM52SP 20in (50.8cm) and BM52MV 17½in (44.4cm).

Tip

To counteract stretching the fabric when machine piecing each column, it is very important to start piecing/machining at alternate ends of your work.

JOINING THE COLUMNS

Stitch into pairs, starting from the top, starting with columns 1and 2. Repeat until all columns apart from 21 are stitched into pairs. Then stitch pairs together, starting with the pairs of 1 and 2 plus 3 and 4, making sure that your pieces are the right way up, but this time machine stitch together from the bottom. Repeat until you have 5 sections. Add column 21 to your last section. Join the sections in the same way, ensuring that machine stitching is started at the bottom each time.

FINISHING THE QUILT

Press the quilt top. Using a ¼in (6mm) seam allowance, seam the backing pieces to form a piece approx. 72in x 88in (183cm x 223.5cm). Layer the quilt top, batting and backing and baste together (see page 148). With machine quilting thread and using the long 'lines' in your quilt, stitch in the ditch and down the centre of each strip. Trim the quilt edges. Attach the binding to the quilt (see page 149).

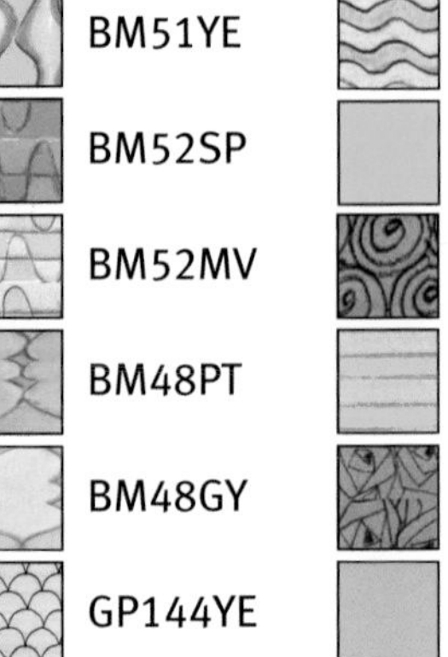

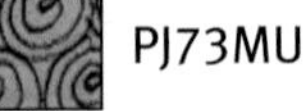
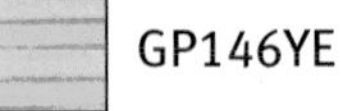
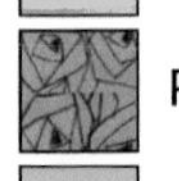

QUILT ASSEMBLY DIAGRAM

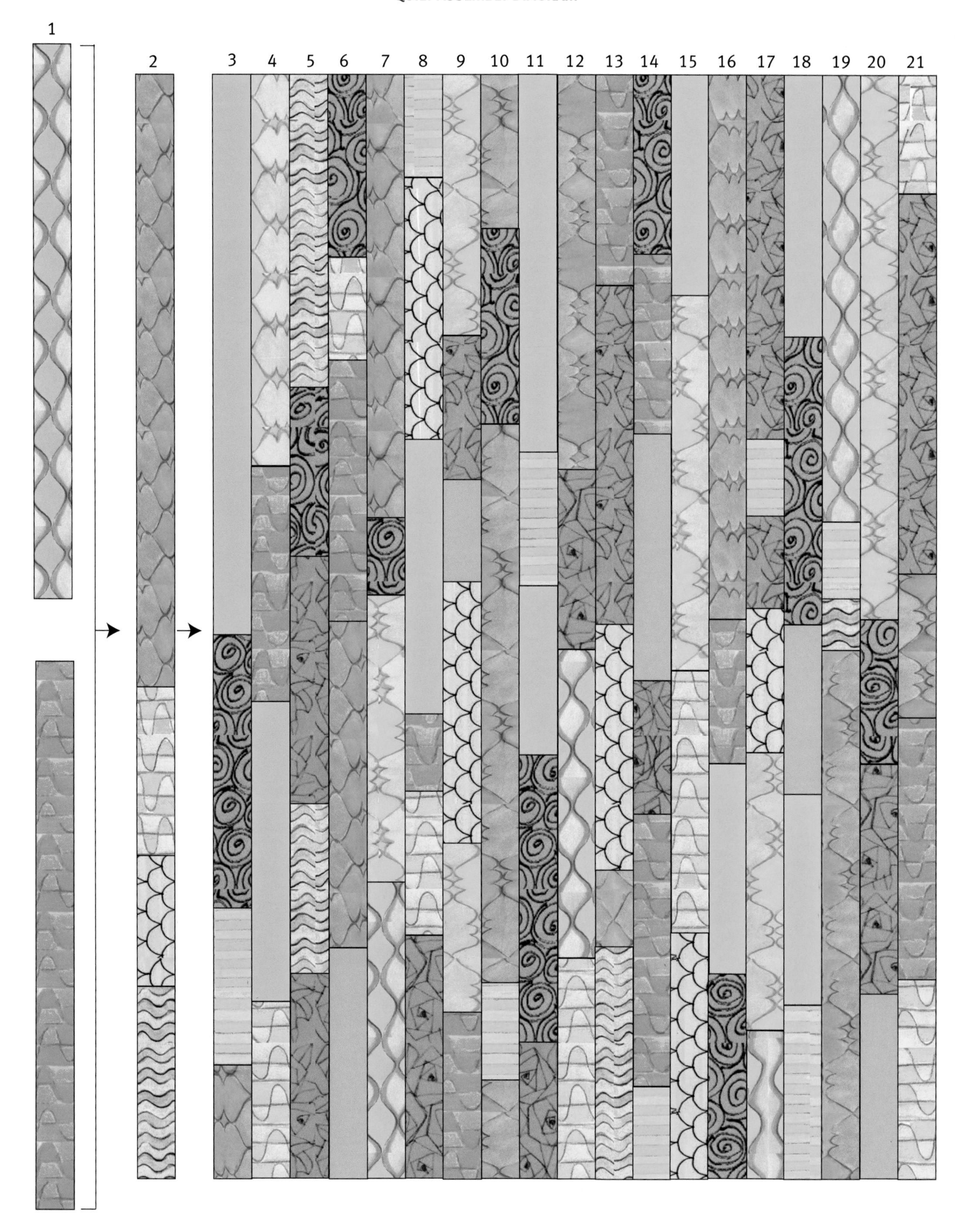

baroque pinwheels **

Brandon Mably

The quilt is made up of on point blocks featuring Brandon's Brocade fabric as the central square, with two triangles attached to each side of the central square.

SIZE OF QUILT
The quilt will measure approximately 58in x 70in (147cm x 178cm)

MATERIALS
Patchwork Fabrics

LABELS		
Tomato	BM45TM	¼yd (25cm)
Purple	BM45PU	¼yd (25cm)
MILLEFIORE		
Blue	GP92BL	¼yd (25cm)
Brown	GP92BR	¼yd (25cm)
ROMAN GLASS		
Byzantine	GP01BY	¼yd (25cm)
CAMOUFLAGE STRIPE		
Summer	BM52SU	¼yd (25cm)
Dark	BM52DK	¼yd (25cm)
ROLLER COASTER		
Purple	BM49PU	½yd (45cm)
SPOT		
Plum	GP70PL	¼yd (25cm)
Orange	GP70OR	¼yd (25cm)
Peacock	GP70PC	¼yd (25cm)
JUMBLE		
Purple	BM53PU	¼yd (25cm)
Orange	BM53OR	¼yd (25cm)
BRANDON'S BROCADE		
Brown	BM48BR	1¼yd (1.15m)
ZIG ZAG		
Cool	BM43CL	¼yd (25cm)
Rare	BM43RR	¼yd (25cm)
FERNS		
Black	GP147BK	⅝yd (60cm)
REGENCY		
Brown	GP146BR	¼yd (25cm)

Border Fabrics

ZIG ZAG		
Jade	BM43JA	1yd (90cm)
ROLLER COASTER		
Purple	BM49PU	(included in yardage for blocks)

Backing Fabric

CAMOUFLAGE STRIPE		
Summer	BM52SU	4⅜yd (4m)

Binding

LABELS		
Tomato	BM45TM	½yd (45cm)

Batting
66in x 78in (168cm x 198cm)

Quilting Thread
Machine quilting thread

Template

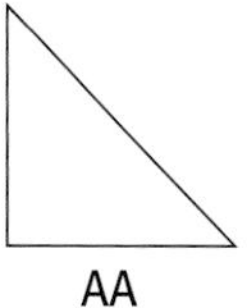

CUTTING OUT

Cut across the width of the fabric unless stated otherwise.
The use of starch will help to stabilize the fabric triangles.
When using triangle template AA, the triangles are cut with the long side aligned with the straight grain. If you prefer to rotary cut, cut strips 7in (17.8cm) wide across the width of the fabric. Then cut 7in (17.8cm) squares from the strips. This will give 5 squares per strip of fabric. Cut the square in half diagonally twice. Do not move the fabric until you have cut both diagonal lines. This will give 4 triangles per square (20 triangles per strip).
Note The numbers in brackets in the following list equal the number of triangles needed for the blocks.

For the triangles Cut 4 squares of GP147BK (14) and sub-cut to give 16 triangles.
Cut 3 squares of BM45TM (12), BM45PU (12), GP92BR (9), GP146BR (11), BM52SU (10), BM49PU (9), GP70OR (12), GP70PC (12), BM53PU (6), BM43RR (10), BM43CL (10). Sub-cut these to give 12 triangles of each fabric.
Cut 2 squares of GP92BL (6), BM52DK (6), GP70PL (8), BM53OR (8), GP01BY (5). Sub-cut these to give 8 triangles of each fabric.

For the central panel squares Cut 5 strips 9in (22.9cm) wide across the width of BM48BR. Cut 20 9in (22.9cm) squares (4 from each strip).

For the border Cut 4 strips of BM43JA parallel with the selvedge, 5½in x 36in (14cm x 90cm), and join in pairs to make 2 strips 60½in (153.5cm) long.
This will give you approx. width of 18in (45.7cm) fabric remaining for the top and bottom borders. Cut 6 strips across this width, 5½in (14cm) wide, and join in threes. Cut to make two strips 48½in (123cm) long. When joined the pattern match will run correctly across the width. There is plenty of fabric to fussy cut these strips.

For the border squares Cut 4 5½in (14cm) squares from BM49PU.

Binding
Cut 7 strips 2½in (6.4cm) across the width of the fabric in BM45TM

Backing
Cut two 78in (198cm) lengths in BM52SU.

MAKING THE QUILT

Use a ¼in (6mm) seam allowance throughout.
Take care when handling the triangles, as there are two bias edges. Spraying with starch will help to stabilize these edges until they are sewn.
Using the quilt assembly diagram as a guide, lay out all the blocks. The use of a design wall will greatly help with the placement.
Join the two triangles at each corner to make one half-square triangle. Sew these to the sides of the large central square as in the block assembly diagram. This forms the block, with the central square on point. Each block should measure 12½in (31.8cm) square.
Keeping to the quilt diagram, sew four blocks together in a row, making sure the seams are aligned. Sew five rows together to make the centre of the quilt.

ADDING THE BORDERS

Sew the side borders and trim to fit if necessary. Sew the corner squares to each end of the top and bottom borders. Sew the top and bottom borders to the quilt centre.

BLOCK ASSEMBLY DIAGRAM

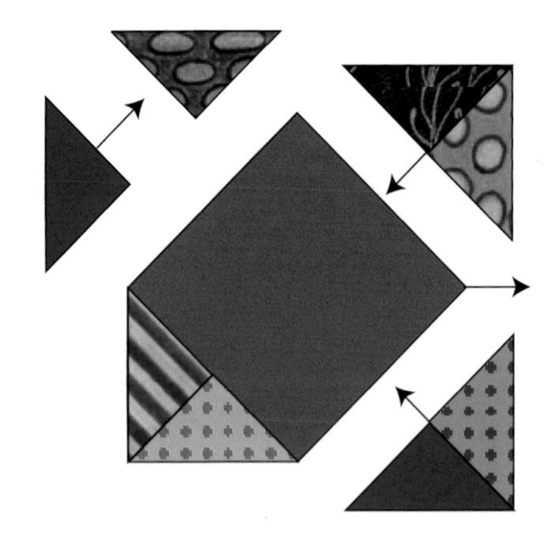

FINISHING THE QUILT.

Press the quilt top.
Seam the backing pieces with a ¼in (6mm) seam allowance to create a piece 66in x 78in (168cm x 198cm).
Layer quilt, batting and backing. Baste, and, using machine quilting thread, quilt as desired (see page 148).
Trim the quilt edges and attach the binding (see page 149).

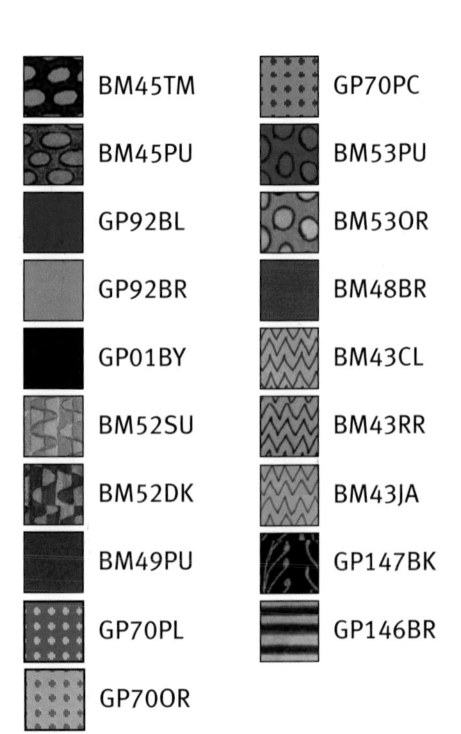

QUILT ASSEMBLY DIAGRAM

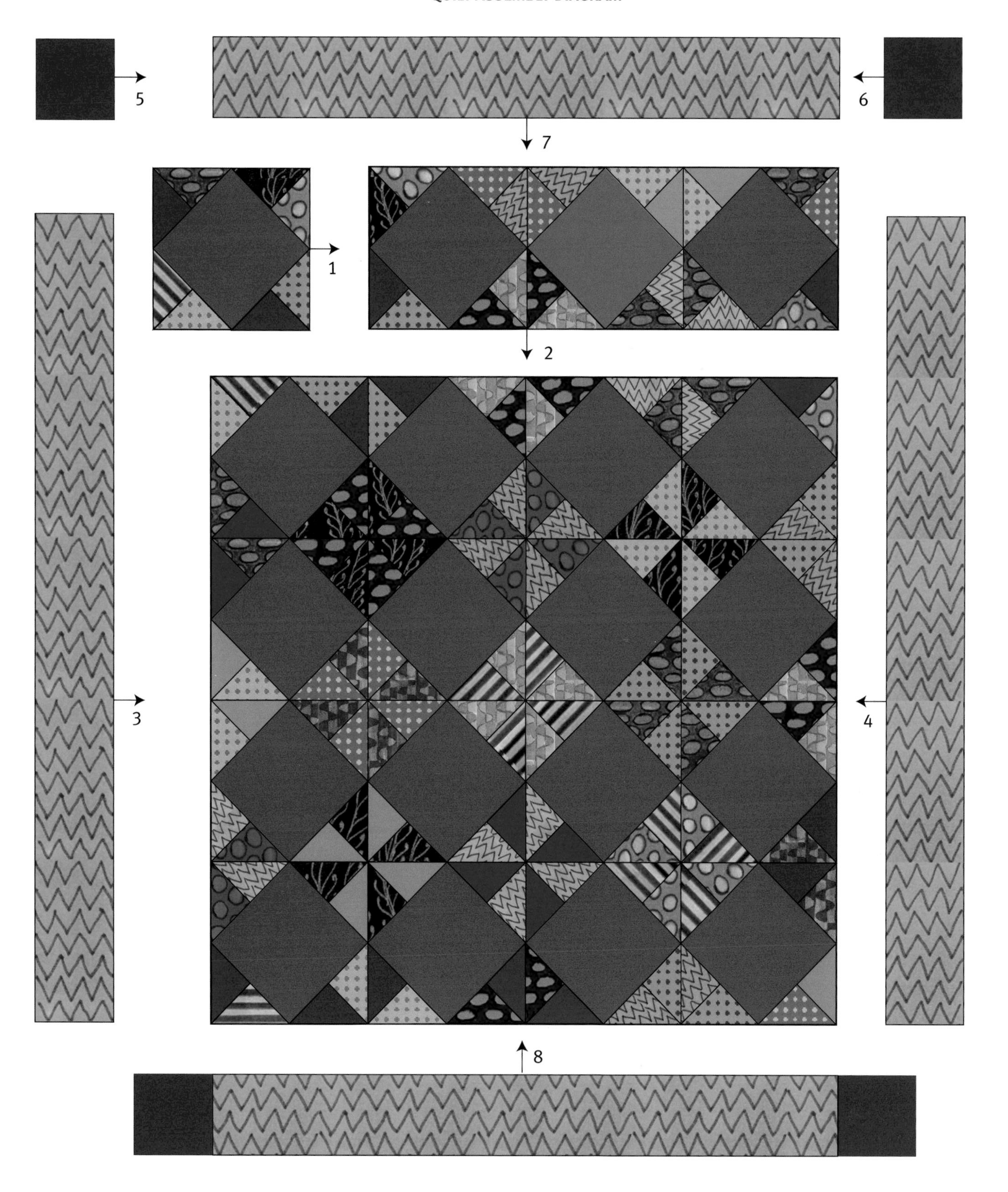

cassetta **

Liza Prior Lucy

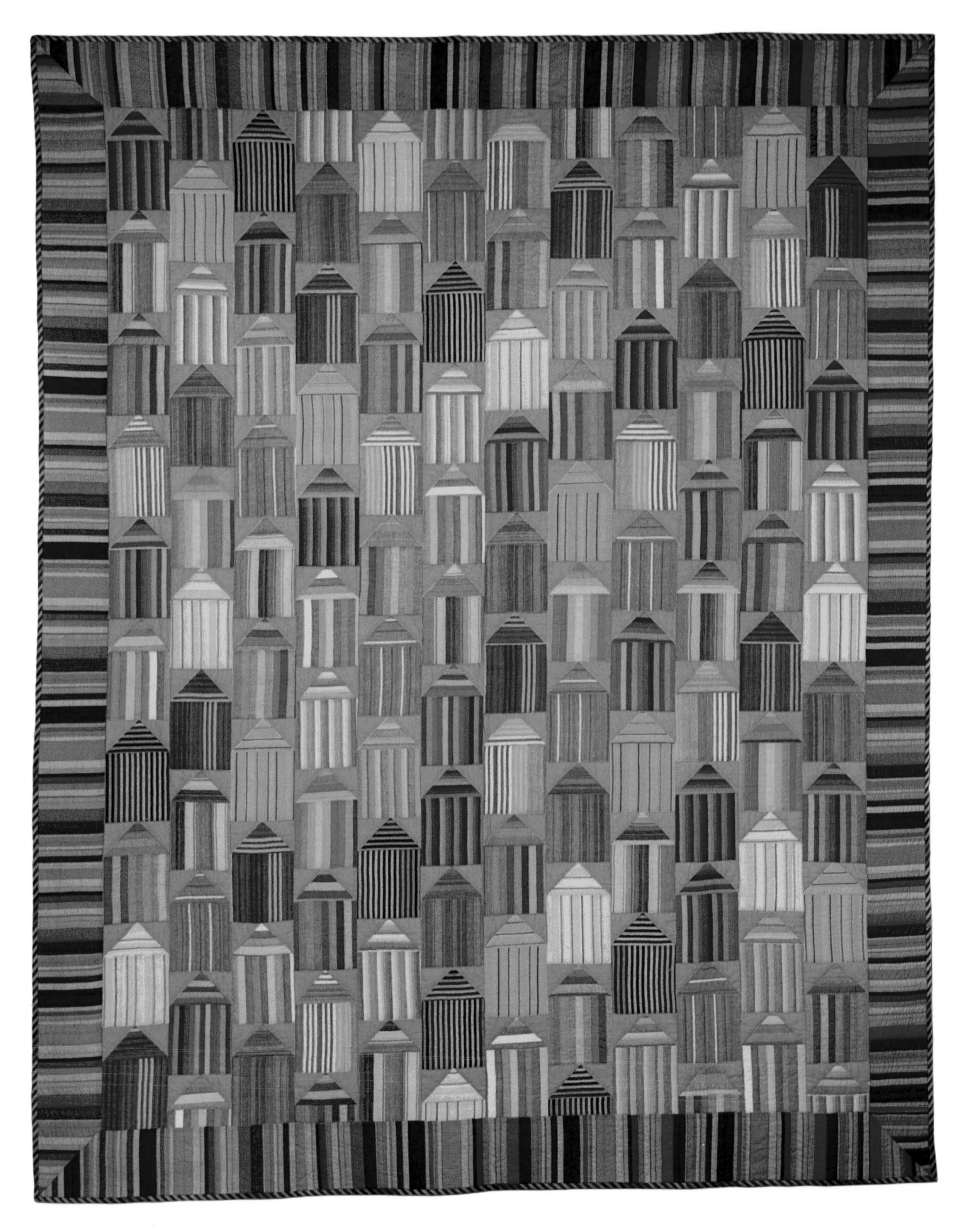

This is a scrappy quilt, so it is not essential to place each house block in exactly the same position as the original. Simply aim to create a pleasing combination of colours.
Note You must pay attention to the direction of the stripes before cutting!

Templates

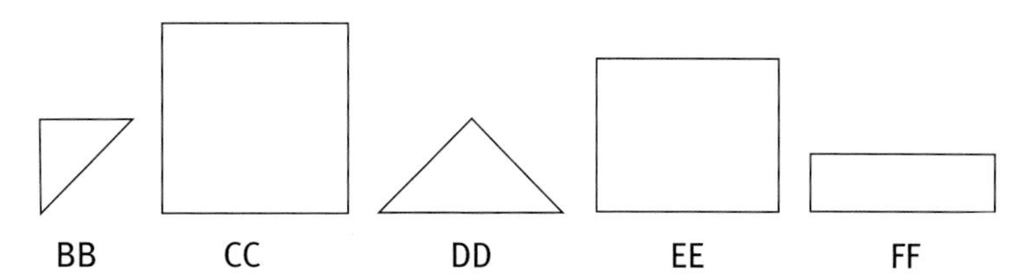

SIZE OF QUILT
The finished quilt will measure approx. 70in x 85in (178cm x 215.9cm)

MATERIALS
Patchwork Fabrics

WOVEN ROMAN STRIPE		
Blood Orange	WRSBO	$1\frac{1}{2}$yd (1.35m)
SHOT COTTON		
Galvanized	SC87	$1\frac{1}{4}$yd (1.2m)
WOVEN BROAD STRIPE		
Subterranean	WBSSA	$\frac{3}{8}$yd (35cm)
Yellow	WBSYE	$\frac{3}{8}$yd (35cm)
Sunset	WBSSS	$\frac{3}{8}$yd (35cm)
Watermelon	WBSWL	$\frac{3}{8}$yd (35cm)
WOVEN NARROW STRIPE		
Spice	WNSSI	$\frac{3}{8}$yd (35cm)
WOVEN CATERPILLAR STRIPE		
Yellow	WCSYE	$\frac{3}{8}$yd (35cm)
Earth	WCSER	$\frac{3}{8}$yd (35cm)
Tomato	WCSTM	$\frac{3}{8}$yd (35cm)
WOVEN ALTERNATING STRIPE		
Yellow	WNSYE	$\frac{3}{8}$yd (35cm)
Orange	WNSOR	$\frac{3}{8}$yd (35cm)
Olive	WNSOV	$\frac{3}{8}$yd (35cm)
WOVEN EXOTIC STRIPE		
Earth	WESER	$\frac{3}{8}$yd (35cm)
Dusk	WESDU	$\frac{3}{8}$yd (35cm)
WOVEN MULTI STRIPE		
Pimento	WMSPI	$\frac{3}{8}$yd (35cm)
Lime	WMSLM	$\frac{3}{8}$yd (35cm)
Toast	WMSTT	$\frac{3}{8}$yd (35cm)

Backing Fabric

ZIG ZAG		
Cool	BM43CL	$5\frac{1}{2}$yd (5m)

Binding

WOVEN CATERPILLAR STRIPE		
Earth	WCSER	$\frac{3}{4}$yd (70cm)

Batting
78in x 93in (198cm x 236cm)

Quilting Thread
Machine quilting thread

CUTTING OUT
For the borders From WRSBO cut 7 strips each $5\frac{1}{2}$in (14cm) wide across the width of the fabric. Remove selvedges and stitch strips together across short ends. Then cut two long borders, each $75\frac{1}{2}$in (192cm), and two shorter borders, each $60\frac{1}{2}$in (153.7cm). Cut two $5\frac{7}{8}$in (15cm) squares and bisect them diagonally to make two triangles from each square.

For the house block backgrounds From SC87 cut 114 squares, each $3\frac{3}{8}$in (8.6cm), and bisect diagonally to make two triangles from each square (228 triangles). Or use template BB.

For the house bases From the 16 other block fabrics, cut $5\frac{1}{2}$in (14cm) squares. Use either template CC or rotary cut. You need 114 squares in total, so cut 8 from each fabric (which will allow extra for the partial house blocks).

For the house roofs The house roof fabrics match the house bases. From each of the 16 block fabrics, cut a $3\frac{1}{8}$in (8cm) wide strip x width of fabric strip. Refer to the roof cutting diagram and with the fabric stripes horizontal use template DD to cut the roofs from each strip as shown, rotating the template alternately along the strip. You need 8 roofs from each strip (although you will get 10 per width) for a total of 114 roofs (plus 6 partial house blocks).

For the partial houses at the top
Cut 6 rectangles $4\frac{1}{2}$in (11.5cm) high x $5\frac{1}{2}$in (14cm) wide, making sure the stripes run parallel to the sides. If you prefer use template EE.

For the partial houses at the bottom
Cut 6 roofs using template DD (as for whole houses) and 6 matching house bases each $1\frac{3}{4}$in (4.4cm) high x $5\frac{1}{2}$in (14cm) wide, making sure the stripes run parallel to the sides. If you prefer, use template FF.

Binding
Cut $2\frac{1}{2}$in (6.4cm) wide strips on the bias of the fabric in WCSER, cutting sufficient to make a length of 325in (825cm) when sewn.

Backing
Cut 2 lengths, 93in (236.2cm) in backing fabric BM43CL.

ROOF CUTTING DIAGRAM

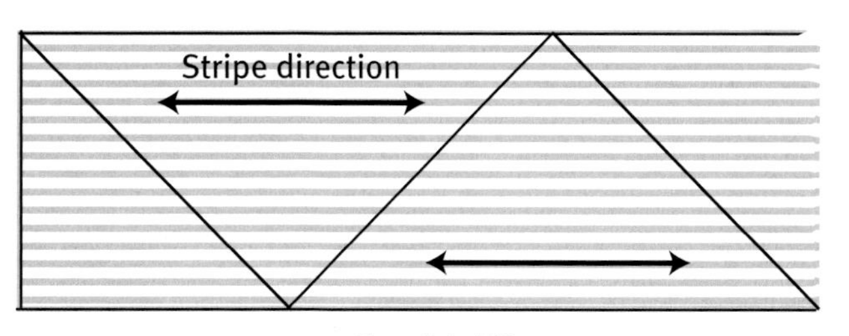

Template DD

HOUSE BLOCK ASSEMBLY DIAGRAM

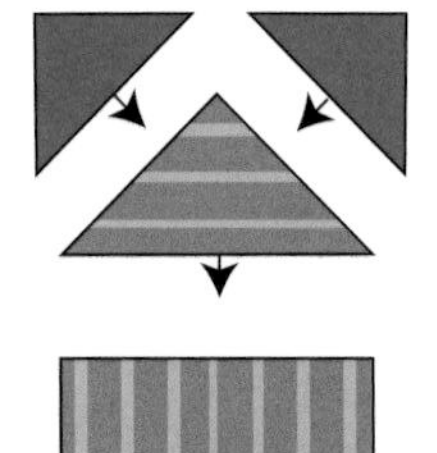

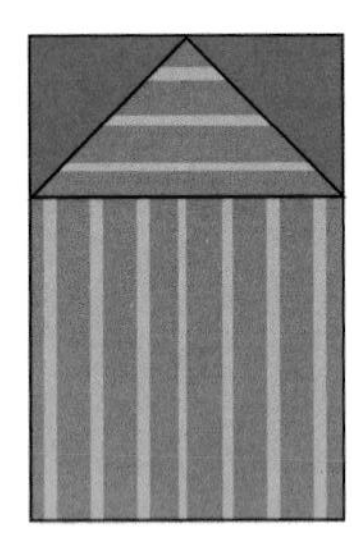

PARTIAL HOUSE BLOCK ASSEMBLY DIAGRAM

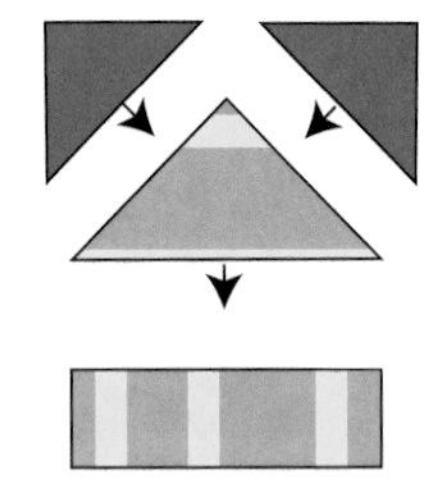

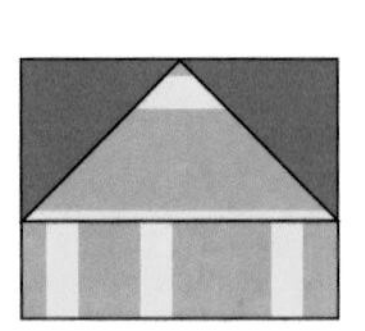

BORDER CORNER BLOCK ASSEMBLY DIAGRAM

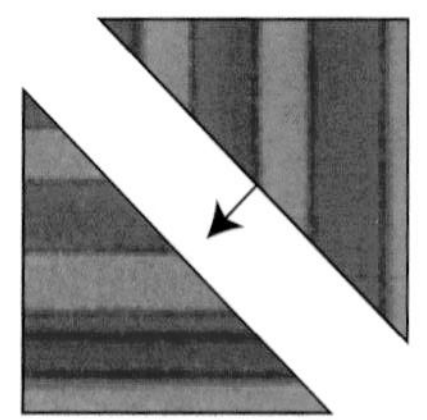

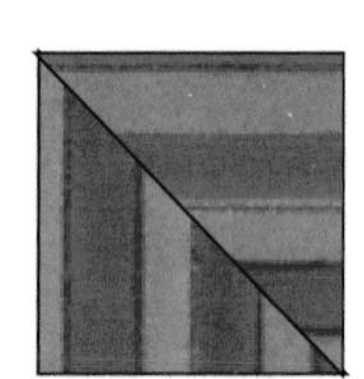

MAKING THE QUILT

Use a 1/4in (6mm) seam allowance throughout.

Assembling the blocks

For each house, take one striped roof and a matching base plus two of the smaller plain triangles (see block assembly diagram). Sew the plain triangles to the striped roof triangle one side at a time. Sew the base to the roof.
Make 114 houses.
Make 6 partial houses with roofs for the bottom row of the quilt.

Assembling the central panel

Place the blocks on a design wall and move them around until you have a pleasing arrangement of houses in columns (see quilt assembly diagram). Column 1 has 10 whole houses. Column 2 has a partial house at the top and at the bottom and 9 whole houses in between. Alternate this arrangement to make 12 columns in total.
Sew the blocks into columns. Sew the columns together.

Assembling the borders

Following the block assembly diagram and photo, flip the half-square trlangles for the border corners so the stripes face correctly. Sew two triangles together (to make a corner square). Make 3 more similar corners.
Sew the longer border lengths to the sides. Sew a corner to each end of the shorter borders. Sew the shorter borders to the top and bottom of the quilt.

FINISHING THE QUILT

Press the quilt top. Seam the backing pieces, using a 1/4in (6mm) seam allowance, to form a piece approx. 78in x 93in (198cm x 236cm). Layer the quilt top, batting and backing and baste together (see page 148).
Using machine quilting thread quilt in the ditch between blocks and also following the stripes of the fabrics within the blocks. Trim the quilt edges and attach the binding (see page 149).

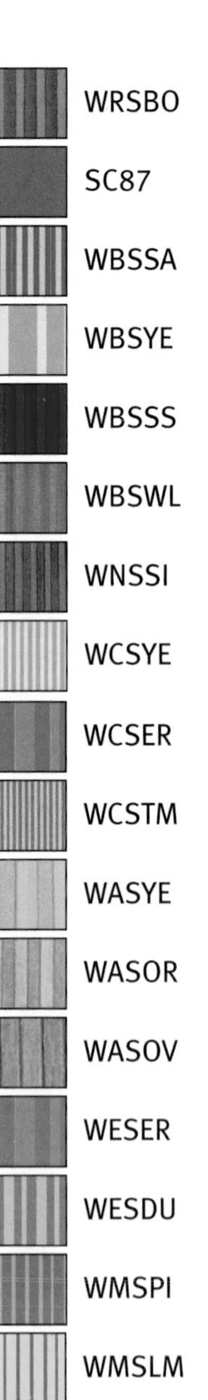

QUILT ASSEMBLY DIAGRAM

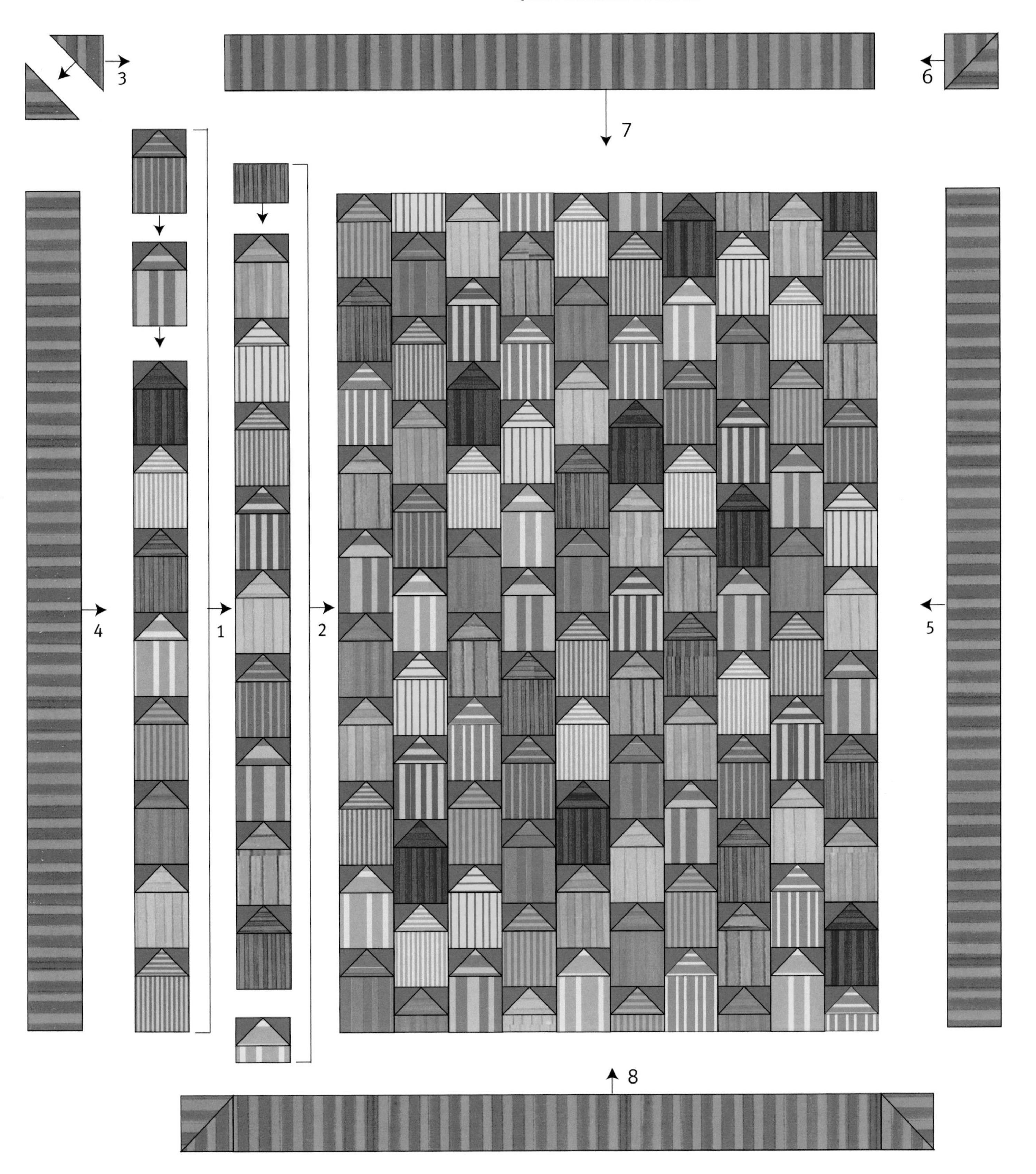

alba *

Liza Prior Lucy

This quilt has a central panel with 50 snowball blocks, each with a fussy cut flower, alternating wih 49 checkerboard 16-patch blocks. Each row in each 16-patch block consists of two ochre-coloured squares alternating with two contrasting 'jewel' colours. The border is also fussy cut to centre a motif along the centre of each border, finished with a 16-patch block at each corner.

SIZE OF QUILT

The finished quilt will measure approx. 66in x 78in (168cm x 198cm)

MATERIALS

CORSAGE		
Gold	GP149GD	3yd (2.85cm)
STRIPED HERALDIC		
Maroon	GP153MR	2yd (1.9cm)
SPOT		
Lichen	GP70LC	⅝yd (60cm)
Ochre*	GP70OC	⅜yd (35cm)
Magenta	GP70MG	¼yd (25cm)
Shocking	GP70SG	¼yd (25cm)
Grape	GP70GP	¼yd (25cm)
Orange	GP70OR	¼yd (25cm)
Red	GP70RD	¼yd (25cm)
ROMAN GLASS		
Gold*	GP01GD	⅜yd (35cm)
FERNS		
Yellow*	GP147YE	⅜yd (35cm)
Purple	GP147PU	¼yd (25cm)
Red	GP147RD	¼yd (25cm)
ABORIGINAL DOTS		
Ochre*	GP71OC	⅜yd (35cm)
Ocean	GP71ON	¼yd (25cm)

Backing Fabric
FERNS

Purple	GP147PU	5yd (4.6m)

Binding Fabric
ROMAN GLASS

Gold	GP01GD	⅝yd (60cm)

Batting
74in x 86in (188cm x 218.5cm)

Quilting Thread
Machine quilting thread

Note * INDICATES 'OCHRE' FABRIC

CUTTING OUT

From GP153MR, cut all four borders, centring a motif down the length of each strip. Cut four strips down the entire 2yd (183cm) length, each 6½in (16.5cm) wide. Then, choosing one of the motifs for the centre of each border, cut two strips 66½in (169cm) long and two strips 54½in (138.5cm) long.

For the snowball blocks From GP149GD, fussy cut 50 6½in (16.5cm) squares, centring a blossom in each square.
From GP70LC, cut 200 2in (5cm) squares.

For the 16-patch blocks You do not need to place each fabric as in the original. The checkerboard 16-patch blocks alternate ochre and jewel tone squares as shown in the assembly diagram. Each checkerboard block is made up of 16 squares, 8 ochre and 8 jewel.
From ochre fabrics GP01GD, GP147YE, GP71OC, GP70OC cut 106 2in (5cm) squares from each different fabric (424 squares in total).
From jewel fabrics GP70MG, GP70SG, GP70GP, GP70OR, GP70RD, GP147PU, GP147RD, GP71ON cut 53 2in (5cm) squares from each different fabric (424 squares).

Binding
Cut 8 strips 2½in (6.4cm) wide across the width of the fabric in GP01GD.

Backing
Cut two lengths 88in (223.5cm) x width of fabric in GP147PU.

ASSEMBLING THE BLOCKS

For each snowball block, choose one fussy cut GP149GD 6½in (16.5cm) square and four GP70LC 2in (5cm) squares.

Sew the small squares to the corners of the large square as in the snowball block assembly diagram. Make 50 snowball blocks in this way.

For each checkerboard block, choose 2 squares from each of the ochre fabrics and 1 square from each of the jewel fabrics. Lay out a checkerboard so that the upper left corner is an ochre, and alternate the ochres with the jewels as in the assembly diagram. Sew each row of 4 squares. Sew the rows together. Make 53 checkerboard blocks.

SNOWBALL BLOCK ASSEMBLY DIAGRAM

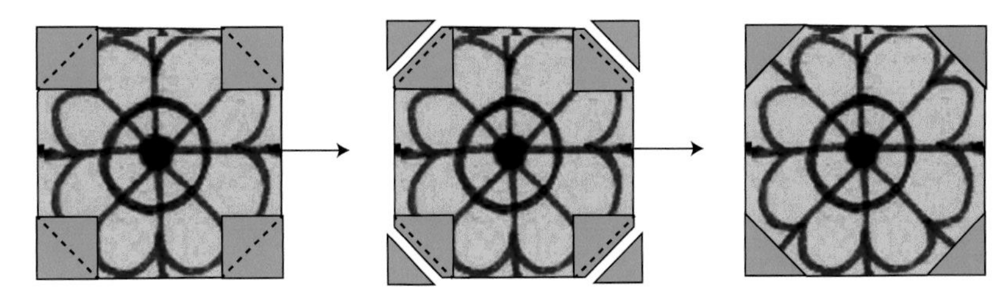

16-PATCH BLOCK ASSEMBLY DIAGRAM

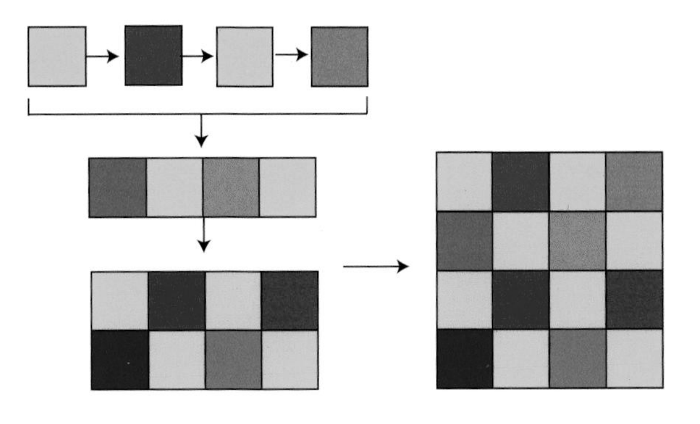

MAKING THE QUILT

Use a ¼in (6mm) seam allowance throughout.

Following the quilt assembly diagram and starting with a snowball block in the upper left, alternate snowballs and checkerboards, 9 blocks across and 11 blocks down. Make sure the snowball flowers are upright.

Sew the 9 blocks into rows. Sew the rows together.

Place the quilt central panel on a design wall and arrange the 4 borders so that the directional motif in the centre of each border seems to be continuous around the centre. Refer to the photo on page 106 to see this. Sew the two side borders to the quilt. Sew a checkerboard block on each end of the shorter borders. Sew the top and bottom borders to the central panel.

FINISHING THE QUILT

Press the quilt top. Remove the selvedge on the two backing pieces. Sew panels together making a back approx. 80in x 88in (203.2cm x 223.5cm). Layer the quilt top, batting and backing and baste together (see page 148).

Using machine quilting thread quilt in the ditch between the blocks. Additionally, quilt straight lines diagonally across the square patches in both directions to create a diamond pattern, and follow the contours of the floral shapes on the snowball blocks. Trim the quilt edges and attach the binding (see page 149).

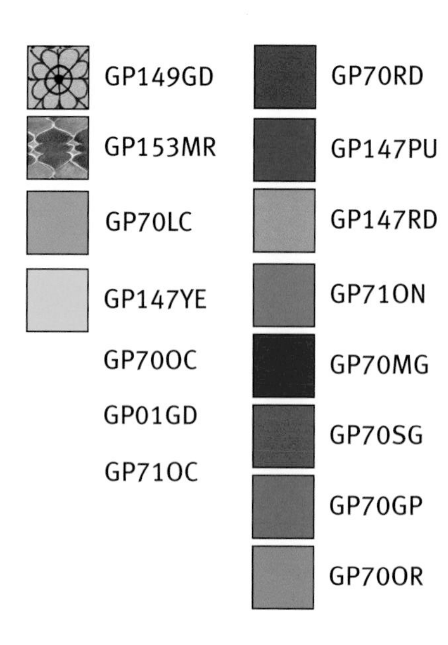

QUILT ASSEMBLY DIAGRAM

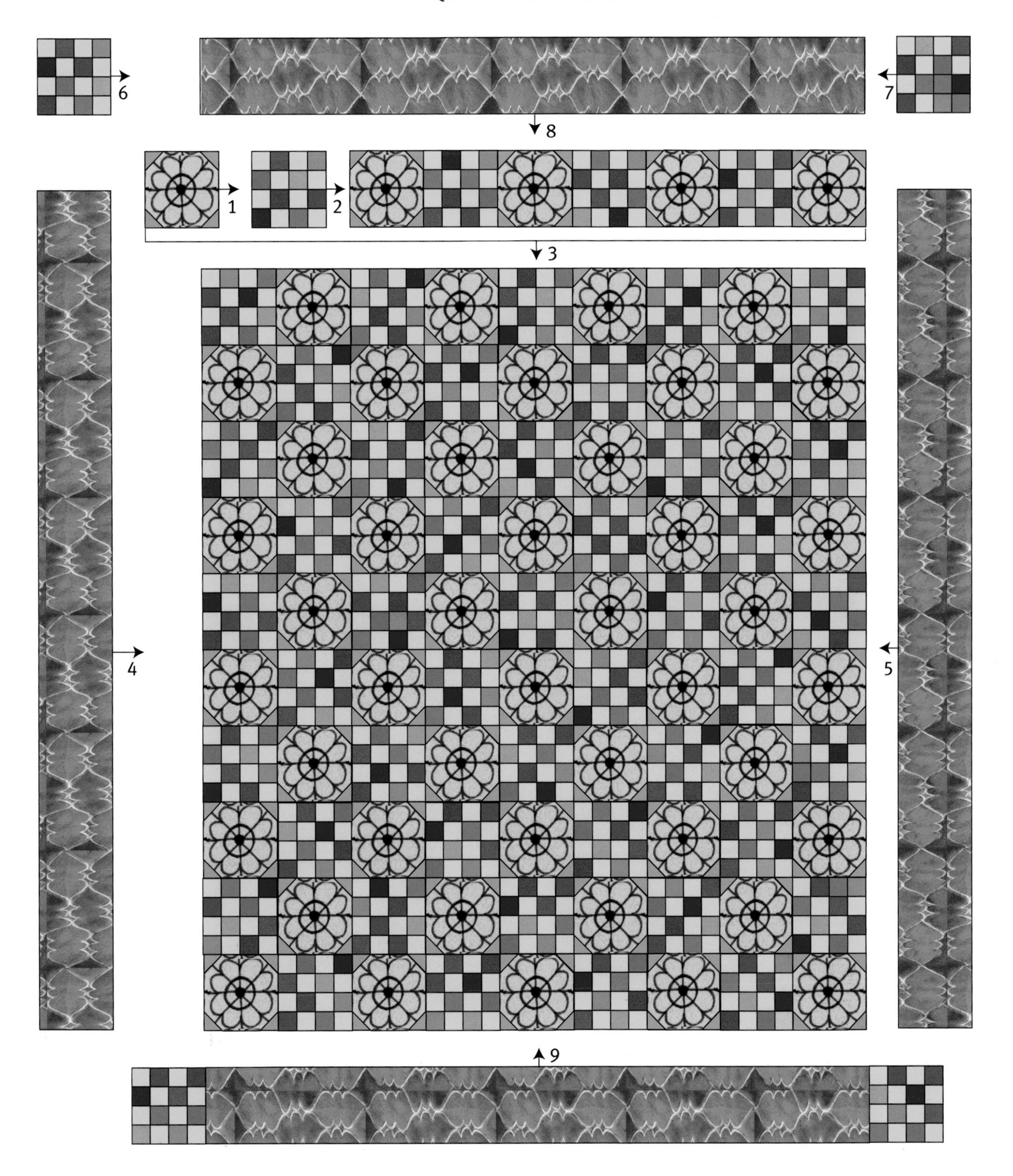

cloudy skies **

Liza Prior Lucy

This is a scrappy quilt. Except for the border, the centre and the very light half-square triangles, it isn't necessary to place each fabric exactly as in the original. Just be sure to use the light fabrics in the light areas, the mediums in the medium areas, and the darks in the dark areas.

SIZE OF QUILT

The finished quilt will measure approx. 80in (203cm) square

MATERIALS

Patchwork Fabrics

For borders and medium-toned block pieces:

FERNS		
Periwinkle	GP147PE	$2\frac{1}{2}$yd (2.3m)

For large light-toned triangles

SPOT		
Sky	GP70SK	$1\frac{1}{4}$yd (1.2m)

For light-toned block pieces

MILLEFIORE		
Pastel	GP92PT	$\frac{1}{4}$yd (25cm)
Lilac	GP92LI	$\frac{1}{4}$yd (25cm)
SPOT		
China Blue	GP70CI	$\frac{1}{4}$yd (25cm)
LAKE BLOSSOMS		
Sky	GP93SK	$\frac{1}{4}$yd (25cm)
CREASED		
Blue	BM50BL	$\frac{1}{4}$yd (25cm)

For medium-toned block pieces

ROMAN GLASS		
Blue	GP01BL	$\frac{3}{8}$yd (35cm)
CURLY BASKETS		
Delft	PJ66DF	$\frac{3}{8}$yd (35cm)
GUINEA FLOWER		
Blue	GP59BL	$\frac{3}{8}$yd (35cm)
ABORIGINAL DOTS		
Delft	GP71DF	$\frac{3}{8}$yd (35cm)

For dark-toned block pieces

PAPERWEIGHT		
Cobalt	GP20CB	$\frac{1}{2}$yd (50cm)
MILLEFIORE		
Blue	GP92BL	$\frac{1}{2}$yd (50cm)
BRASSICA		
Blue	PJ51BL	$\frac{1}{2}$yd (50cm)
ABORIGINAL DOTS		
Periwinkle	GP71PE	$\frac{1}{2}$yd (50cm)
Iris	GP71IR	$\frac{1}{2}$yd (50cm)
SPOT		
Sapphire	GP79SP	$\frac{1}{2}$yd (50cm)

For centre medallion

BRANDON'S BROCADE		
Blue	BM48BL	1yd (90cm)

Note The medallion must be cut from one of the centre motifs of the printed fabric. It will be cut to a $16\frac{1}{2}$in (41.8cm) square. It may be possible to achieve this from as little as $\frac{1}{2}$yd (45cm) but to be safe you need a 1yd (90cm) piece.

Backing Fabric

CREASED		
Blue	BM50BL	6yd (5.5m)

Binding

CREASED		
Blue	BM50BL	$\frac{3}{4}$yd (70cm)

Batting

88in x 88in (224cm x 224cm)

Quilting Thread

Machine quilting thread

CUTTING OUT

Borders

From GP147PE (cutting along the fabric length) cut two equal rectangles of $8\frac{1}{2}$in x $80\frac{1}{2}$in (21.6cm x 204.5cm) for the top and bottom borders. Cut two equal rectangles of $8\frac{1}{2}$in x $64\frac{1}{2}$in (21.6cm x 164cm) for the two sides.

Blocks

The quilt is made up of two shades of block: 28 light and 32 dark blocks. From GP70SK cut 60 $4\frac{7}{8}$in (12.4cm) squares. Cut each square diagonally (corner to corner) to make two triangles from each square (120 triangles).

For each of the 28 light blocks, choose one of the medium-toned fabrics, cut one $4\frac{7}{8}$in (12.4cm) square and then cut diagonally to make two triangles. Then from the same fabric cut four squares, each measuring $2\frac{1}{2}$in (6.4cm). From one of the light fabrics, cut four squares, each measuring $2\frac{1}{2}$in (6.4cm).

For each of the 32 dark blocks, choose one of the dark fabrics, cut one $4\frac{7}{8}$in (12.4cm) square and cut diagonally to make two triangles. From the same fabric, cut four squares, each $2\frac{1}{2}$in (6.4cm). From one of the light fabrics, cut four squares, each measuring $2\frac{1}{2}$in (6.4cm).

BLOCK ASSEMBLY DIAGRAMS

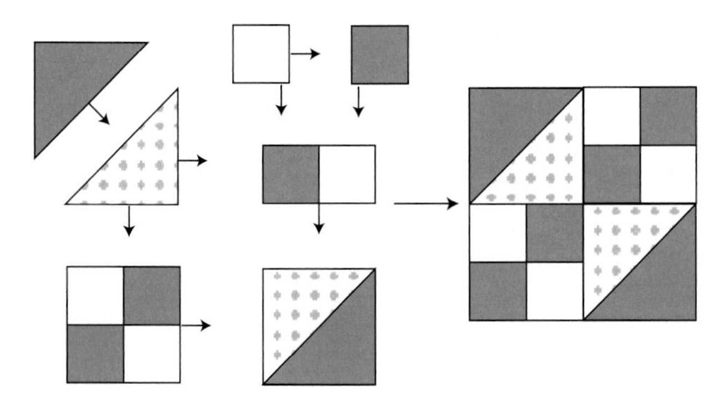

Light Block

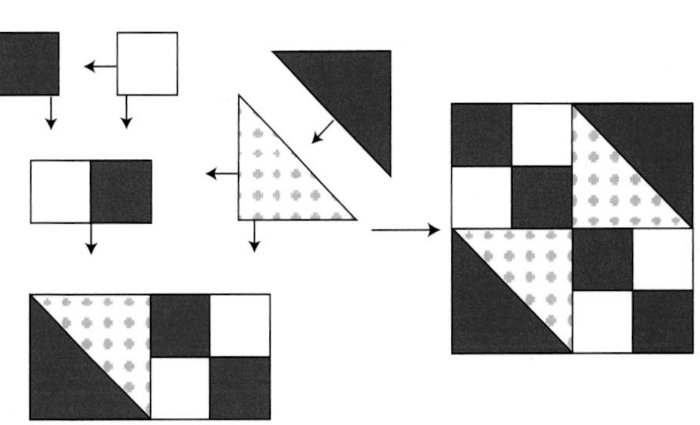

Dark Block

Centre medallion
Fussy cut one of the motifs from the centre of BM48BL. Cut one 16½in (42cm) square.

Binding
Cut 2½in (6.4cm) wide strips on the bias of the fabric in BM50BL, cutting sufficient strips to make a sewn length of at least 336in (854cm).

Backing
In BM50BL, cut 2 pieces 90in (228.6cm) and 1 piece 31in (78.7cm), cut into 3 pieces each 12in x 31in (30.5cm x 78.7cm). Sew end to end to create a piece 12in x 93in (30.5cm x 236.2cm), trimmed to 90in (228.6cm). Remove selvedges and sew one wide piece to the pieced panel, and the other wide piece on the other side of the pieced panel. The stitched panel measures approx 92in x 90in (233.7cm x 228.6cm).

MAKING THE QUILT
Use a ¼in (6mm) seam allowance throughout. The dark and light blocks are made in the same way using the fabrics described earlier. To make the half-square triangle units for the light blocks, take one triangle of GP70SK and one triangle of a medium fabric and sew them together along the long side. Press. To make the half-square triangle units for the dark blocks, repeat this with a GP70SK triangle and a dark triangle. Repeat the process to make 120 half-square triangle units in total.

For a light block, take two matching half-square triangle units, four medium 2½in (6.4cm) squares (to match the half-square triangle medium fabric) and four light 2½in (6.4cm) squares. Arrange and sew together the units as shown in the block assembly diagram on page 111. Make 28 blocks like this in total. Repeat this process to make 32 dark blocks.

Lay out the dark and light blocks and the centre panel following the order shown in the block layout diagram. Note that the design requires that some blocks are rotated 90 degrees. The blocks must be placed so that the overall effect is chains of dark-coloured squares criss-crossing with medium-coloured squares.

BLOCK LAYOUT DIAGRAM

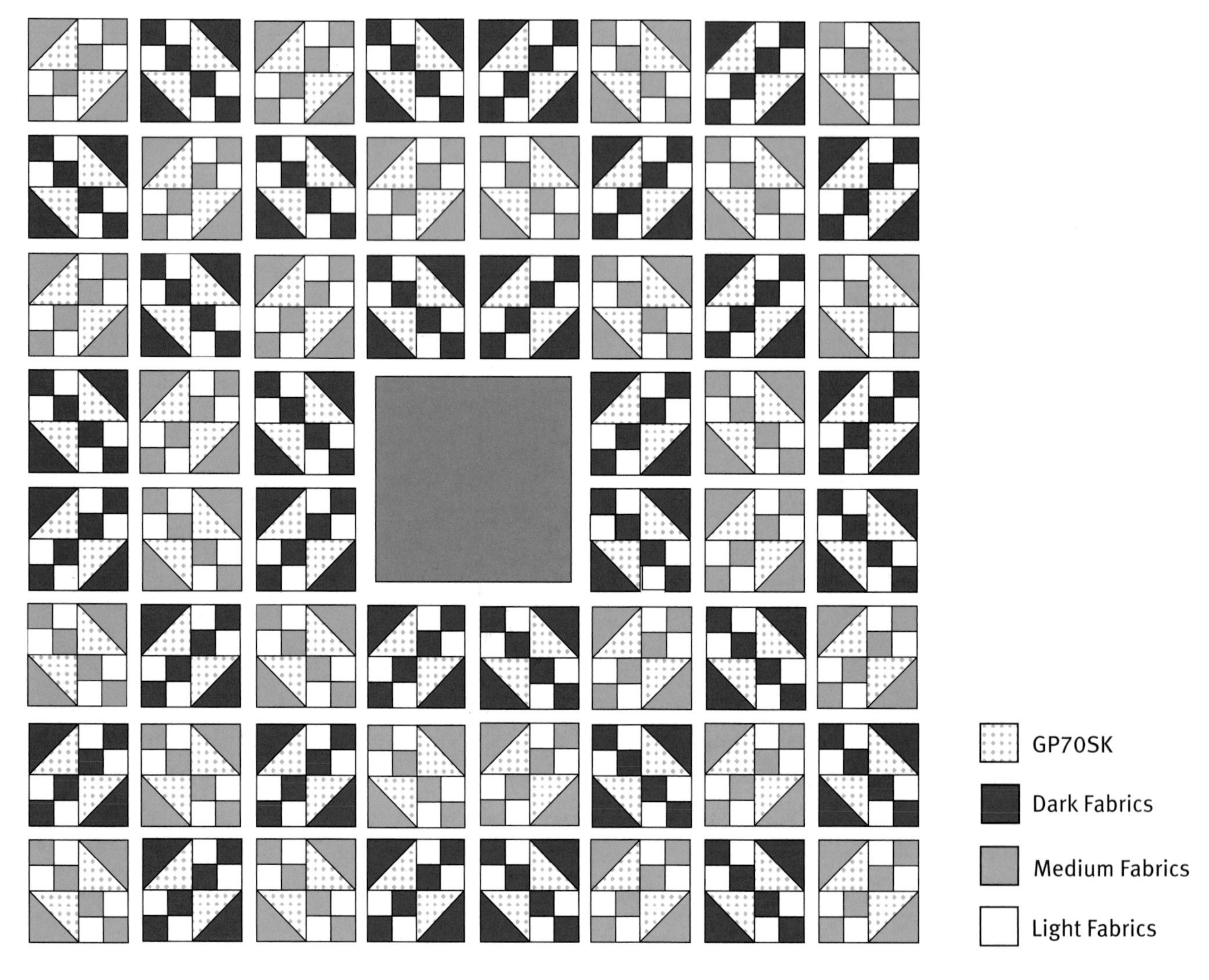

Follow the quilt assembly diagram to sew the blocks into rows. Note that 2 short rows (6 blocks in total) need to be pieced first before being sewn to the right-hand and left-hand sides of the central panel.

Add the borders by sewing the side borders first, followed by the top and bottom borders.

FINISHING THE QUILT
Press the quilt top. Trim the backing to form a piece approx. 88in x 88in (223.5cm x 223.5cm). Layer the quilt top, batting and backing and baste together (see page 148).

Using machine quilting thread quilt in the ditch between the patches and also following the contours of the fabric patterns within the blocks. Trim the quilt edges and attach the binding (see page 149).

QUILT ASSEMBLY DIAGRAM

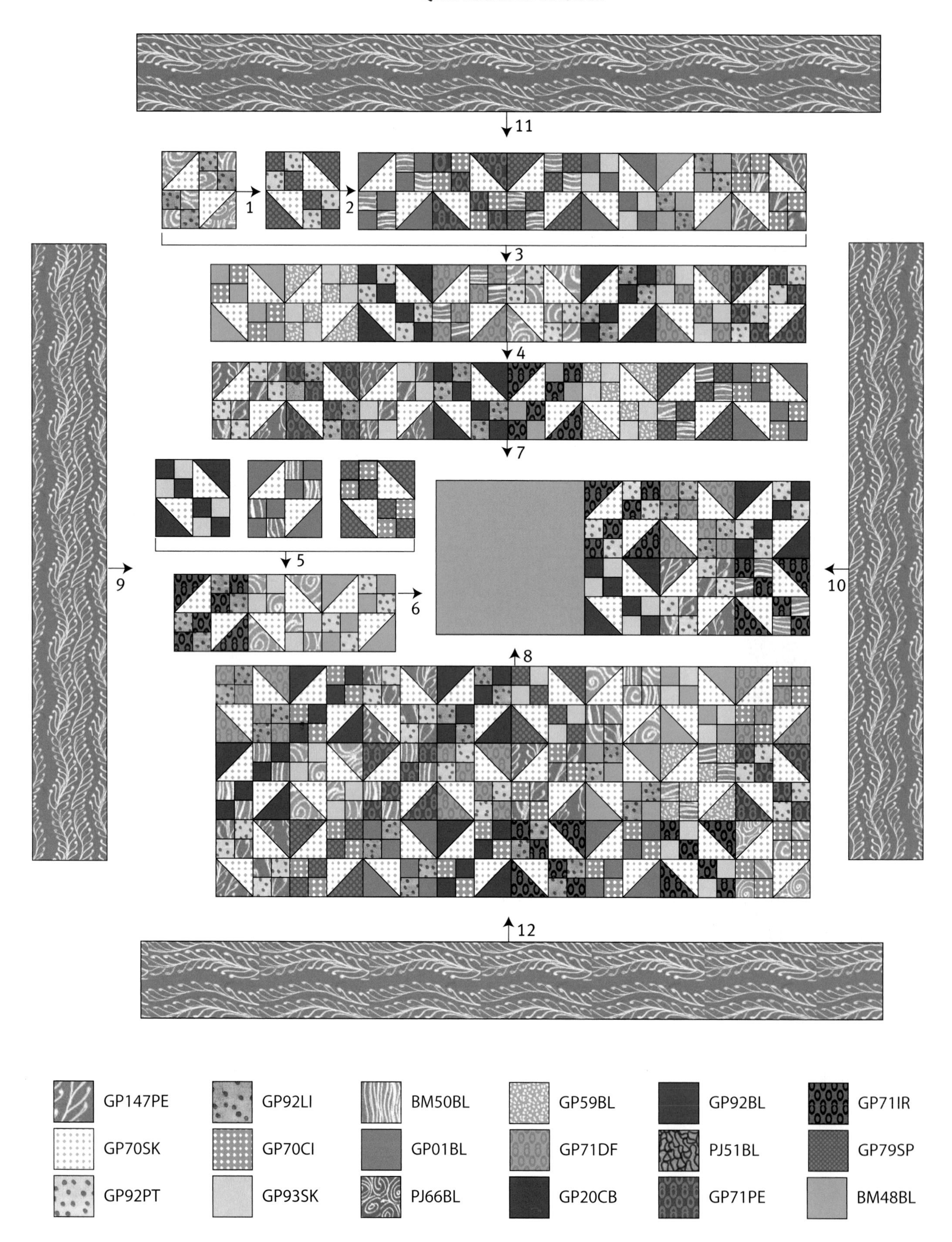

losing my marbles **

Julie Stockler

This quilt consists of 289 squares, each 3½in (8.9cm) finished. There are also 115 circles appliquéd to the centre of some of the squares. By its very nature, this is a scrappy quilt, so you can choose how many circles to appliqué. Those shown here were hand appliquéd. The quilt could be made with far fewer fabrics as long as you choose a wide assortment of colours.

SIZE OF QUILT

The finished quilt will measure 59½in x 59½in (151cm x 151cm).

MATERIALS

Patchwork Fabrics

ABORIGINAL DOTS		
Iris	GP71IR	⅛yd (15cm)
Periwinkle	GP71PE	⅛yd (15cm)
Red	GP71RD	⅛yd (15cm)
Sweet Pea	GP71SW	⅛yd (15cm)
Terracotta	GP71TC	⅛yd (15cm)
WOVEN ALTERNATING STRIPE		
Orange	WASOR	⅛yd (15cm)
WOVEN BROAD STRIPE		
Bliss	WBSBS	⅛yd (15cm)
Subterranean	WBSSA	¼yd (25cm)
Watermelon	WBSWL	⅛yd (15cm)
WOVEN CATERPILLAR STRIPE		
Aqua	WCSAQ	⅛yd (15cm)
Sprout	WCSST	⅛yd (15cm)
CREASED		
Black	BM50BK	¼yd (25cm)
Orange	BM50OR	⅛yd (15cm)
JUPITER		
Blue	GP131BL	⅛yd (15cm)
Malachite	GP131MA	⅛yd (15cm)
Red	GP131RD	⅛yd (15cm)
MAD PLAID		
Candy	BM37CD	⅛yd (15cm)
Pastel	BM37PT	⅛yd (15cm)
Red	BM37RD	⅛yd (15cm)
MILLEFIORE		
Blue	GP92BL	¼yd (25cm)
Jade	GP92JA	⅛yd (15cm)
Tomato	GP92TM	⅛yd (15cm)
WOVEN NARROW STRIPE		
Blue	WNSBL	⅛yd (15cm)
Heliotrope	WNSHL	⅛yd (15cm)
Spring	WNSSP	⅛yd (15cm)
OMBRE		
Blue	GP117BL	¼yd (25cm)
Pink	GP117PK	¼yd (25cm)
Red	GP117RD	¼yd (25cm)
PAPERWEGHT		
Cobalt	GP20CB	⅛yd (15cm)
Jewel	GP20JE	⅛yd (15cm)
Lime	GP20LM	⅛yd (15cm)
Pink	GP20PK	¼yd (25cm)
Purple	GP20PU	⅛yd (15cm)
Teal	GP20TE	⅛yd (15cm)
ROMAN GLASS		
Pastel	GP01PT	⅛yd (15cm)
Pink	GP01PK	⅛yd (15cm)
Purple	GP01PU	⅛yd (15cm)
Red	GP01RD	¼yd (25cm)
SHOT COTTON		
Lime	SC43	⅛yd (15cm)
Pink	SC83	⅛yd (15cm)
Pool	SC71	⅛yd (15cm)
Scarlet	SC44	⅛yd (15cm)
Persimmon	SC07	⅛yd (15cm)
SPOT		
Apple	GP70AL	⅛yd (15cm)
Charcoal	GP70CC	¼yd (25cm)
Fuchsia	GP70FU	⅛yd (15cm)
Green	GP70GN	⅛yd (15cm)
Ochre	GP70OC	¼yd (25cm)
Paprika	GP70PP	⅛yd (15cm)
Peacock	GP70PC	¼yd (25cm)
Periwinkle	GP70PE	⅛yd (15cm)
Plum	GP70PL	⅛yd (15cm)
Red	GP70RD	⅛yd (15cm)
Royal	GP70RY	⅛yd (15cm)
Sapphire	GP70SP	¼yd (25cm)
Shocking	GP70SG	⅛yd (15cm)
ZIG ZAG		
Cool	BM43CL	⅛yd(15cm)
Jade	BM43JA	⅛yd (15cm)
Pink	BM43PK	⅛yd (15cm)
Warm	BM43WM	⅛yd (15cm)

Backing Fabric

ROMAN GLASS		
Red	GP01RD	4yd (3.75m)

Binding

BROAD WOVEN STRIPE		
Watermelon	WBSWL	¾yd (70cm)

Batting

68in x 68in (173cm x 173cm)

Quilting Thread

Machine quilting thread

Other Materials

Cardboard or template plastic

Templates

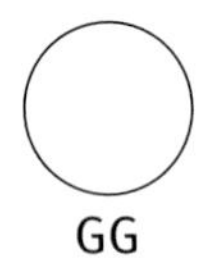

GG

CUTTING OUT

This is a scrappy quilt and it is more enjoyable to simply cut the squares randomly from your selection of fabrics. If you want to make the quilt look more like the original, the quilt assembly diagram provides a plan to follow when arranging the squares and the circle placement diagram for placing your circles. You will need 289 squares in total and 115 circles, but you can change the latter if you wish. Before you start, it will help if you sort your fabrics into basic colour groups, as shown on the quilt assembly diagram on page 118.

Using a rotary cutter and ruler, cut 4in (10.2cm) squares to create a total of 289 squares.

Using the outer circle of Template GG, cut out 1 cardboard or plastic template. Using the inner circle of template GG cut out several template circles. Using the larger template, mark and cut out the required number of 3in (7.6cm) circles from various fabrics. The circle placement diagram shows the basic colours of the circles used in the quilt.

Binding

Cut 2½in (6.4cm) wide strips on the bias using WBSWL sufficient to make a sewn length of at least 255in (648cm).

Backing

Cut 2 pieces 34½in x 68in (87.6cm x 173cm) in backing fabric GP01RD.

MAKING THE QUILT

Lay out the squares in 17 rows of 17 blocks: you can choose your own random arrangement or follow the rough guide shown in the quilt assembly diagram. Place the circles in the centres of the appropriate squares, following the suggested pattern in the circle placement

diagram if you wish. When you're happy with the placement, take a photo of the layout to refer to later.
Using a ¼in (6mm) seam allowance throughout, join the squares into 17 rows of 17 blocks, pressing seams in opposite directions on alternate rows so they will fit together neatly. Then sew the rows together.

To prepare the circle appliqués, run a line of basting stiches ⅛in (3mm) from the outside edge of the fabric circle. Place one of the inner GG templates against the centre of the wrong side of the fabric and pull the basting thread ends to draw up the fabric around the template. Press with starch and then remove the template. Repeat with all of the circles. Following your layout plan, use matching thread and small slipstitches to appliqué the circles to the relevant squares. Press the work.
Note If you prefer, you can appliqué the circles in place before you piece the rows together.

FINISHING THE QUILT
Press the quilt top. Using a ¼in (6mm) seam allowance, seam the backing pieces to form a piece approx. 68in x 68in (173cm x 173cm). Layer the quilt top, batting and backing and baste together (see page 148).
Using machine quilting thread, quilt as desired.
Trim the quilt edges and attach the binding (see page 149).

Tip
If you don't want to stitch very long rows, sew the quilt together in four quarters (approx.) and then sew the four quarters together.

QUILT ASSEMBLY DIAGRAM

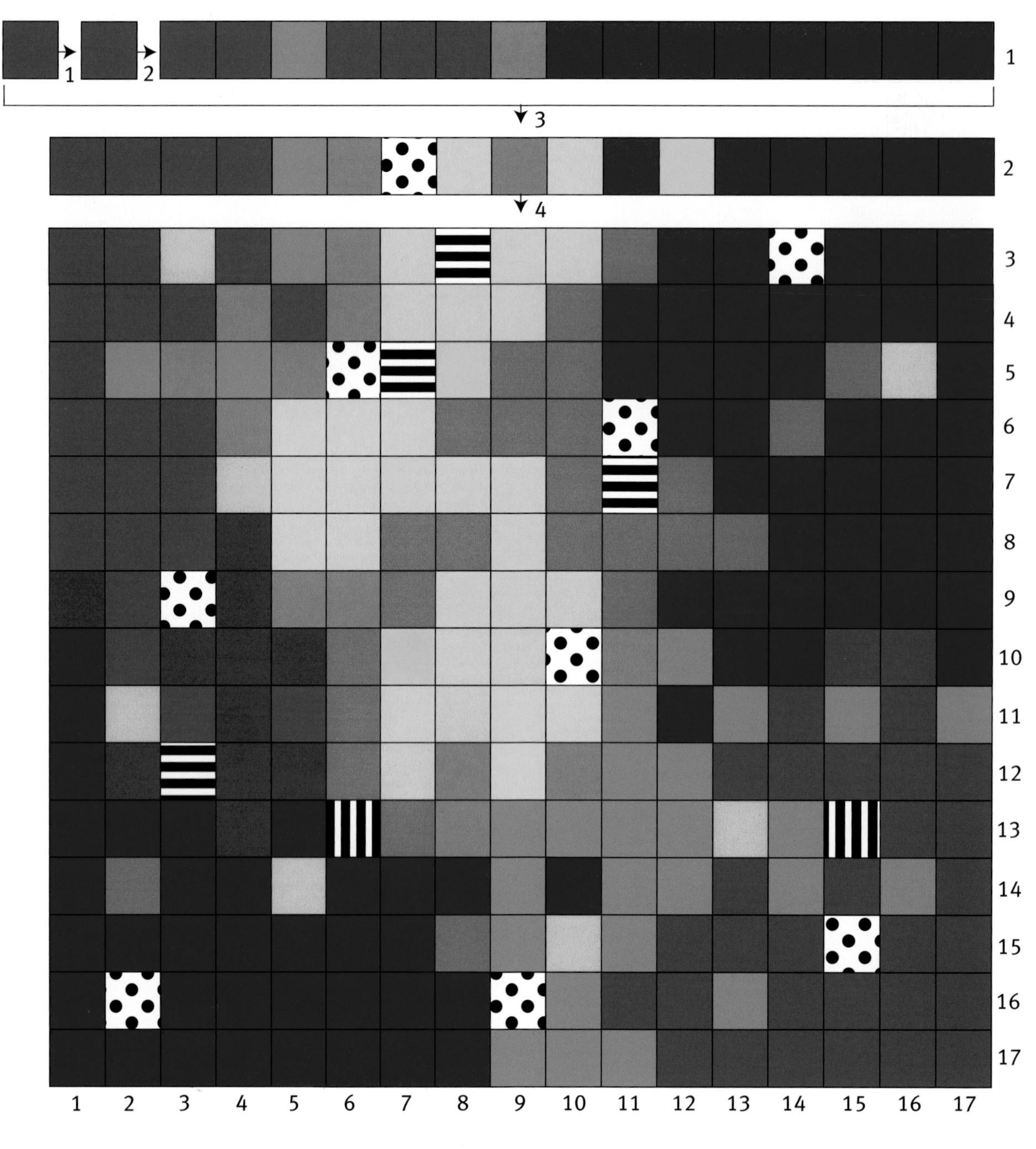

GP71IR
GP71PE
WBSBS
WBSSA
GP131BL
GP92BL
WNSBL
GP117BL
GP20CB
GP20TE
GP01PU

GP71RD
GP71TC
WASOR
WBSWL
BM50OR
GP131RD
BM37RD
GP92TM
GP117RD
GP01RD
SC44
SC07
GP70PP
GP70RD
BM43WM

WCSST
WNSSP
SC43

WNSHL
GP20PU
GP70FU
GP70PE
GP70PL
GP70RY

WCSAQ
GP131MA
GP9JA
GP20JE
SC71
GP70GN
GP70PC
GP70SP
BM43CL
BM43JA

BM37CD
GP117PK
GP20PK
GP70SG
BM43PK

BM37PT
GP20LM
GP01PT
GP70AL

GP71SW
GP01PK
SC83

GP70CC

BM50BK

GP70OC

CIRCLE PLACEMENT DIAGRAM

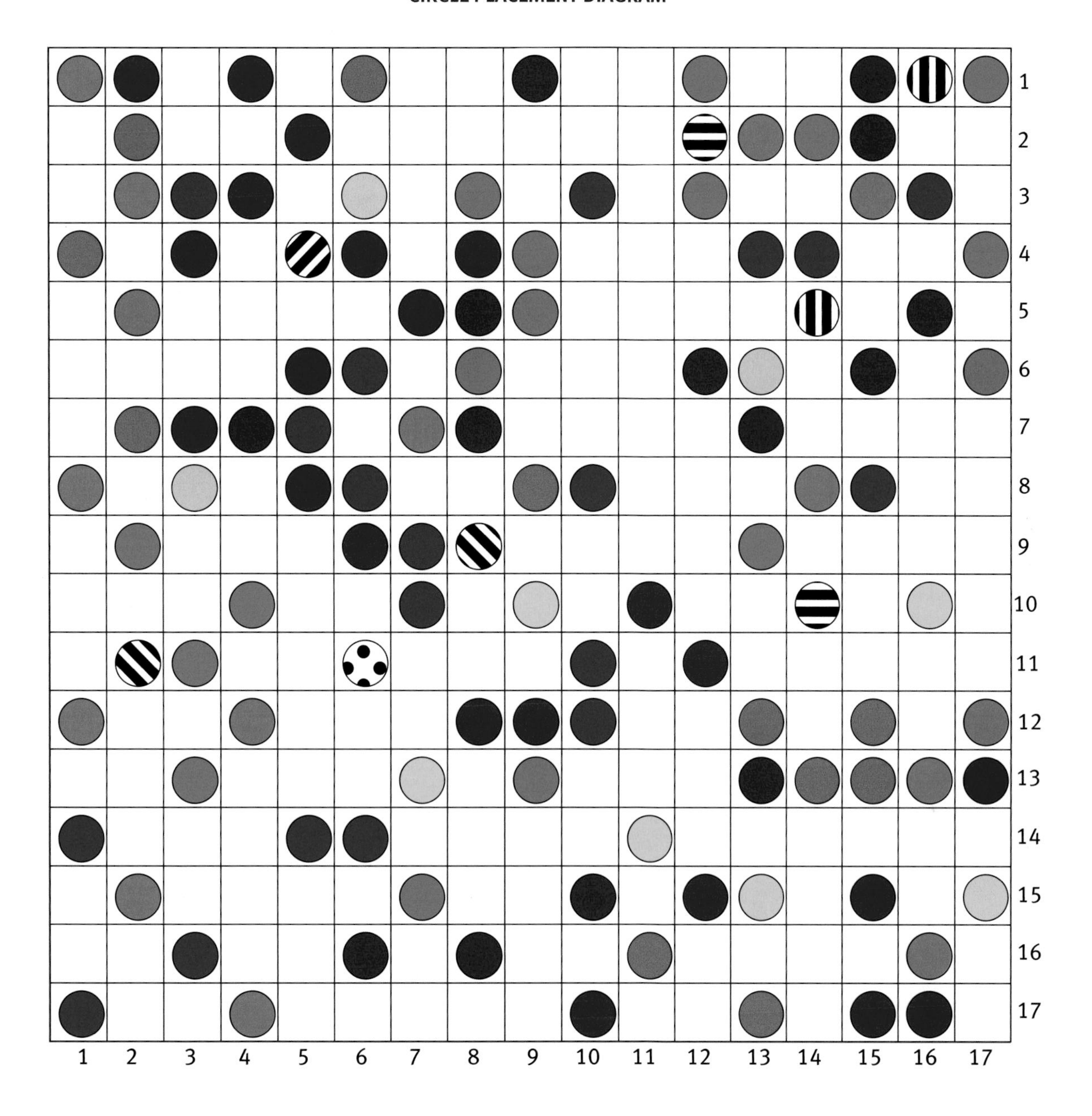

embers *

Sally Davis

This quilt is composed of 35 blocks, of which 18 are solid and 17 are pieced. In the pieced blocks, each block has 16 squares, of which eight squares are always Fern Black (GP147BK). Note that the solid squares, outer borders and binding are all cut from the same fabric Dream Brown (GP148BR), though the amount required for the binding is listed separately. As this is a scrappy quilt, you do not need to place each red and gold toned fabric as in the original.

SIZE OF QUILT

The finished quilt will measure approx. 63in x 83in (160cm x 211cm).

MATERIALS

Patchwork Fabrics

DREAM		
Brown	GP148BR	2½yd (2.3m)
ABORIGINAL DOTS		
Leafy	GP71LF	⅝yd (60cm)
Forest	GP71FO	⅛yd (15cm)
FERN		
Black	GP147BK	1yd (90cm)
BROCADE PEONY		
Wine	PJ62WN	¾yd (70cm)
BRASSICA		
Brown	PJ51BR	¼yd (25cm)
Rust	PJ51RU	¼yd (25cm)
BIG BLOOMS		
Brown	GP91BR	¼yd (25cm)
MILLEFIORE		
Orange	GP92OR	⅜yd (35cm)
Red	GP92RD	¼yd (25cm)
Tomato	GP92TM	⅛yd (15cm)
Brown	GP92BR	⅛yd (15cm)
CURLY BASKETS		
Brown	PJ66BR	⅛yd (15cm)
GUINEA FLOWER		
Yellow	GP59YE	⅛yd (15cm)
THOUSAND FLOWERS		
Red	GP144RD	⅛yd (15cm)
GLOXINIA		
Umber	PJ71UM	⅛yd (15cm)
ROMAN GLASS		
Gold	GP01GD	⅛yd (15cm)

Backing Fabric

MILLEFIORE		
Tomato	GP92TM	5⅛yd (4.7m)

Binding

DREAM		
Brown	GP148BR	¾yd (70cm)

Batting
72in x 92in (183cm x 234cm).

Quilting Thread
Machine quilting thread

CUTTING OUT

Cut the fabrics in the order stated.

Solid squares and outer borders The solid squares and outer borders are all cut in fabric GP148BR.

Outer borders Cutting down the length of fabric GP148BR, cut 2 strips 74½in (189.3cm) long x 5in (12.7cm) wide, and 2 strips 63½in (161.5cm) long x 5in (12.7cm) wide.

Solid squares Cutting across the remaining width of fabric GP148BR, cut 18 squares each 10½in (26.7cm).

Inner borders In fabric GP71LF, cut 6 strips 2½in (6.4cm) wide across the width of the fabric. Join these together with ¼in (6mm) seams and cut 2 borders 70½in (179cm) long and 2 borders 54½in (138.5cm) long.

Pieced squares Cut the remaining 16 fabrics across the width into 3in (7.6cm) wide strips. From each of these strips cut 9 squares 3in (7.6cm). This will give 144 squares and you will need 136. If you prefer to follow the quilt assembly diagram more closely, cut 14 squares from each strip, which will allow you to use some colours more than others.

Binding
Cut 8 strips 2½in (6.4cm) wide across the width of the fabric in GP148BR.

Backing
Cut 2 pieces 35½in x 92in (90cm x 234cm) in GP92TM.

MAKING THE PIECED BLOCKS

Use a ¼in (6mm) seam allowance throughout.

Each pieced block is a 16-patch made up of 3in (7.6cm) squares. Each row of each block has 2 squares in GP147BK and 2 in another fabric/colour. You can choose the other colours from the list of materials.

Following the block assembly diagram, lay out the 16 squares for each pieced block, alternating GP147BK squares with squares in other fabrics. Start rows 1 and 3 with a GP147BK square and rows 2 and 4 with a square in another fabric. In this quilt, the same two fabrics were used in each row, but you could place them completely randomly. Stitch the 4 squares in each row together, then stitch the 4 rows together to complete the block, as shown. Make up all the pieced blocks (17 in total).

BLOCK ASSEMBLY DIAGRAM

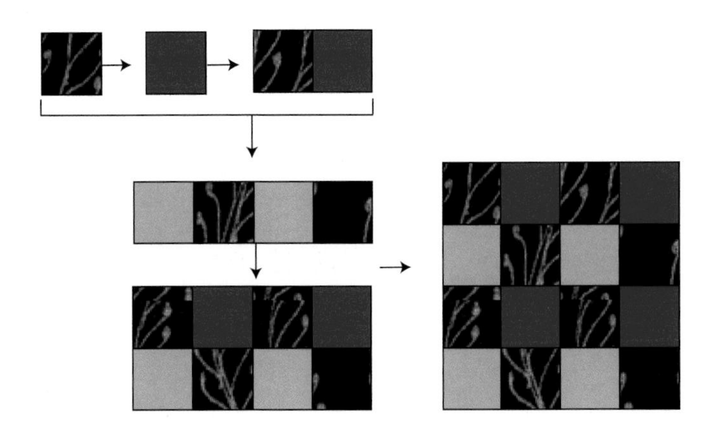

MAKING THE QUILT
Starting with a solid square in the top left corner and alternating solid squares and pieced blocks, lay out 7 rows of 5 blocks each. Stitch the 5 blocks in each row together, then stitch the 7 rows together to complete the quilt centre, as shown in the quilt assembly diagram.

Stitch the side inner borders to the quilt centre first, then add the top and bottom inner borders. Add the outer borders in the same way.

FINISHING THE QUILT
Press the quilt top. Using a ¼in (6mm) seam allowance, seam the backing pieces to form a piece approx. 72in x 92in (183cm x 234cm). Layer the quilt top, batting and backing and baste together (see page 148).

Using machine quilting thread, quilt in the ditch for the squares with outlining of the flowers. Use meander quilting on the border. Trim the quilt edges and attach the binding (see page 149).

GP148BR

GP71LF

GP147BK

GP71FO
PJ62WN
PJ51RU
GP92RD
GP92TM
GP144RD

PJ51BR
GP91BR
GP92OR
GP92BR
PJ66BR
GP59YE
PG71UM
GP01GD

QUILT ASSEMBLY DIAGRAM

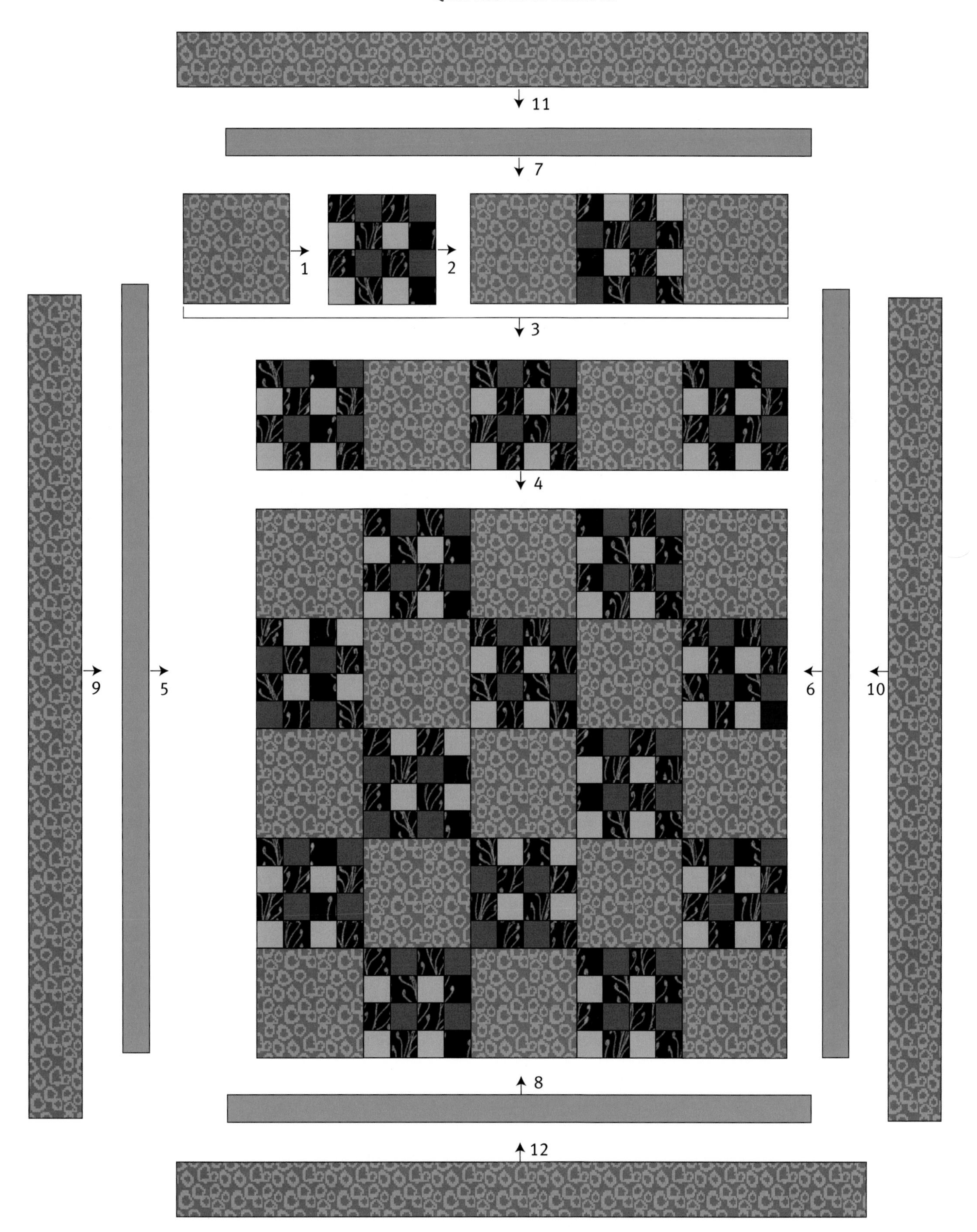

whirligig **

Judy Baldwin

This quilt is composed of blue and red/pink pinwheel blocks, set on point against a background of a vibrant blue floral fabric. The outer sections of each block are all cut from the same pale blue fabric (Lake Blossom Sky: GP93SK) to provide continuity across the quilt and allow the darker colours of the pinwheels to stand out.

SIZE OF QUILT
The finished quilt will measure approx. 70in (178cm) square.

MATERIALS
Patchwork Fabrics

LAKE BLOSSOMS		
Sky	GP93SK	1½yd (1.4m)
Blue	GP93BL	¼yd (25cm)
DREAM		
Blue	GP148BL	1¾yd (1.6m)
SPOT		
Shocking	GP70SG	¼yd (25cm)
Fuchsia	GP70FU	¼yd (25cm)
Sapphire	GP70SP	¼yd (25cm)
GLOXINIA		
Pink	PJ71PK	¼yd (25cm)
CURLY BASKETS		
Cobalt	PJ66CB	¼yd (25cm)
Red	PJ66RD	¼yd (25cm)
BRASSICA		
Red	PJ51RD	¼yd (25cm)
Blue	PJ51BL	¼yd (25cm)
MILLEFIORE		
Blue	GP92BL	¼yd (25cm)
SERPENTINE		
Magenta	GP145MG	¼yd (25cm)
BOUFFANT		
Red	PJ61RD	¼yd (25cm)
Inner Border		
SPOT		
Fuchsia	GP70FU	½yd (50cm)
Outer Border		
REGENCY DAISY		
Blue	GP146BL	1½yd (1.4m)

Backing fabric

MILLEFIORE		
Blue	GP92BL	4½yd (4.2m)

Binding

CURLY BASKETS		
Cobalt	PJ66CB	⅝yd (60cm)

Batting
78in x 78in (198cm x 198cm)

Quilting thread
Machine quilting thread

Template

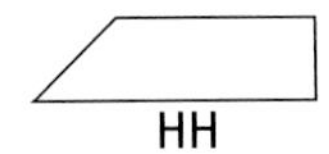

CUTTING OUT
The pinwheel blocks are pieced from three different fabrics – a dark blue and a red or pink print for the inner sections of the pinwheels and a pale blue (GP93SK) for all the outer sections. GP93SK is used on all the blocks; for the inner sections, choose one dark blue and one pink/red fabric for each block. In total, there are 23 whole pinwheels and 4 half pinwheels. Cut the fabrics in the order stated.

Pinwheel blocks
For small triangles from GP93SK: cut 4 strips 5¼in (13.4cm) wide across the width of the fabric. Sub-cut each strip into 5¼in (13.4cm) squares. Each strip will give you 7 squares and you need 25 squares. Sub-cut each square in half diagonally in both directions to yield 100 triangles.
For small triangles from each of the five blue fabrics available (GP93BL, GP70SP, PJ66CB, PJ51BL, GP92BL): cut 1 strip 5¼in (13.4cm) wide across the width of the fabric. From each strip cut 5 squares each 5¼in (13.4cm) square. Sub-cut each square in half diagonally in both directions. This will give a total of 100 triangles. Keep the triangles in matching sets of four.

Tip
I based my outer border width on the size of the fabric pattern repeat, cutting the border strips about 5⅞in (15cm) wide. This enabled me to cut midway between every other row of daisies, so that the space between the inner border and the line of daisies was the same on every side.

For small triangles from each of the seven red/pink fabrics available (GP70SG, GP70FU, PJ71PK, PJ66RD, PJ51RD, GP145MG, PJ61RD): cut a strip 5¼in (13.4cm) wide x 21in (53.4cm) long. Sub-cut each strip into 4 squares each 5¼in (13.4cm) square. Sub-cut each square in half diagonally in both directions (16 triangles per strip). This will give a total of 112 triangles and you will need 100. Keep the triangles in matching sets of four.
From GP93SK cut 12 strips 1⅝in (4.1cm) wide across the width of the fabric. Using Template HH, sub-cut each strip into 9 shapes, rotating the template 180 degrees along the fabric as shown in the template HH cutting diagram for the most economical cuts. Be sure to only rotate the template – don't flip it. You need 100 shapes in total.

Setting triangles
For the larger triangles that act as background to the pinwheel blocks, from GP148BL cut 1 strip 6¼in (15.9cm) wide across the width of the fabric. Sub-cut this strip into 6 squares each 6¼in (15.9cm). Sub-cut each square in half diagonally once to yield 12 triangles.
From GP148B cut 6 strips 9in (22.9cm) wide across the width of the fabric. Sub-cut each strip into 4 squares, to yield 24 9in (22.9cm) squares. Sub-cut each

TEMPLATE HH CUTTING DIAGRAM

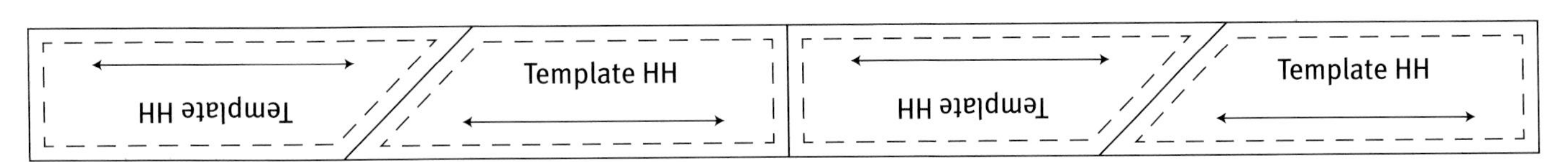

BLOCK ASSEMBLY DIAGRAMS

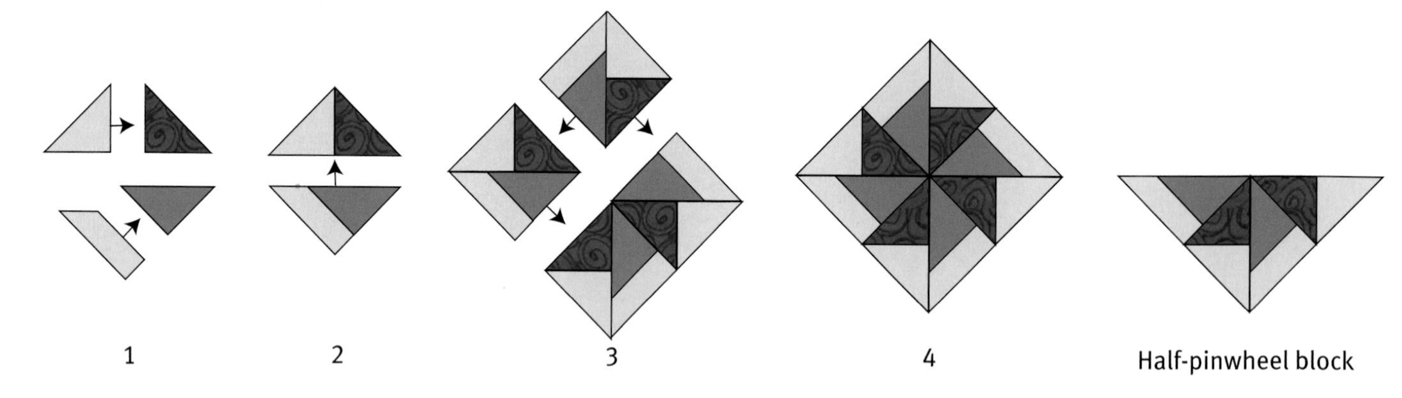

square in half diagonally once to yield 48 triangles. You will need 44.

Inner borders
In GP70FU cut 6 strips each 2in (5cm) wide across the width of the fabric.

Outer borders
In GP146BL cut 7 strips each 5⅞in (15cm) wide across the width of the fabric.

Binding
Cut 8 strips 2½in (6.4cm) wide across the width of the fabric in PJ66CB.

Backing fabric
Cut 2 pieces 40in x 78in (101.5cm x 198cm) in backing fabric GP92BL.

MAKING THE PINWHEEL BLOCKS
Use a ¼ in (6mm) seam allowance throughout.
Sew each GP93SK triangle to a darker blue triangle along one short side, as shown in the block assembly diagrams.
Sew each GP93SK Template HH shape to one short side of each red/pink triangle, aligning the units at the lower points to ensure straight sides on the unit.
For each pinwheel block, take 4 blue sections in the same fabric and 4 red.

Stitch a blue and a red section together along their long edges to make up one quarter of the block. Repeat 3 more times. Stitch together in pairs, making sure that the colours alternate, then stitch the two halves together to complete the block. Construct 23 full pinwheel blocks in this way.

Then make up 4 half pinwheel blocks, each comprising 2 blue and 2 red sections.

ASSEMBLING THE QUILT
Referring to the quilt assembly diagram, arrange the blocks in your chosen order, setting them on point in 5 vertical columns of 5, 4, 5, 4 and 5 full blocks respectively, with the background GP148BL triangles, as shown. Position the half pinwheel blocks at the top and bottom of columns 2 and 4.

Stitch the background setting triangles to the pinwheel blocks in the order shown to make diagonal segments, taking care to maintain straight sides where pieces are joined. Stitch the segments together to complete each column. Finally, join the columns together.

Join the 6 strips of GP70FU for the inner border along their short edges to make one continuous length. Measure the height of the quilt down the middle of the completed top. From the continuous strip, cut 2 borders to this length and attach 1 to each side. Then measure the width of the quilt, including both side borders, to determine the length of the top and bottom borders. Cut 2 borders to this size and attach to the top and bottom of the quilt.
Piece, cut and attach the GP146BL outer border strips in the same way.

FINISHING THE QUILT
Press the quilt top. Using a ¼in (6mm) seam allowance, seam the backing pieces to form a piece approx. 78in x 78in (198cm x 198cm). Layer the quilt top, batting and backing and baste together (see page 000).

Using machine quilting thread, quilt as preferred. Trim the quilt edges and attach the binding (see page 000).

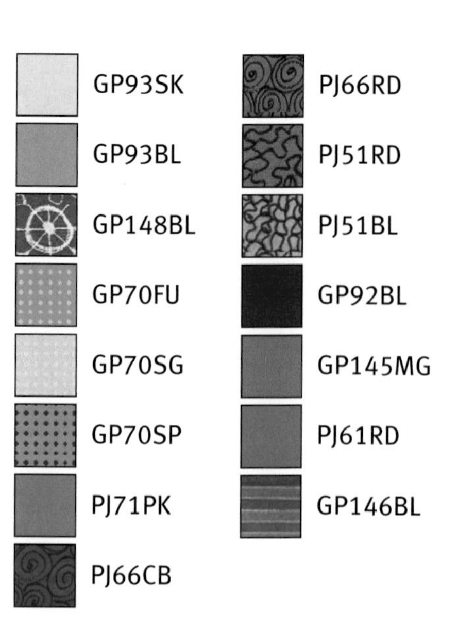

QUILT ASSEMBLY DIAGRAM

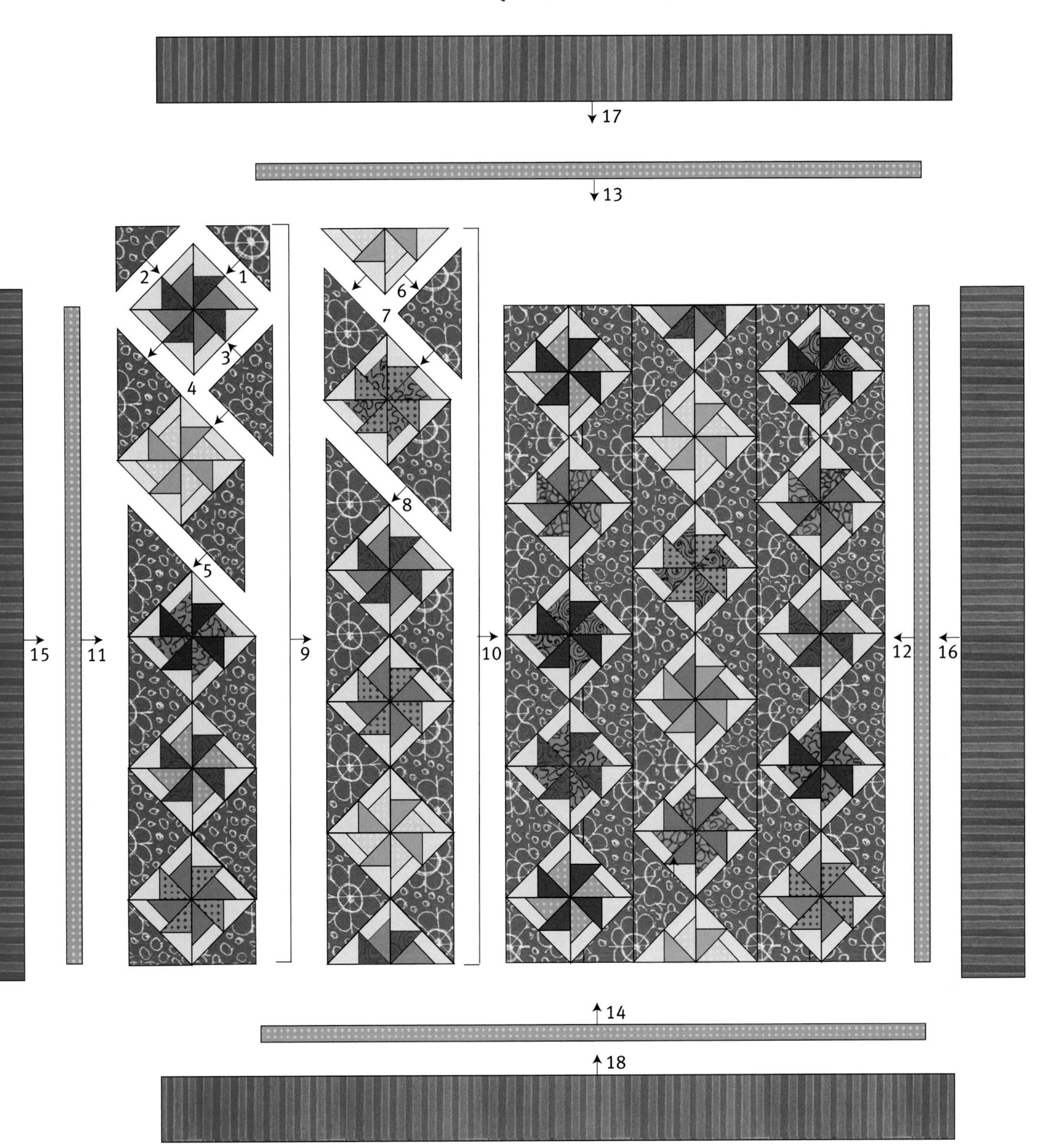

wagon wheels **

Corienne Kramer

This quilt features 36 quarter-circle blocks, each 8in (20.3cm) square (finished); when combined they make up 9 'wagon wheels'. It's a great way of using up scraps, as the individual 'spokes' of the wheels are very small. The spokes are pieced using the individual wedge template provided. The inner and outer curves are added after the spokes have been pieced.

SIZE OF QUILT

The finished quilt will measure approx. 64½in x 64½in (164cm x (164cm).

MATERIALS

Patchwork Fabrics

SHOT COTTON		
Brick	SC058	⅜yd (35cm)
Dill	SC0102	⅜yd (35cm)
Bordeaux	SC054	½yd (45cm)
Ecru	SSC024	⅛yd (15cm)
Eucalyptus	SC090	¼yd (25cm)
Galvanized	SC087	⅜yd (35cm)
Granite	SC066	⅜yd (35cm)
Lilac	SC036	⅜yd (35cm)
Moor	SC052	¼yd (25cm)
WOVEN ROMAN STRIPES		
Moss	WRSMS	¼yd (25cm)
Shadow	WRSSHD	¼yd (25cm)
Blood orange	WRSBO	¼yd (25cm)
ABORIGINAL DOTS		
Taupe	GP71TA	⅜yd (35cm)
WOVEN BROAD STRIPE		
Blue	WBSBL	¼yd (25cm)
WOVEN EXOTIC STRIPE		
Purple	WESPU	¼yd (25cm)
OMBRE		
Purple	GP117PU	¼yd (25cm)
SPOT		
Grey	GP70GY	⅜yd (35cm)
Silver	GP70SV	⅜yd (35cm)
Brown	GP70BR	¼yd (25cm)
Lichen	GP70LC	⅜yd (35cm)
PAPERWEIGHT		
Grey	GP20GY	¼yd (25cm)
PANSIES		
Purple	PJ76PU	¼yd (25cm)
THOUSAND FLOWERS		
Smoke	GP144SM	¼yd (25cm)
LOTUS LEAF		
Mauve	GP29MV	⅜yd (35cm)

Border

LOTUS LEAF		
Mauve	GP29MV	2yd (1.9m)

Backing Fabric

THOUSAND FLOWERS		
Smoke	GP144SM	4¼yd (3.8m)

Binding

SHOT COTTON		
Brick	SC058	½yd (45cm)

Batting

72in x 72in (183cm x 183cm)

Quilting thread

Machine quilting thread

Templates

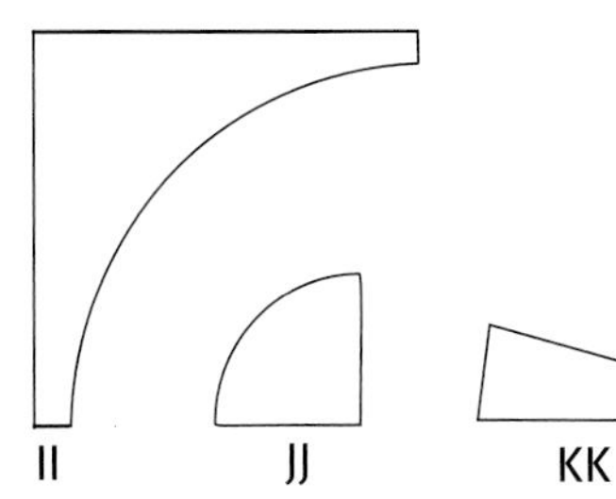

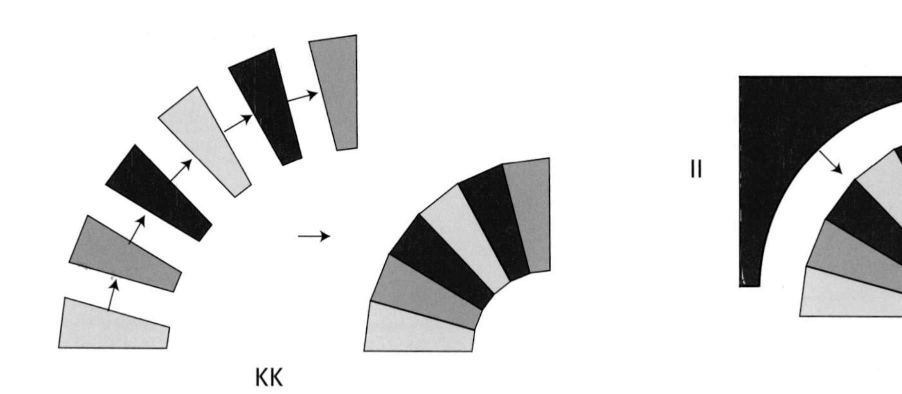

CUTTING OUT

A 9in (23cm) square of fabric is sufficient to cut 1 II template and 1 JJ template, with some left over for wedges. The fabrics used in the spokes can be used randomly as you choose.

Blocks For 1 quarter block, cut 1 of template JJ (inner curve of wheel). You will need to cut 4 for a whole wheel and 36 for the 9-wheel quilt shown here. Different fabrics were used for each section.

For 1 quarter block, cut 1 of template II (outer curve of wheel). You will need to cut 4 for a whole wheel and 36 for the 9-wheel quilt shown here. Different fabrics were used for each section.

For 1 quarter block you will need six of the wedge shapes cut using template KK. For a whole wheel you will need 24 wedges; for the whole quilt, you will need 216.

Note When cutting striped fabrics for the spokes bear in mind the stripe direction – having the stripes horizontal will enhance the wheel effect.

Outer borders

In GP29MV, cut 2 strips 8½in (21.6cm) wide x 48½in (123.2cm) long and 2 strips 8½in (21.6cm) wide x 64½in (163.8cm) long down the length of the fabric.

Binding

Cut 7 strips 2½in (6.4cm) wide across the width of the fabric in SC058.

Backing fabric

Cut 2 pieces 37in x 72in (94cm x 183cm) in backing fabric GP90LC.

PIECING THE PATCHWORK SECTIONS

Lay out all of the wedges in quarter circle blocks, each with six wedges. When you are satisfied with the arrangement, piece one patchwork section at a time. Sew the wedges together along their long sides and press seams open (see patchwork assembly diagram). Repeat to create 36 quarter-wheel wedge patchworks in total.

COMPLETING THE QUARTER BLOCKS

Add the inner and outer sections to complete each quarter block, as follows. Fold the wedge quarter-wheel section in half, matching the straight edges, and finger press to find the centre of the curved edge. Take a template II fabric shape and finger press the centre point of its curve in the same way. Place this piece and quarter-wheel wedge section right sides together, aligning and pinning at the centre creases. Pin at each side edge, aligning the straight edges. Now pin in between, easing the fabric to fit, and machine stitch the pieces together using a scant ¼in (6mm) seam. Snip ⅛in (3mm) into the curved seam at intervals and then press the seam away from the wedges (see block assembly diagram). Using the same process, attach the template JJ fabric shape to the inner curved edge of the quarter-wheel wedge section. Press the block.

Repeat to complete all 36 blocks.

ASSEMBLING THE QUILT

Lay out the blocks in your chosen order, in 6 rows of 6 blocks each, so that 4 quarter blocks placed together make up an individual wheel. Assemble each wheel in turn by stitching the top 2 blocks of each pair together, and then the bottom 2. Now stitch the two halves together to complete the wheel (see quilt assembly diagram). Finally, sew the wheels in 3 rows of 3.

Sew the 48½in (123.2cm) long borders to the sides of the quilt and press seams outwards (see quilt assembly diagram). Sew the remaining two border strips to the top and bottom of the quilt and press.

FINISHING THE QUILT

Using a ¼in (6mm) seam allowance, seam the backing fabric pieces to form a piece about 72in x 72in (183cm x 183cm). Layer the quilt top, batting and backing and baste together (see page 148).

Using machine quilting thread, quilt as desired. The quilt shown was machine quilted with a long cross through each wheel 'spoke', echo quilting on the outer curve of each quarter block, with lines about ½in (1.3cm) apart, and a double line heart motif in the inner curve. Trim the quilt edges and attach the binding (see page 149).

QUILT ASSEMBLY DIAGRAM

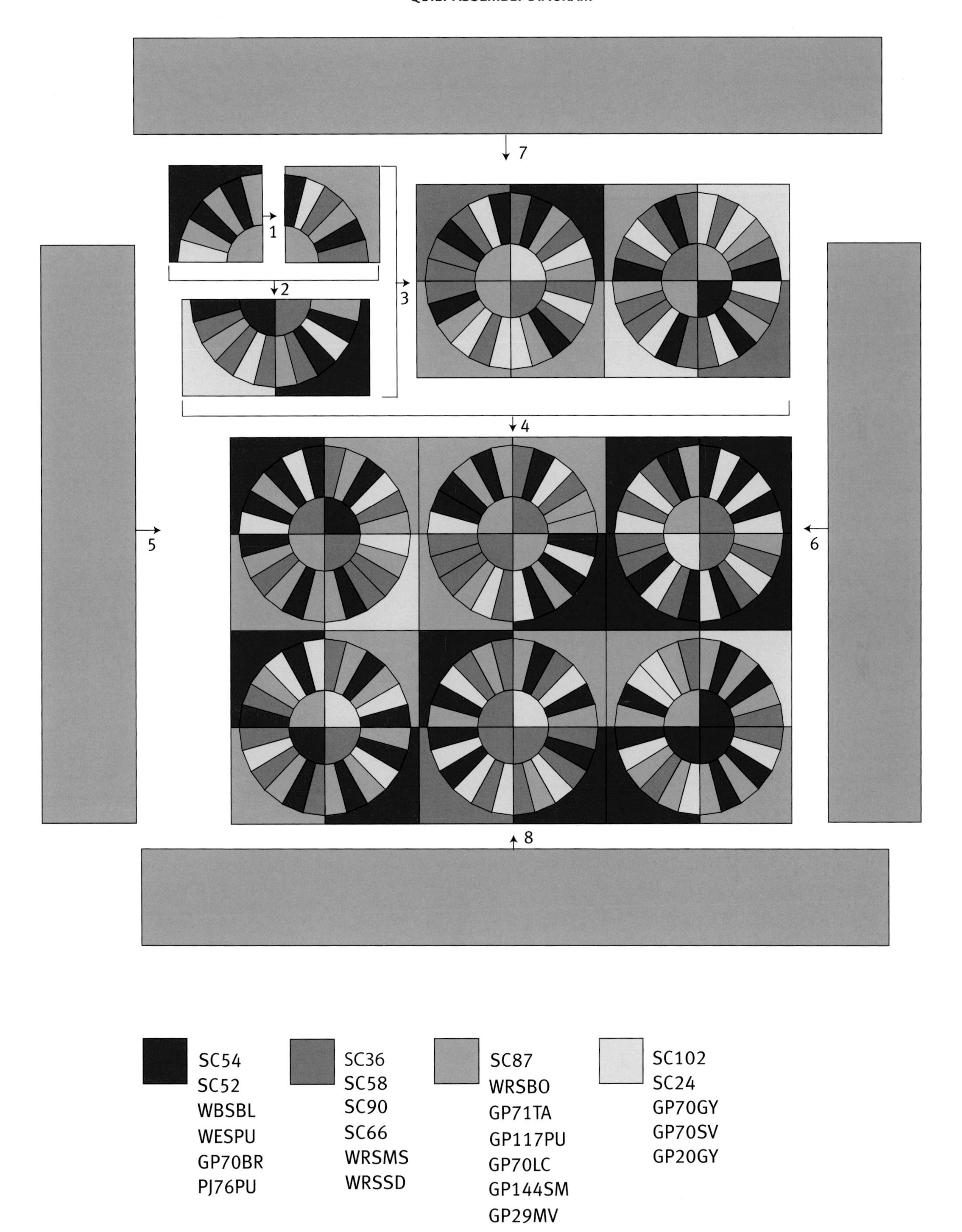

templates

Please refer to the individual instructions for the templates required for each quilt as some templates are used in several projects. The arrows on the templates should be lined up with the straight grain of the fabric, which runs either along the selvedge or at 90 degrees to the selvedge. Following the marked grain lines is important to prevent patches having bias edges along block and quilt edges which can cause distortion. In some quilts the arrows also denote stripe direction.

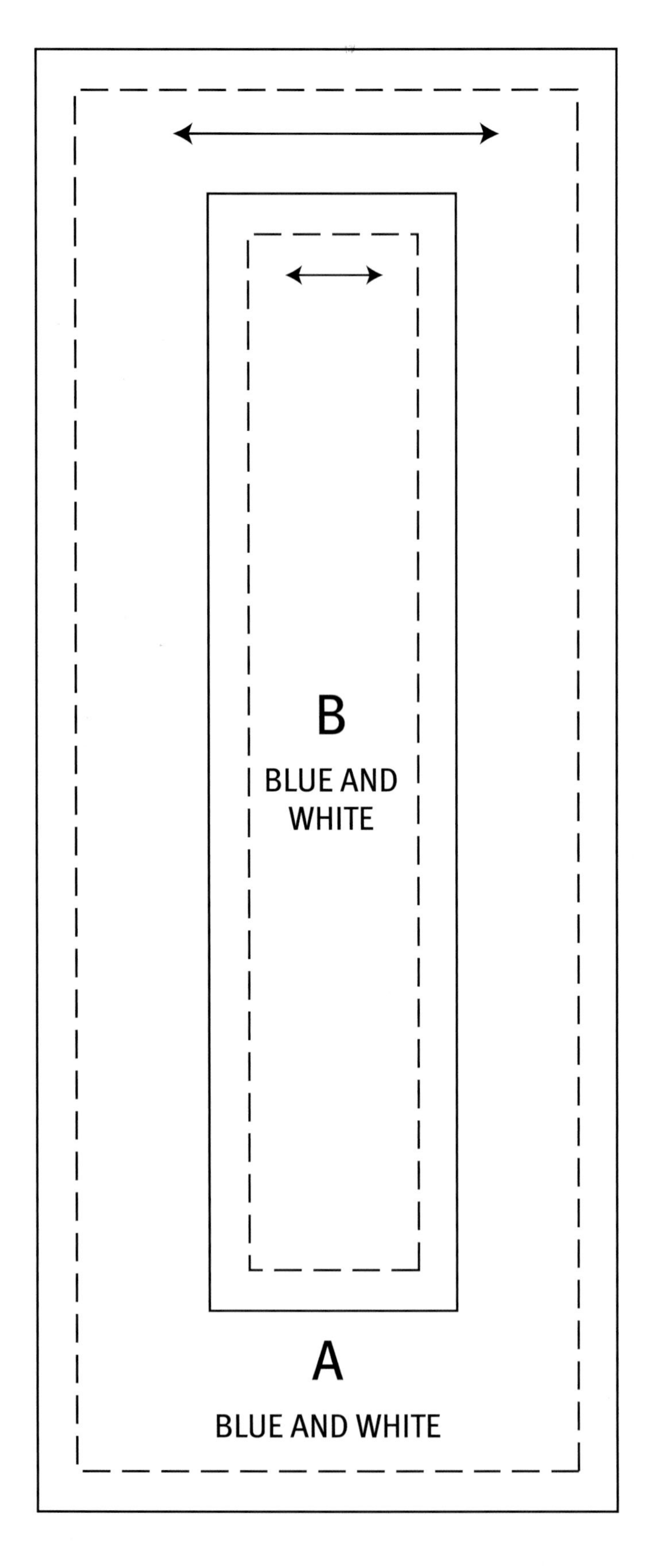

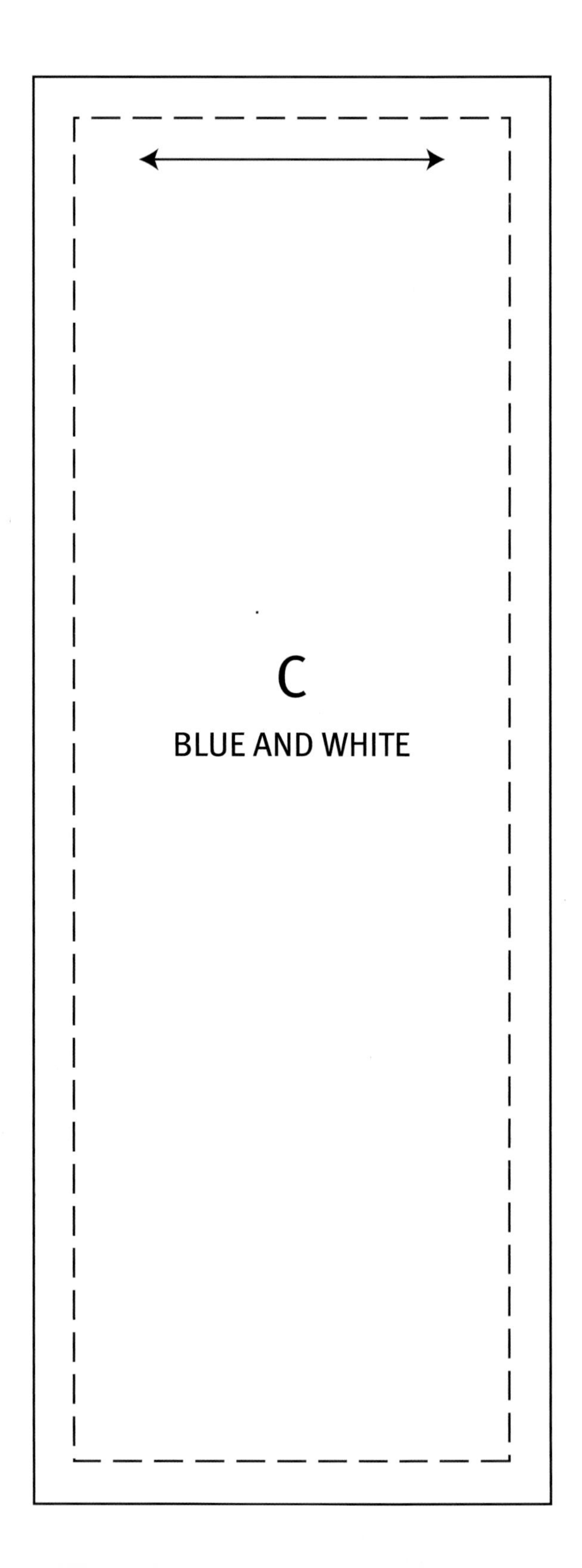

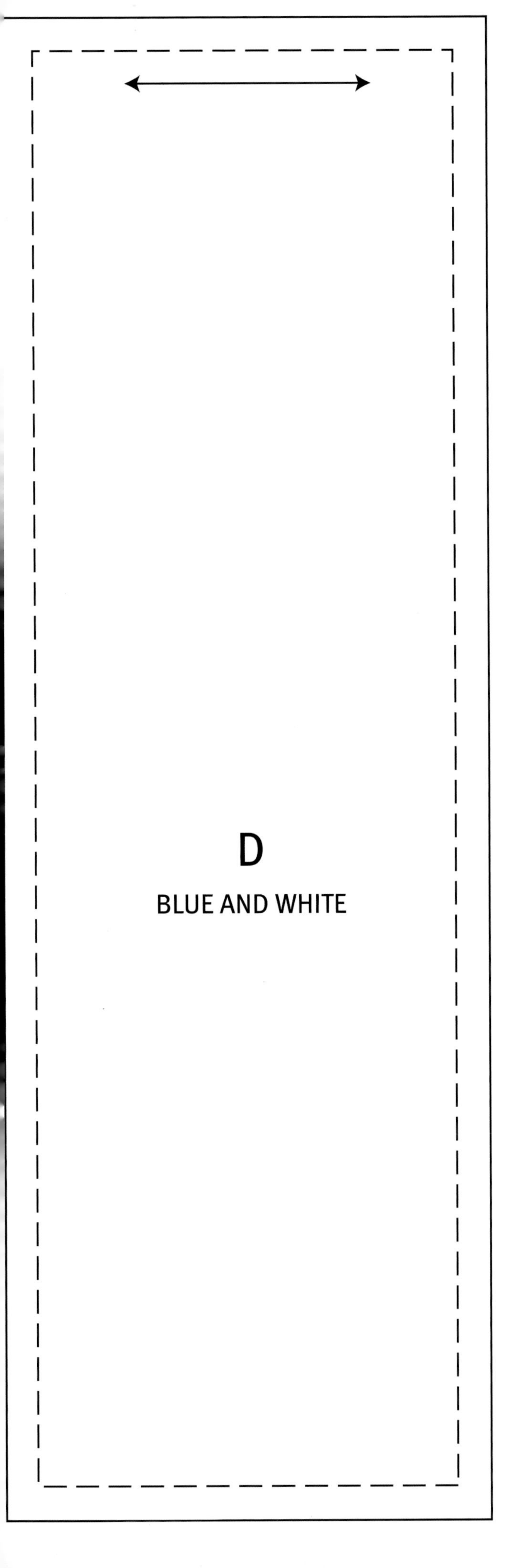
D
BLUE AND WHITE

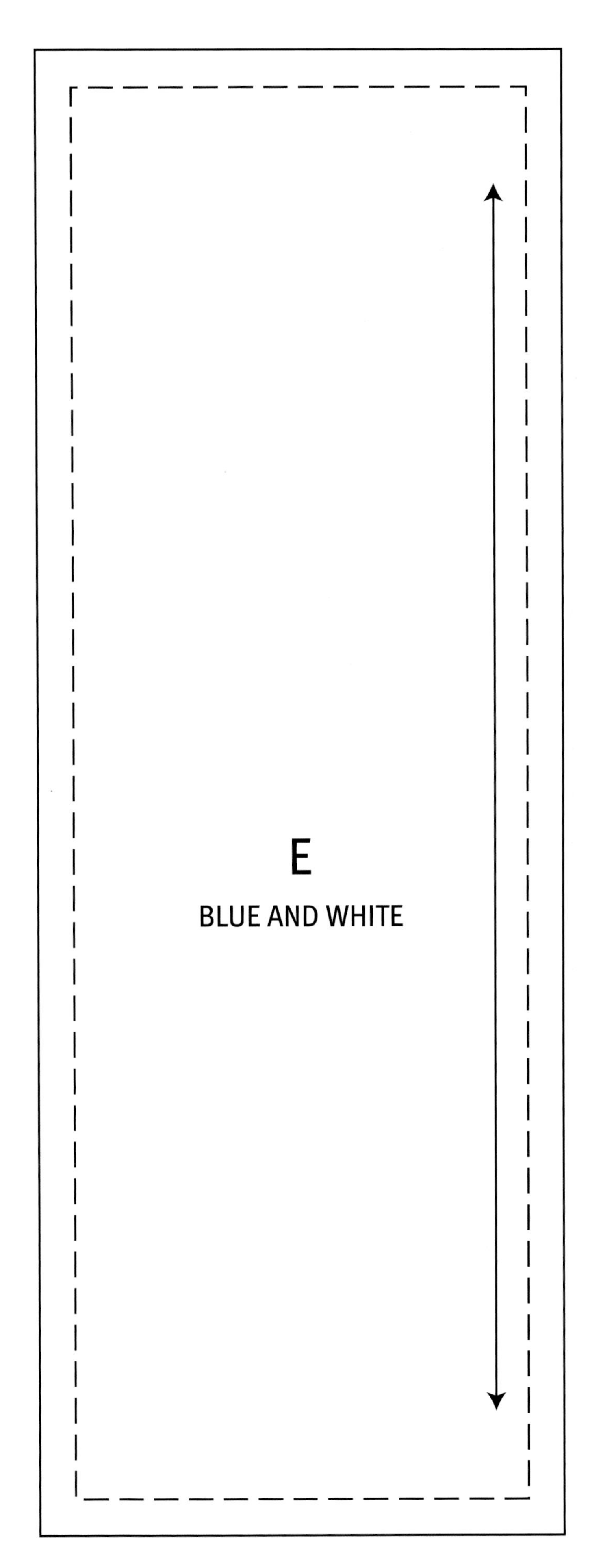
E
BLUE AND WHITE

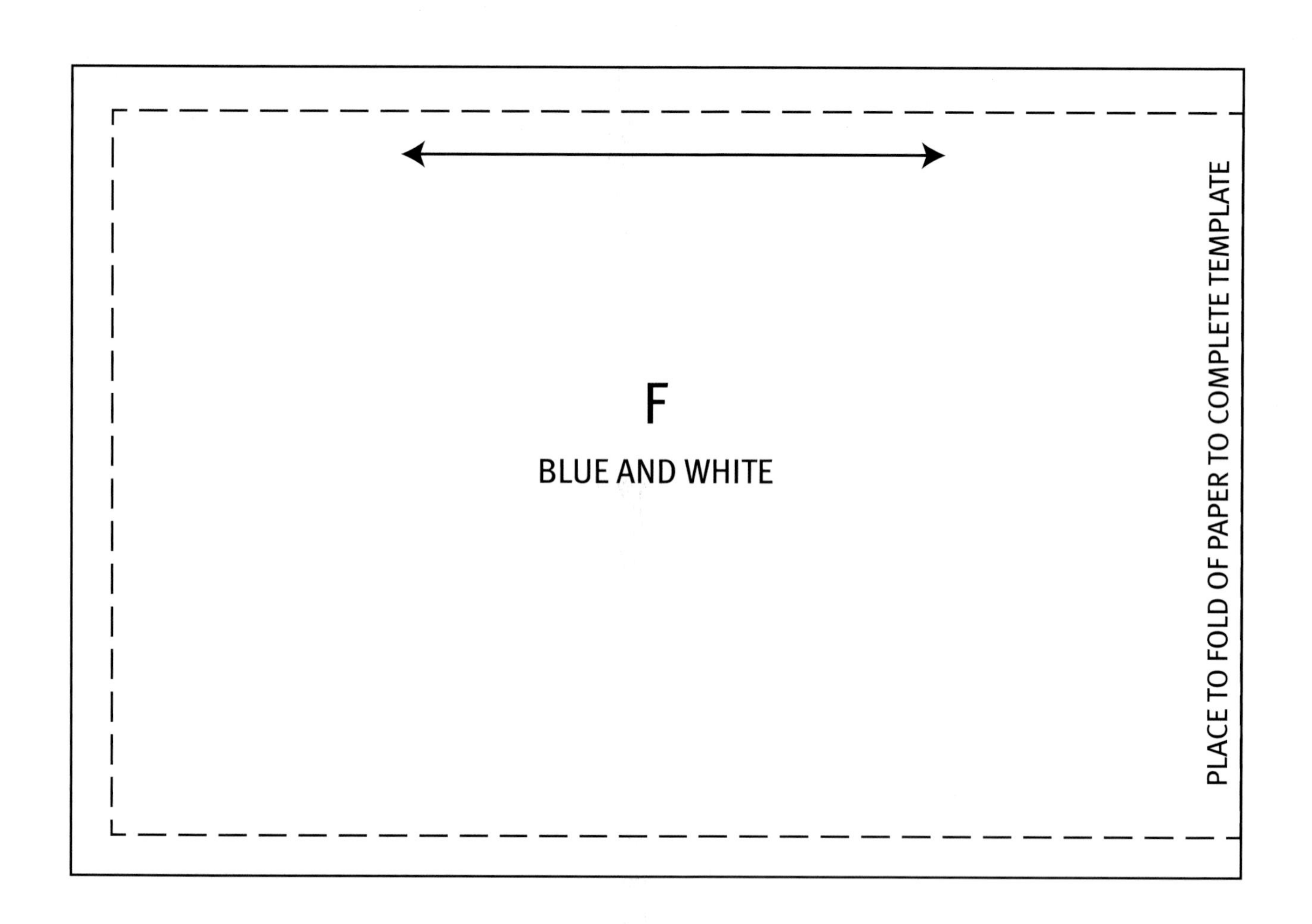
F
BLUE AND WHITE
PLACE TO FOLD OF PAPER TO COMPLETE TEMPLATE

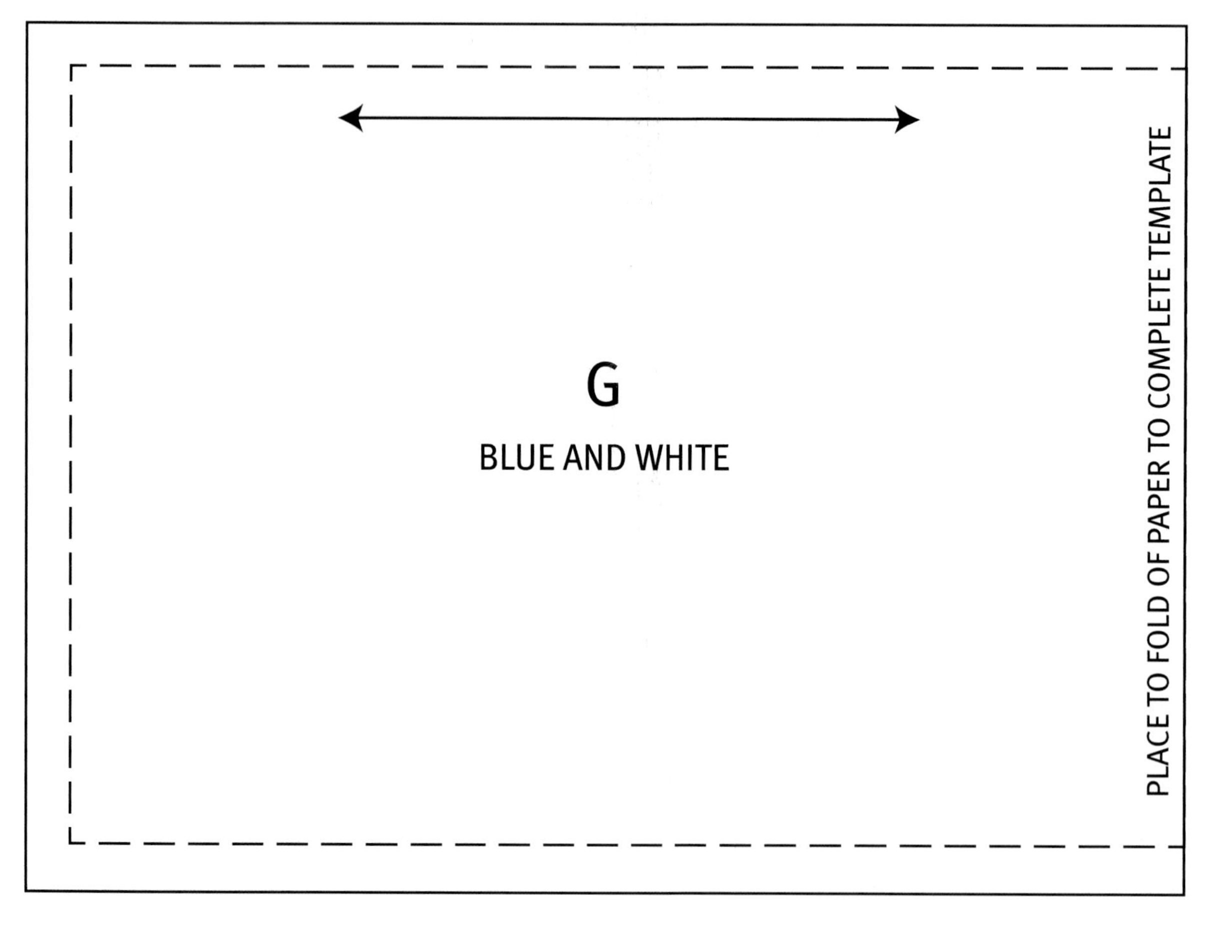
G
BLUE AND WHITE
PLACE TO FOLD OF PAPER TO COMPLETE TEMPLATE

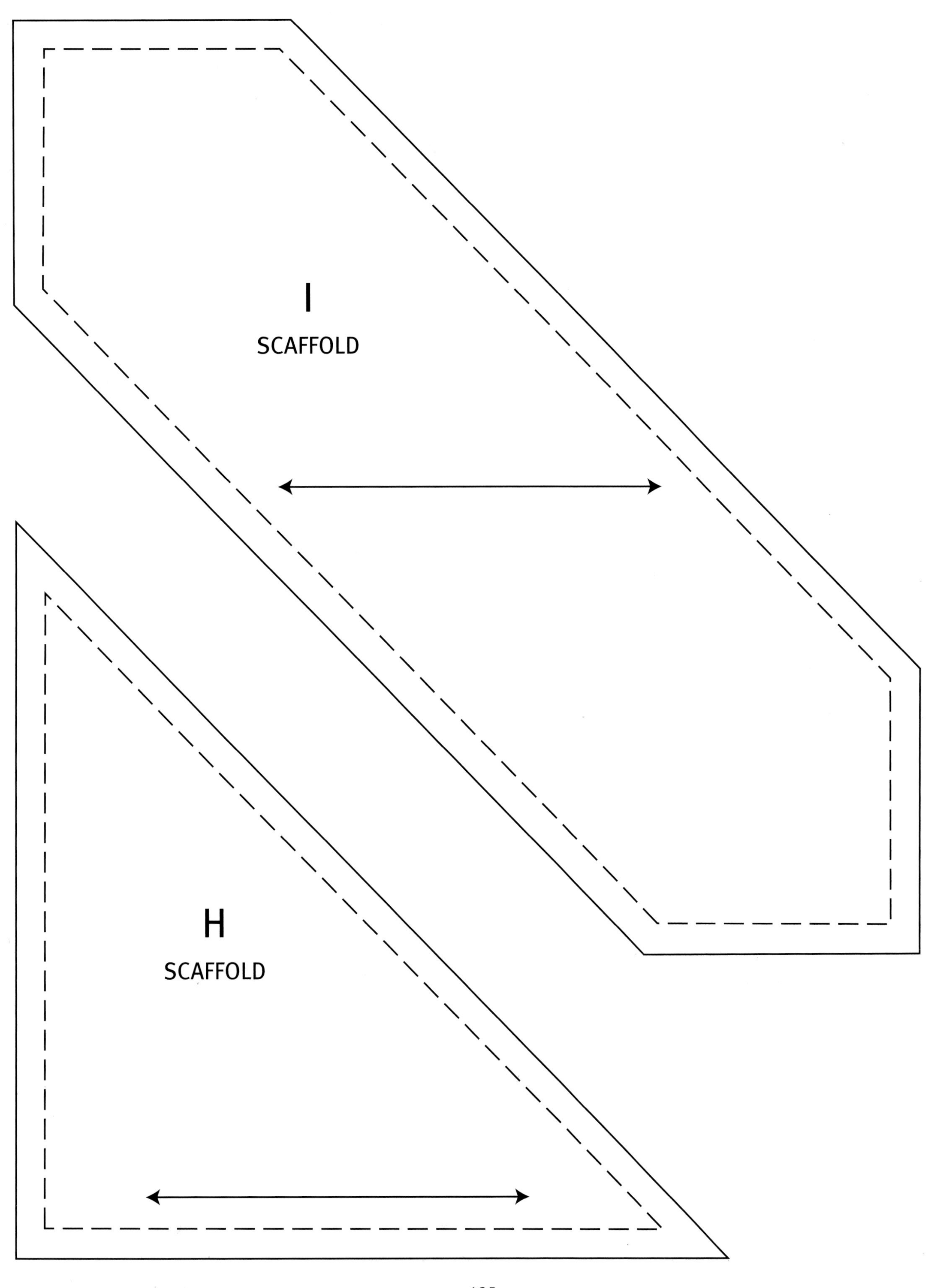
I
SCAFFOLD
H
SCAFFOLD

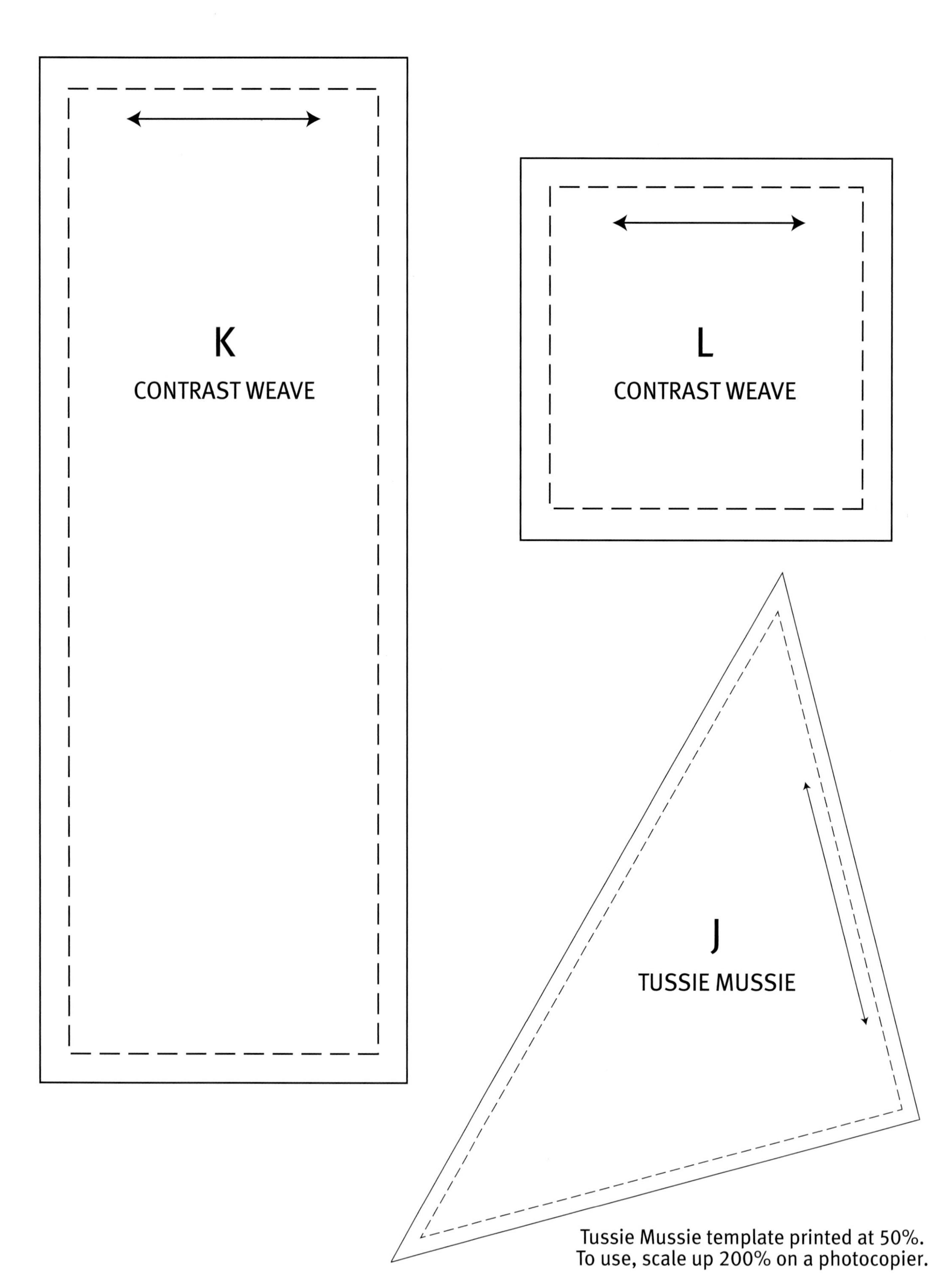

Tussie Mussie template printed at 50%.
To use, scale up 200% on a photocopier.

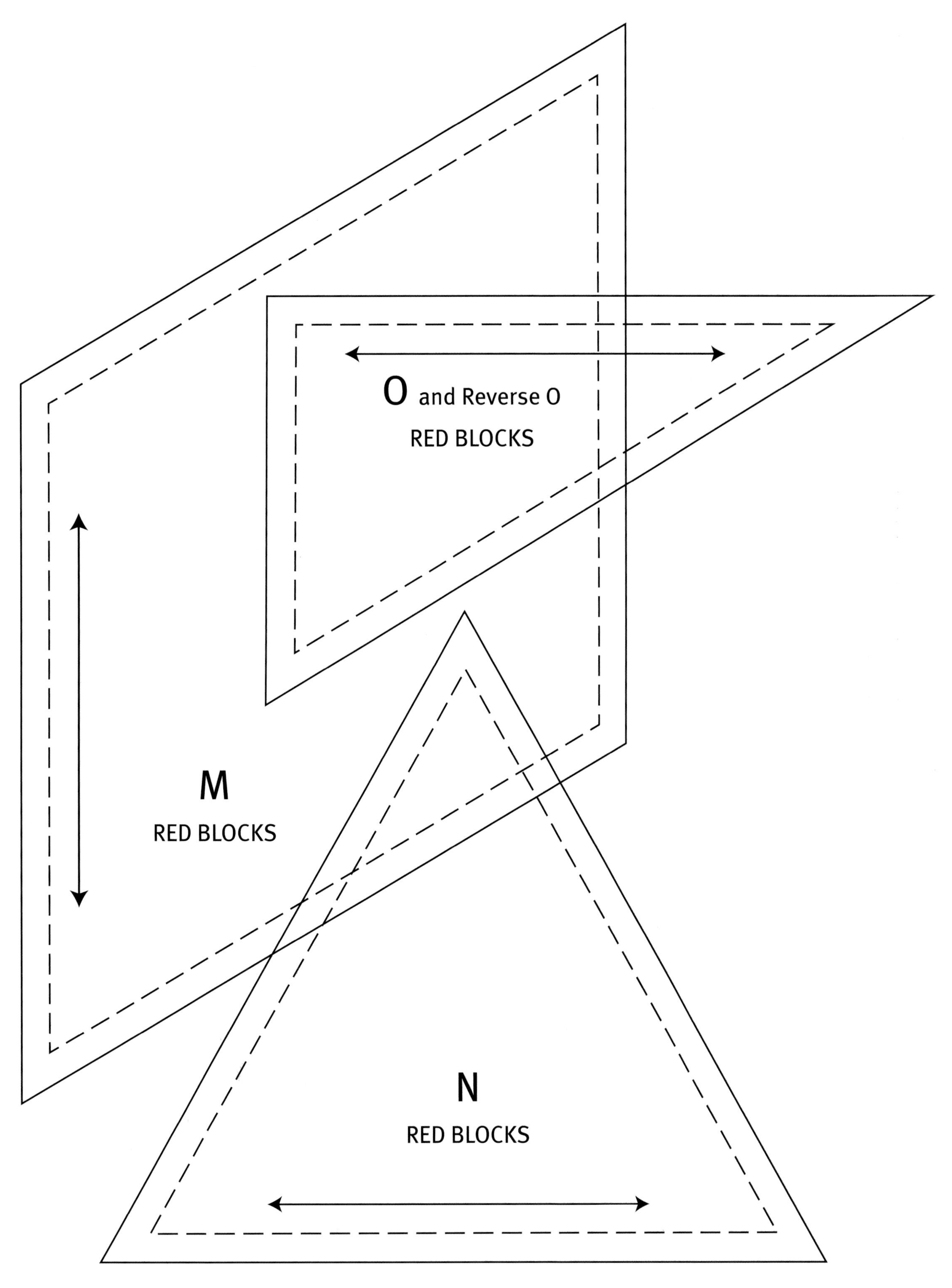
O and Reverse O
RED BLOCKS
M
RED BLOCKS
N
RED BLOCKS

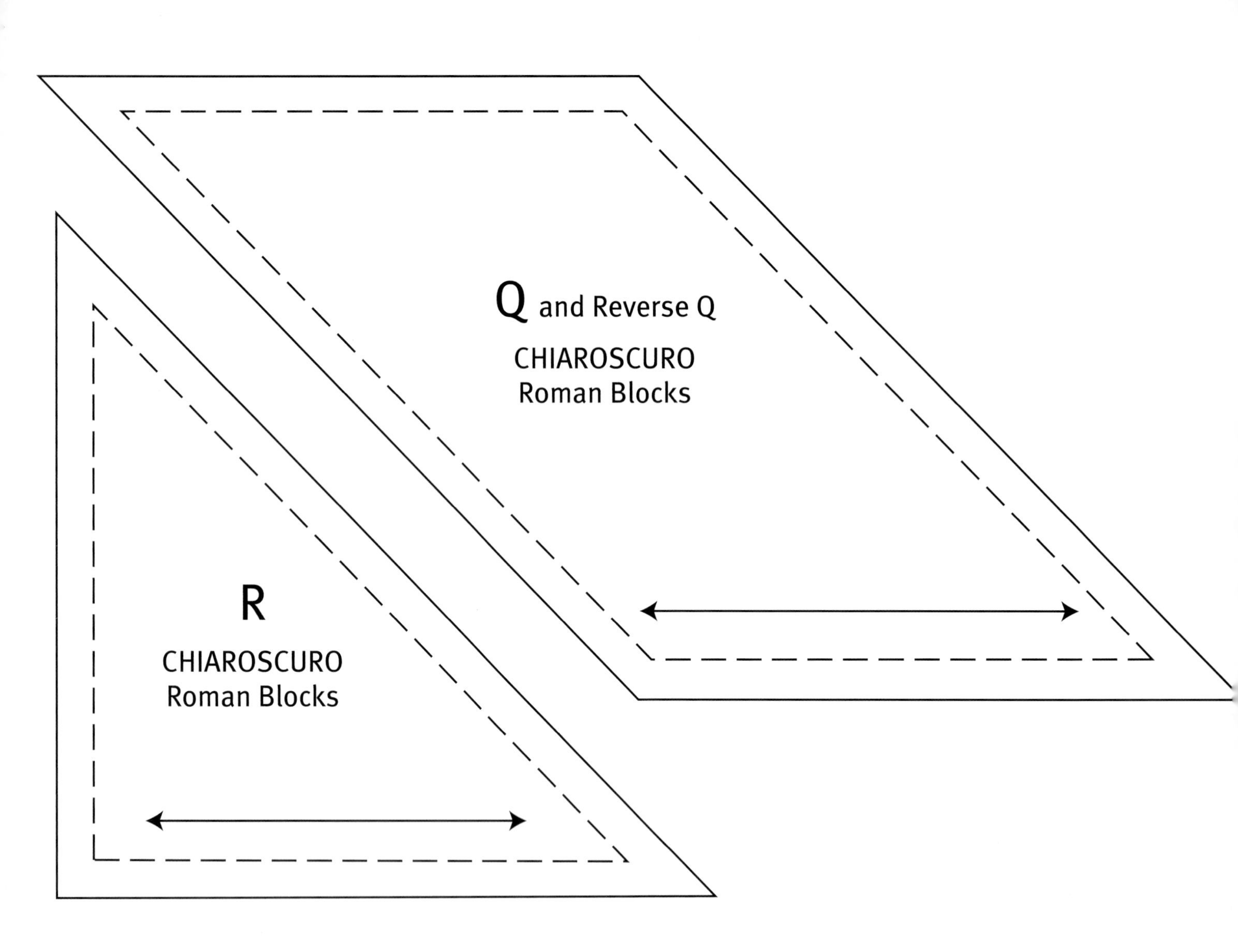
Q and Reverse Q
CHIAROSCURO
Roman Blocks
R
CHIAROSCURO
Roman Blocks

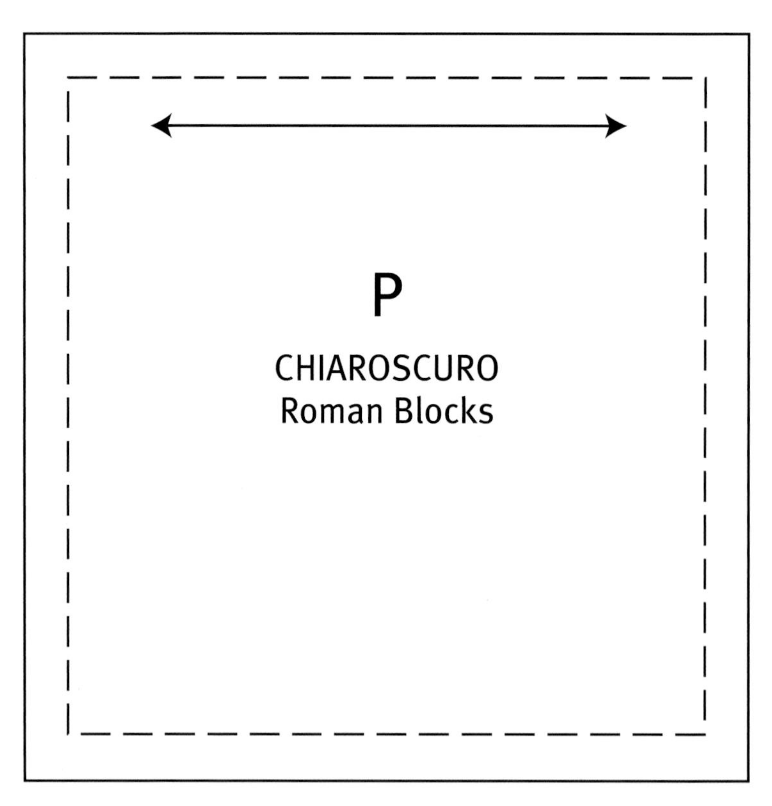
P
CHIAROSCURO
Roman Blocks

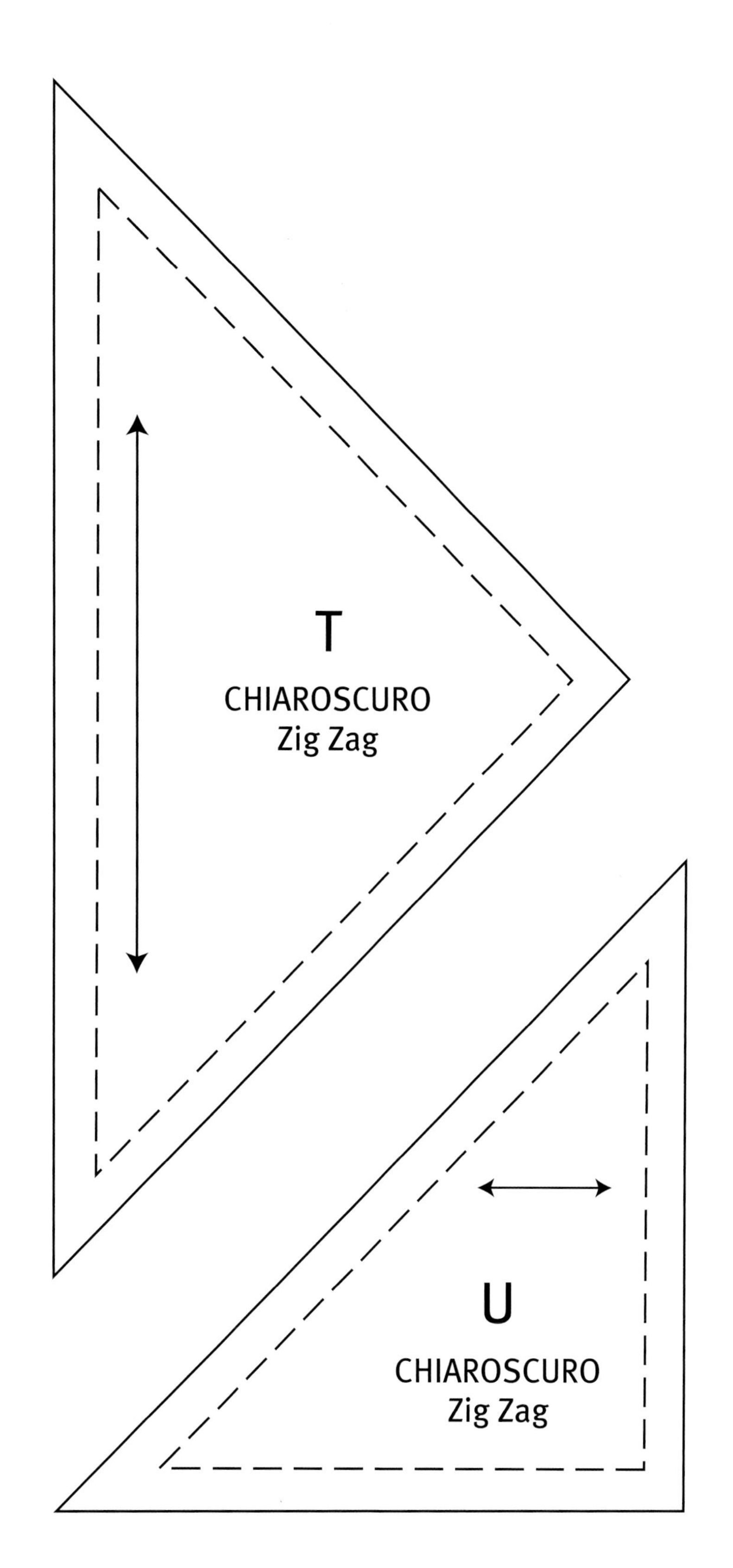
T
CHIAROSCURO
Zig Zag
U
CHIAROSCURO
Zig Zag

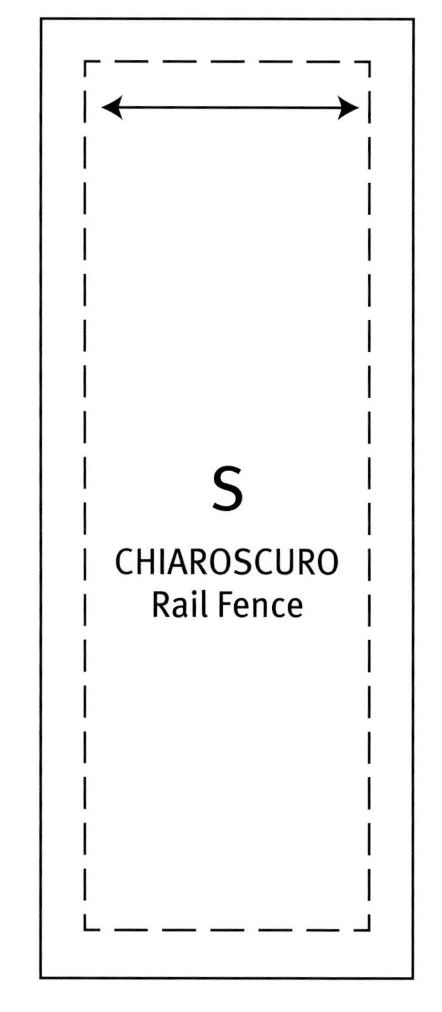
S
CHIAROSCURO
Rail Fence

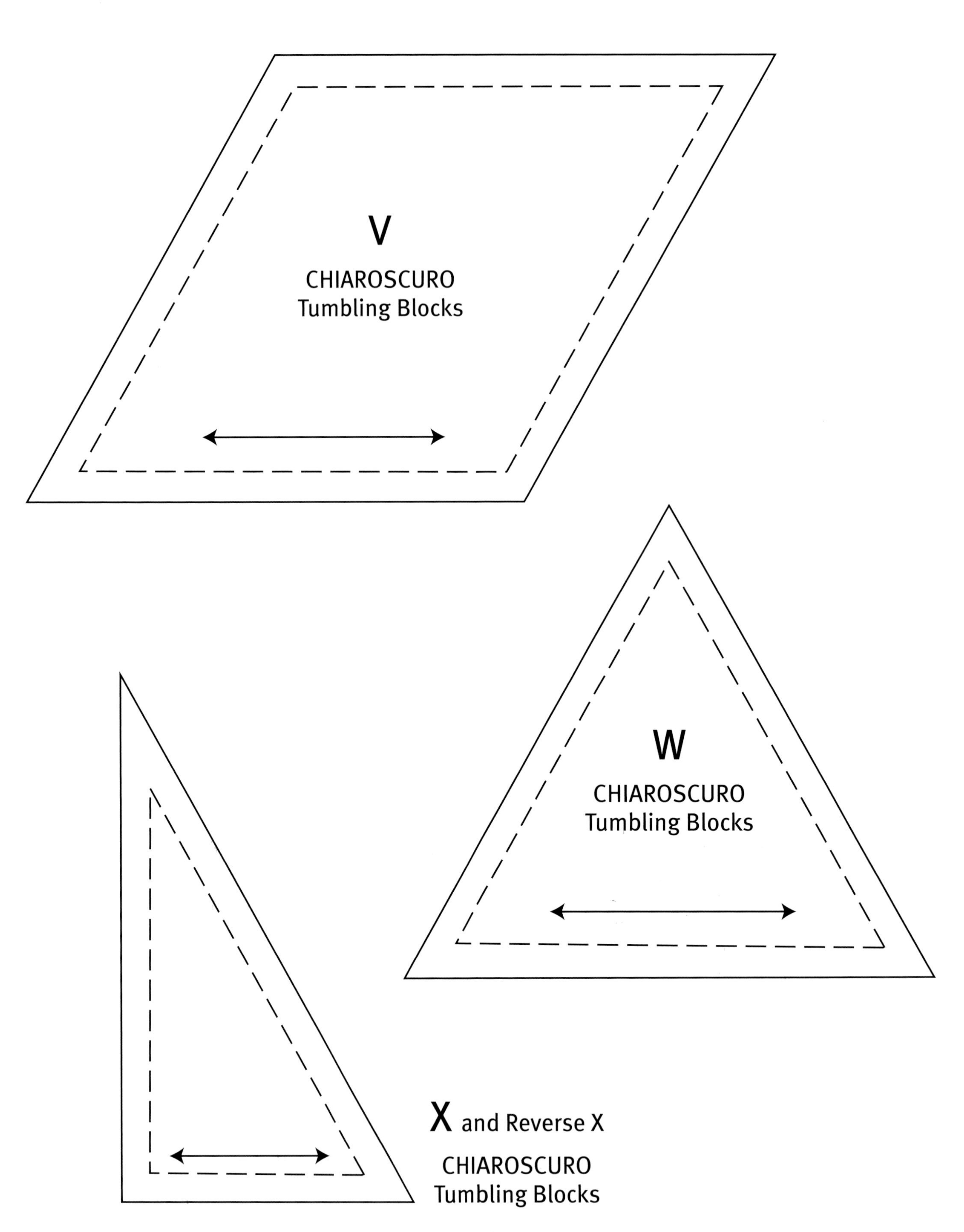
V
CHIAROSCURO
Tumbling Blocks
W
CHIAROSCURO
Tumbling Blocks
X and Reverse X
CHIAROSCURO
Tumbling Blocks

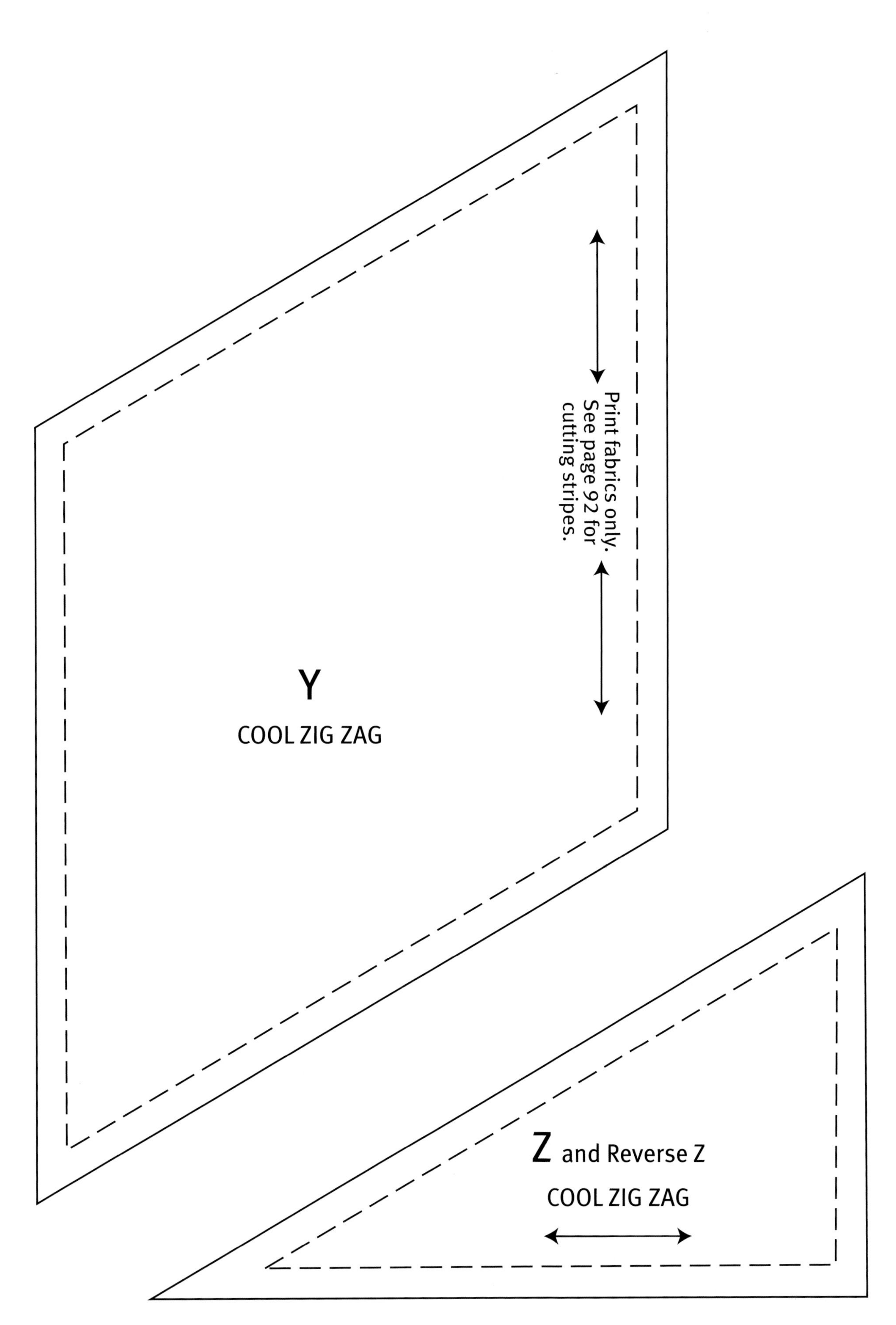
Print fabrics only.
See page 92 for
cutting stripes.
Y
COOL ZIG ZAG
Z and Reverse Z
COOL ZIG ZAG

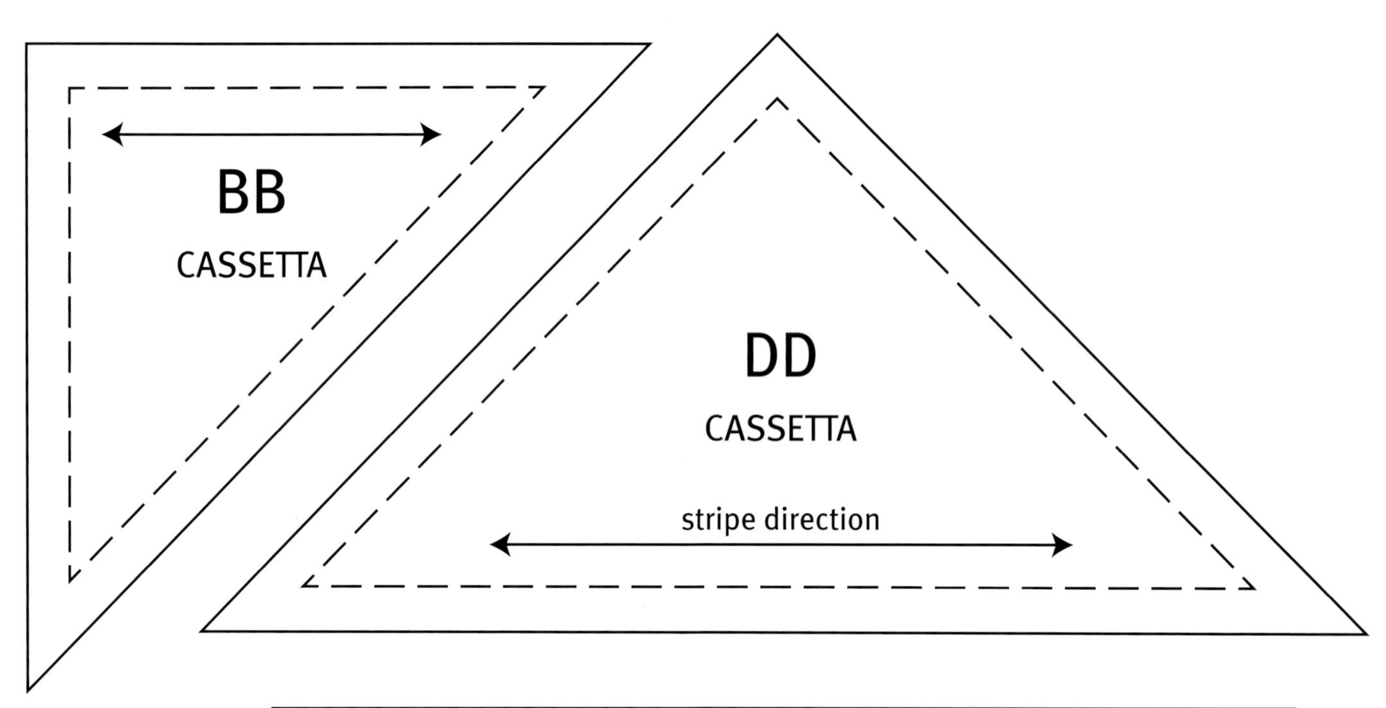
BB
CASSETTA
DD
CASSETTA
stripe direction

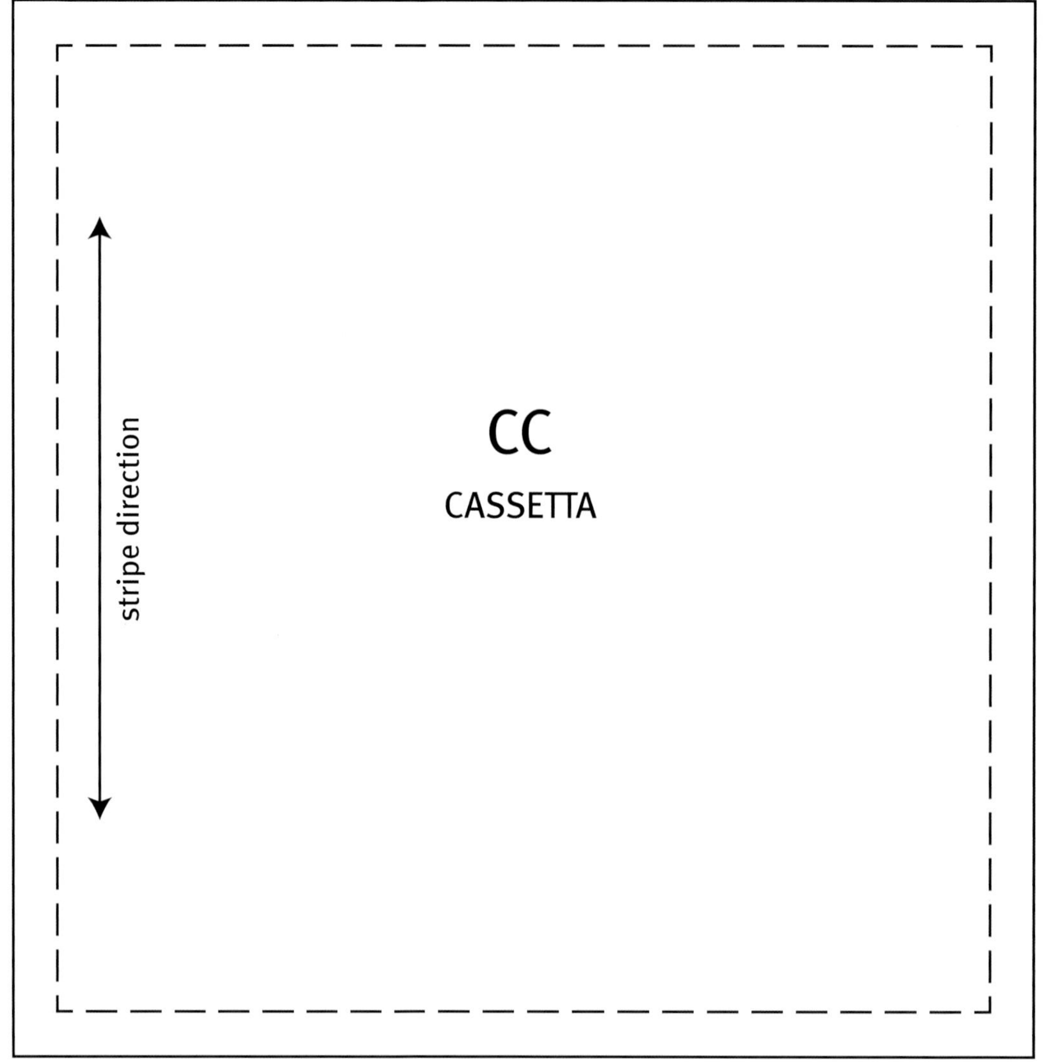
stripe direction
CC
CASSETTA

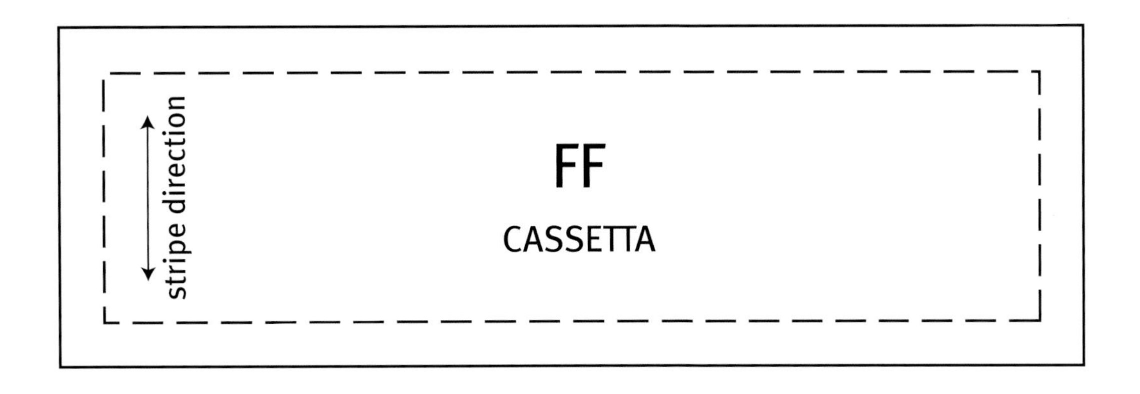
stripe direction
FF
CASSETTA

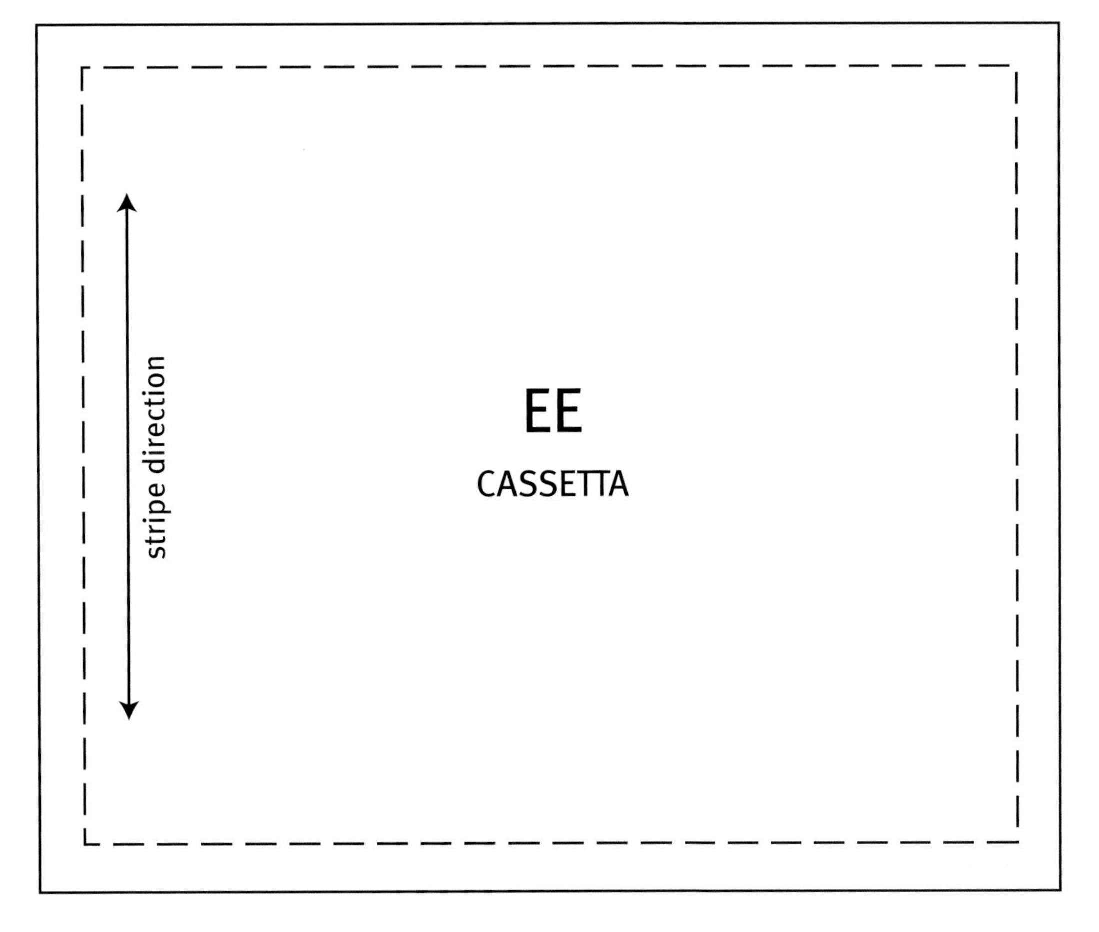
stripe direction
EE
CASSETTA

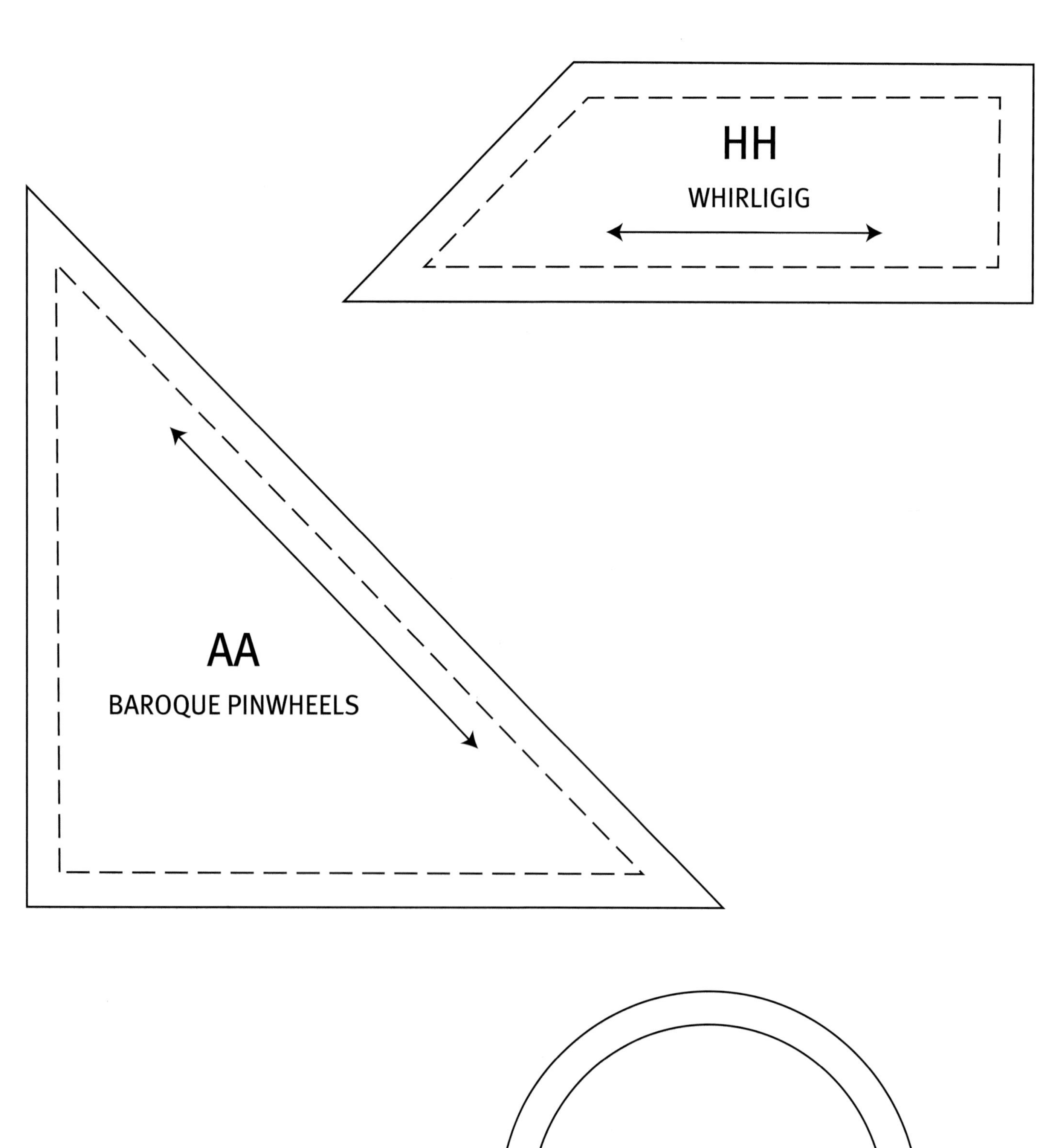
HH
WHIRLIGIG
AA
BAROQUE PINWHEELS

GG
LOSING MY MARBLES

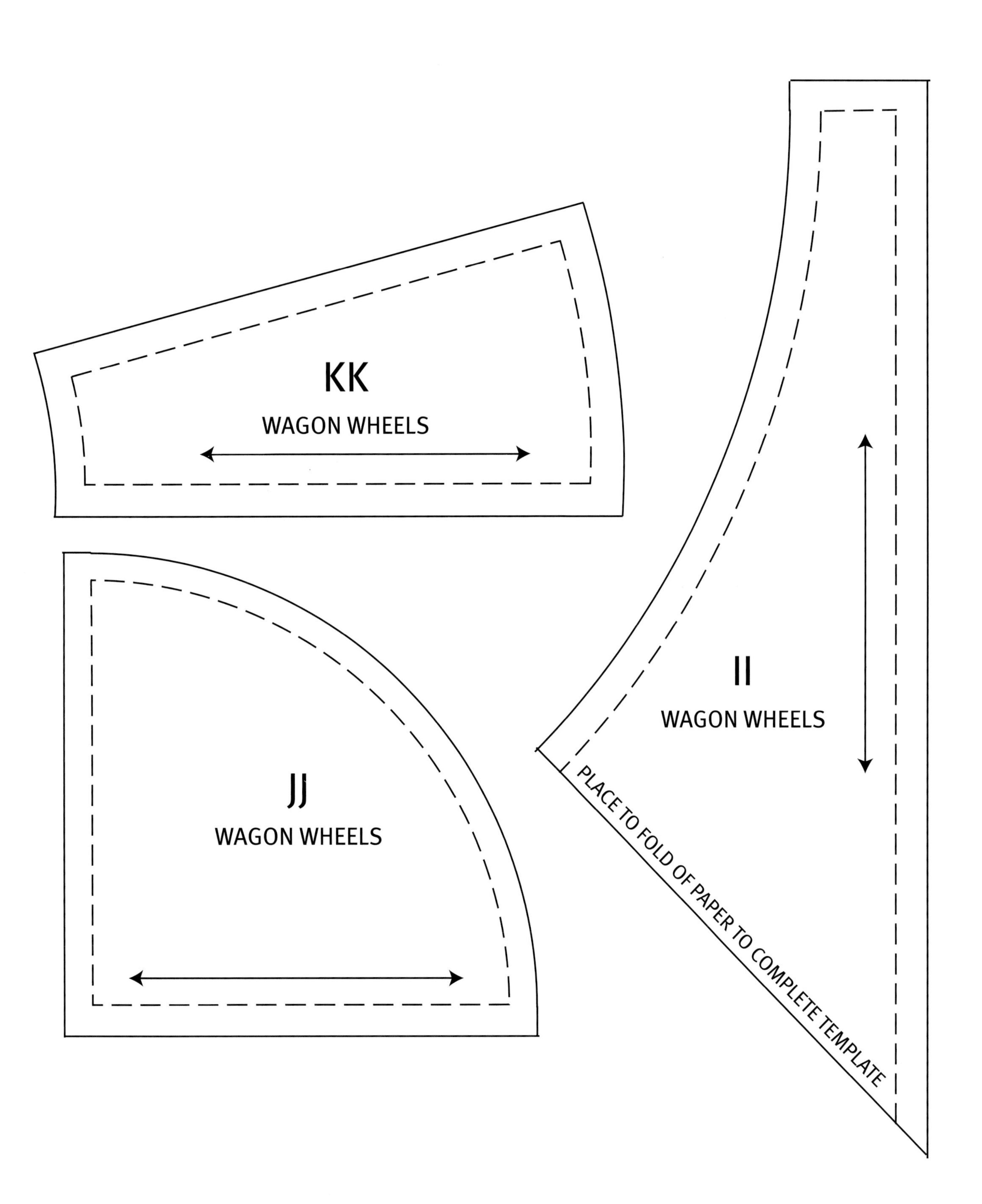
KK
WAGON WHEELS
JJ
WAGON WHEELS
II
WAGON WHEELS
PLACE TO FOLD OF PAPER TO COMPLETE TEMPLATE

patchwork know-how

These instructions are intended for the novice quilt maker, providing the basic information needed to make the projects in this book, along with some useful tips.

EXPERIENCE RATINGS
* Easy, straightforward, suitable for a beginner.
** Suitable for the average patchwork and quilter.
*** For the more experienced patchwork and quilter.

ABOUT THE FABRICS
The fabrics used for the quilts in this book are from Kaffe Fassett Collective. The first two letters of the fabric codes denote the designer:
GP is the code for the Kaffe Fassett collection
PJ is the code for the Philip Jacobs collection
BM is the code for the Brandon Mably collection.

PREPARING THE FABRIC
Prewash all new fabrics before you begin, to ensure that there will be no uneven shrinkage and no bleeding of colours when the finished quilt is laundered. Press the fabric whilst it is still damp to return crispness to it. All fabric requirements in this book are calculated on a 40in (101.5cm) usable fabric width, to allow for shrinkage and selvedge removal.

MAKING TEMPLATES
Transparent template plastic is the best material to use: it is durable and allows you to see the fabric and select certain motifs. You can also use thin stiff cardboard.

Templates for machine piecing
1 Trace off the actual–sized template provided either directly on to template plastic, or tracing paper, and then on to thin cardboard. Use a ruler to help you trace off the straight cutting line, dotted seam line and grain lines.

Some of the templates in this book were too large to print complete. Transfer the template onto the fold of a large sheet of paper, cut out and open out for the full template.
2 Cut out the traced off template using a craft knife, a ruler and a self-healing cutting mat.
3 Punch holes in the corners of the template, at each point on the seam line, using a hole punch.

Templates for hand piecing
• Make a template as for machine piecing, but do not trace off the cutting line. Use the dotted seam line as the outer edge of the template.

• This template allows you to draw the seam lines directly on to the fabric. The seam allowances can then be cut by eye around the patch.

CUTTING THE FABRIC
On the individual instructions for each project, you will find a summary of all the patch shapes used.

Always mark and cut out any border and binding strips first, followed by the largest patch shapes and finally the smallest ones, to make the most efficient use of your fabric. The border and binding strips are best cut using a rotary cutter.

Rotary cutting
Rotary cut strips are usually cut across the fabric from selvedge to selvedge, but some projects may vary, so please read through all the instructions before you start cutting the fabrics.

1 Before beginning to cut, press out any folds or creases in the fabric. If you are cutting a large piece of fabric, you will need to fold it several times to fit the cutting mat. When there is only a single fold, place the fold facing you. If the fabric is too wide to be folded only once, fold it concertina-style until it fits your mat. A small rotary cutter with a sharp blade will cut up to six layers of fabric; a large cutter up to eight layers.

2 To ensure that your cut strips are straight and even, the folds must be placed exactly parallel to the straight edges of the fabric and along a line on the cutting mat.

3 Place a plastic ruler over the raw edge of the fabric, overlapping it about ½in (1.25cm). Make sure that the ruler is at right angles to both the straight edges and the fold to ensure that you cut along the straight grain. Press down on the ruler and wheel the cutter away from you along the edge of the ruler.

4 Open out the fabric to check the edge. Don't worry if it's not perfectly straight – a little wiggle will not show when the quilt is stitched together. Re-fold fabric, then place the ruler over the trimmed edge, aligning the edge with the markings on the ruler that match the correct strip width. Cut strip along the edge of the ruler.

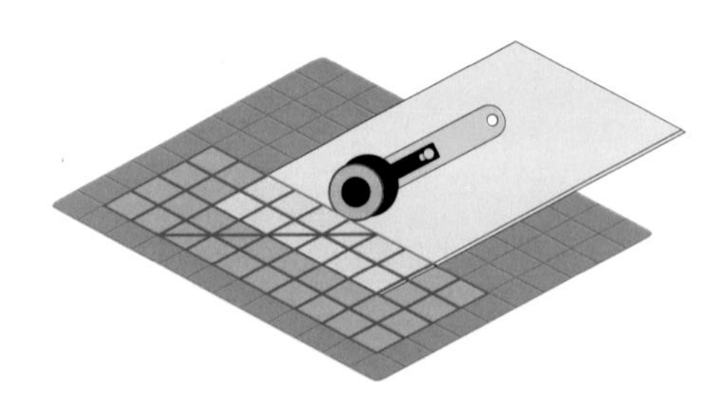

USING TEMPLATES
The most efficient way to cut out templates is by first rotary cutting a strip of fabric to the width stated for your template, and then marking off your templates along the strip, edge to edge at the required angle. This method leaves hardly any waste and gives a random effect to your patches.

A less efficient method is to 'fussy cut' them, where the templates are cut individually by placing them on particular motifs or stripes, to create special effects. Although this method is more wasteful, it yields very interesting results.

1 Place the template face down, on the wrong side of the fabric, with the grain-line arrow following the straight grain of the fabric, if indicated. Be careful though – check with your individual instructions, as some instructions may ask you to cut patches on varying grains.

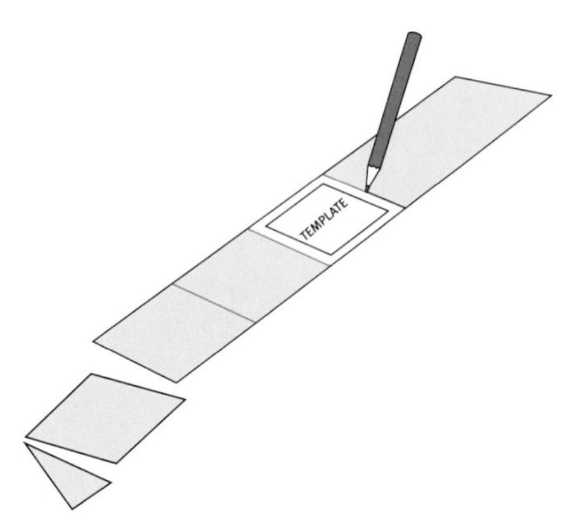

2 Hold the template firmly in place and draw around it with a sharp pencil or crayon, marking in the corner dots or seam lines. To save fabric, position patches close together or even touching. Don't worry if outlines positioned on the straight grain when drawn on striped fabrics do not always match the stripes when cut – this will add a degree of visual excitement to the patchwork!

3 Once you've drawn all the pieces needed, you are ready to cut the fabric, with either a rotary cutter and ruler or a pair of sharp sewing scissors.

BASIC HAND AND MACHINE PIECING
Patches can be stitched together by hand or machine. Machine stitching is quicker, but hand assembly allows you to carry your patches around with you and work on them in every spare moment. The choice is yours. For techniques that are new to you, practise on scrap pieces of fabric until you feel confident.

Machine piecing
Follow the quilt instructions for the order in which to piece the individual patchwork blocks and then assemble the blocks together in rows.

1 Seam lines are not marked on the fabric for simple shapes, so stitch ¼in (6mm) seams using the machine needle plate, a ¼in (6mm) wide machine foot, or tape stuck to the machine as a guide. Pin two patches with right sides together, matching edges.

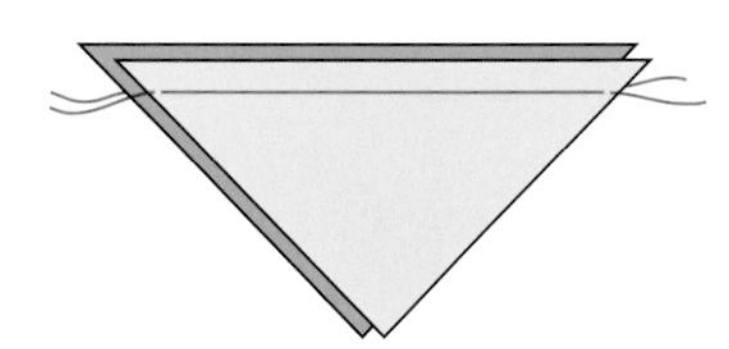

For some shapes, particularly diamonds you need to match the sewing lines, not the fabric edges. Place 2 diamonds right sides together but offset so that the sewing lines intersect at the correct position. Use pins to secure for sewing.

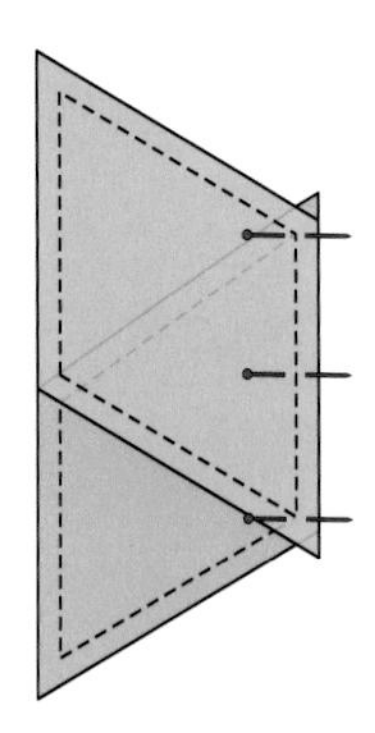

Set your machine at 10–12 stitches per inch (2.5cm) and stitch seams from edge to edge, removing pins as you feed the fabric through the machine.

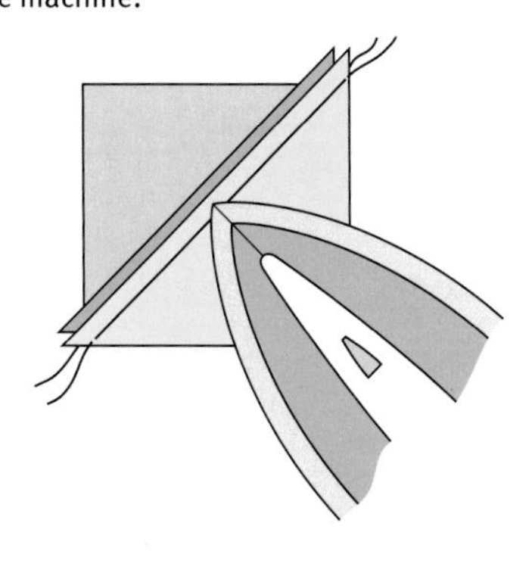

2 Press the seams of each patchwork block to one side before attempting to join it to another block. When joining diamond shaped blocks you will need to offset the blocks in the same way as diamond shaped patches, matching the sewing lines, not the fabric edges.

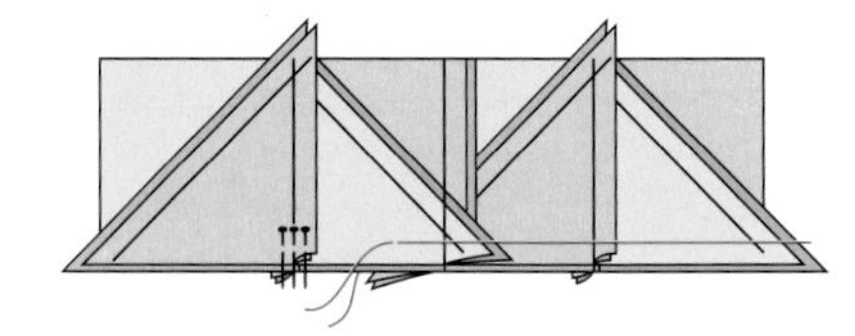

3 When joining rows of blocks, make sure that adjacent seam allowances are pressed in opposite directions to reduce bulk and make matching easier. Pin pieces together directly through the stitch line and to the right and left of the seam. Remove pins as you sew. Continue pressing seams to one side as you work.

Hand piecing
1 Pin two patches with right sides together, so that the marked seam lines are facing outwards.

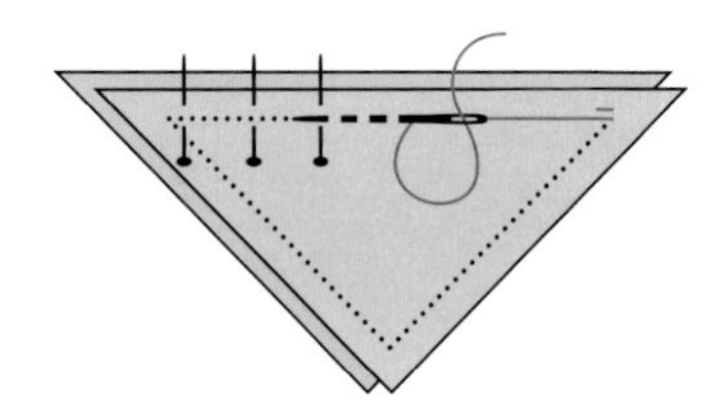

2 Using a single strand of strong thread, secure the corner of a seam line with a couple of back stitches.

3 Sew running stitches along the marked line, working 8–10 stitches per inch (2.5cm) and ending at the opposite seam line corner with a few back stitches. When hand piecing never stitch over the seam allowances.

4 Press the seams to one side, as shown in machine piecing (Step 2).

MACHINE APPLIQUÉ WITH ADHESIVE WEB
To make appliqué very easy you can use adhesive web (which comes attached to a paper backing sheet) to bond the motifs to the background fabric. There are two types of web available: the first keeps the pieces in place while they are stitched, the second permanently attaches the pieces so that no sewing is required. Follow steps 1 and 2 for the non-sew type and steps 1–3 for the type that requires sewing.

1 Trace the reversed appliqué design onto the paper side of the adhesive web leaving a ¼in (6mm) gap between all the shapes. Roughly cut out the motifs ⅛in (3mm) outside your drawn line.

2 Bond the motifs to the reverse of your chosen fabrics. Cut out on the drawn line with very sharp scissors. Remove the backing paper by scoring the centre of the motif carefully with a scissor point and peeling the paper away from the centre out (to prevent damage to the edges). Place the motifs onto the background, noting any which may be layered. Cover with a clean cloth and bond with a hot iron (check instructions for temperature setting as adhesive web can vary depending on the manufacturer).

3 Using a contrasting or toning coloured thread in your machine, work small close zigzag stitches (or a blanket stitch if your machine has one) around the edge of the motifs; the majority of the stitching should sit on the appliqué shape. When stitching up to points stop with the machine needle in the down position, lift the foot of your machine, pivot the work, lower the foot and continue to stitch. Make sure all the raw edges are stitched.

HAND APPLIQUÉ
Good preparation is essential for speedy and accurate hand appliqué. The finger-pressing method is suitable for needle-turning application, used for simple shapes like leaves and flowers. Using a card template is the best method for bold simple motifs such as circles.

Finger–pressing method
1 To make your template, transfer the appliqué design using carbon paper on to stiff card, and cut out the template. Trace around the outline of your appliquéd shape on to the right side of your fabric using a well sharpened pencil. Cut out shapes, adding by eye a ¼in (6mm) seam allowance all around.

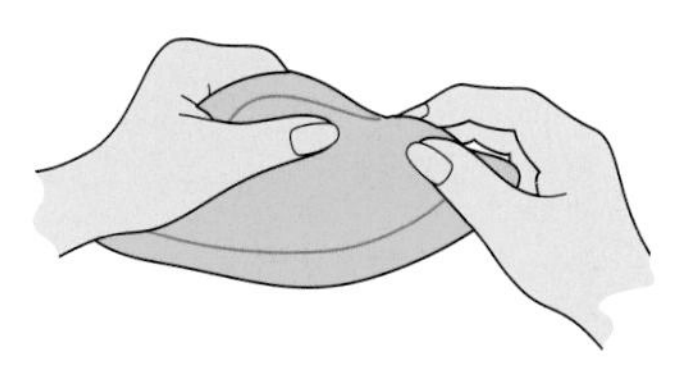

2 Hold shape right side up and fold under the seam, turning along your drawn line, pinch to form a crease. Dampening the fabric makes this very easy. When using shapes with 'points' such as leaves, turn in the seam allowance at the 'point' first, as shown in the diagram. Then continue all round the shape. If your shapes have sharp curves, you can snip the seam allowance to ease the curve. Take care not to stretch the appliqué shapes as you work.

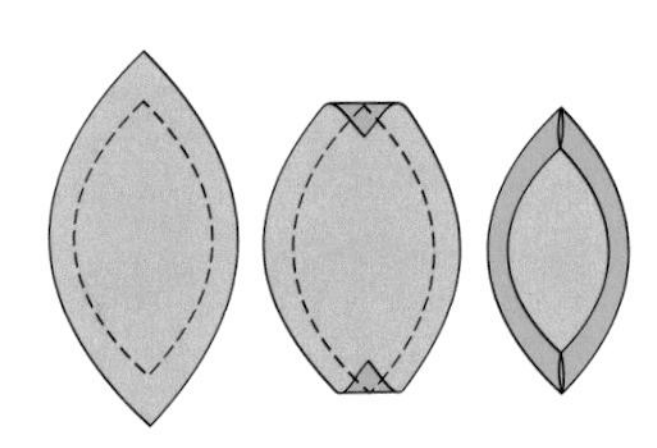

Card template method
1 Cut out appliqué shapes as shown in step 1 of finger-pressing. Make a circular template from thin cardboard, without seam allowances.

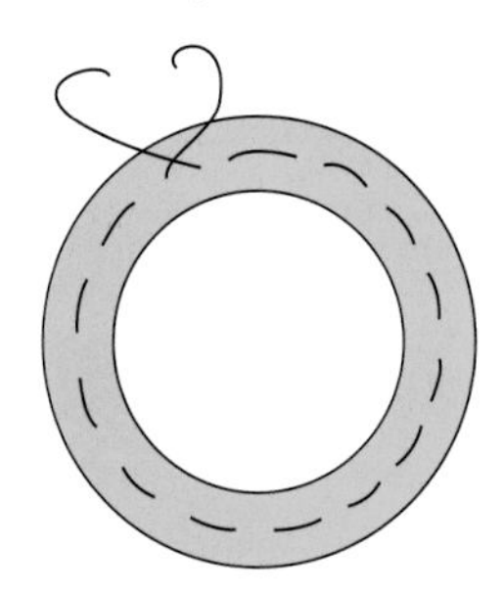

2 Using a matching thread, work a row of running stitches close to the edge of the fabric circle. Place a thin cardboard template in the centre of the fabric circle on the wrong side of the fabric.

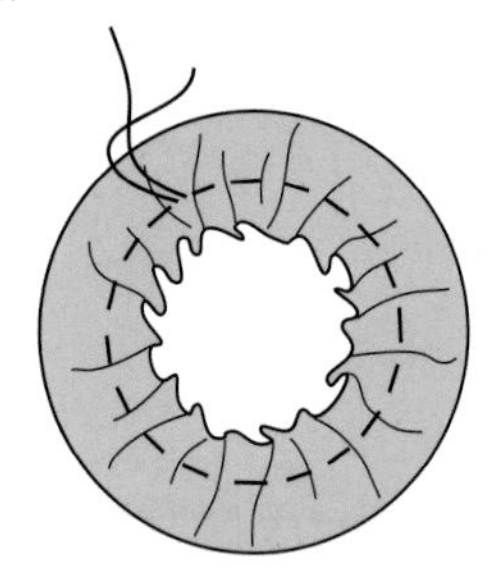

3 Carefully pull up the running stitches to gather up the edge of the fabric circle around the cardboard template. Press, so that no puckers or tucks appear on the right side. Then, carefully pop out the cardboard template without distorting the fabric shape.

Straight stems

Place fabric face down and simply press over the ¼in (6mm) seam allowance along each edge. You don't need to finish the ends of stems that are layered under other appliqué shapes. Where the end of the stem is visible, simply tuck under the end and finish neatly.

Needle-turning application

Take the appliqué shape and pin in position. Stroke the seam allowance under with the tip of the needle as far as the creased pencil line, and hold securely in place with your thumb. Using a matching thread, bring the needle up from the back of the block into the edge of the shape and proceed to blind-hem in place. (This stitch allows the motifs to appear to be held on invisibly.) To do this, bring the thread out from below through the folded edge of the motif, never on the top. The stitches must be small, even and close together to prevent the seam allowance from unfolding and from frayed edges appearing. Try to avoid pulling the stitches too tight, as this will cause the motifs to pucker up. Work around the whole shape, stroking under each small section before sewing.

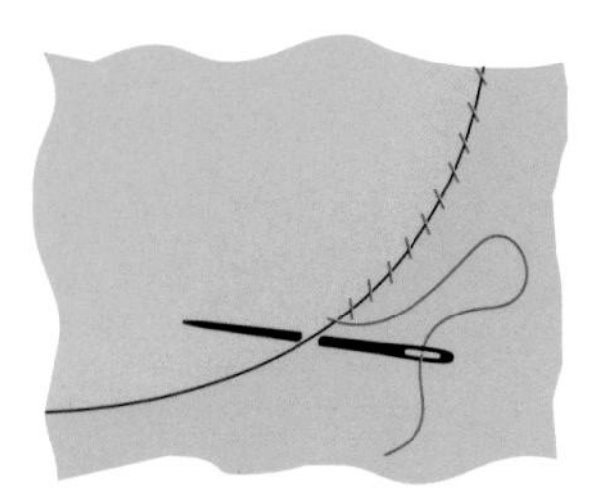

QUILTING

When you have finished piecing your patchwork and added any borders, press it carefully. It is now ready for quilting.

Marking quilting designs and motifs

Many tools are available for marking quilting patterns, check the manufacturer's instructions for use and test on scraps of fabric from your project. Use an acrylic ruler for marking straight lines.

Stencils

Some designs require stencils, these can be made at home, by transferring the designs on to template plastic, or stiff cardboard. The design is then cut away in the form of long dashes, to act as guides for both internal and external lines. These stencils are a quick method for producing an identical set of repeated designs.

Preparing the backing and batting

• Remove the selvedges and piece together the backing fabric to form a backing at least 4in (10cm) larger all round than the patchwork top.

• Choose a fairly thin batting, preferably pure cotton, to give your quilt a flat appearance. If your batting has been rolled up, unroll it and let it rest before cutting it to the same size as the backing.

• For a large quilt it may be necessary to join two pieces of batting to fit. Lay the pieces of batting on a flat surface so that they overlap by around 8in (20cm). Cut a curved line through both layers.

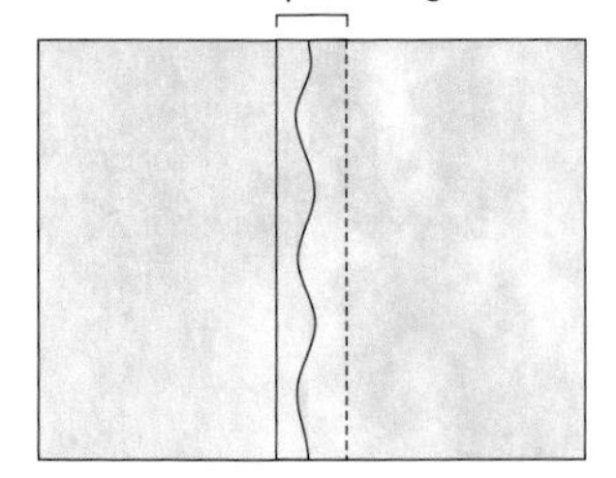

• Carefully peel away the two narrow pieces and discard. Butt the curved cut edges back together. Stitch the two pieces together using a large herringbone stitch.

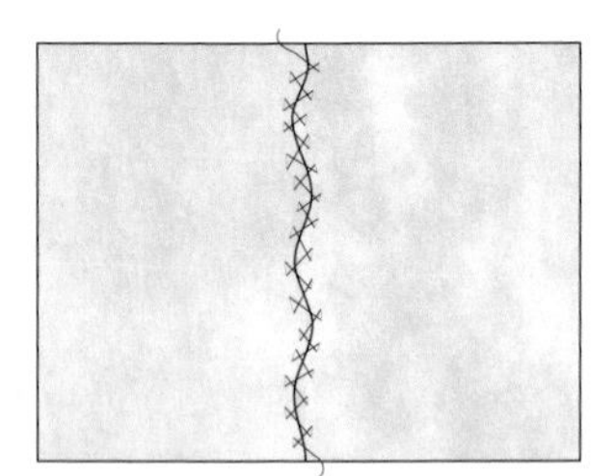

BASTING THE LAYERS TOGETHER

1 On the floor or on a large work surface, lay out the backing with wrong side uppermost. Use weights along the edges to keep it taut.

2 Lay the batting on the backing and smooth it out gently. Next lay the patchwork top, right side up, on top of the batting and smooth gently until there are no wrinkles. Pin at the corners and at the midpoints of each side, close to the edges.

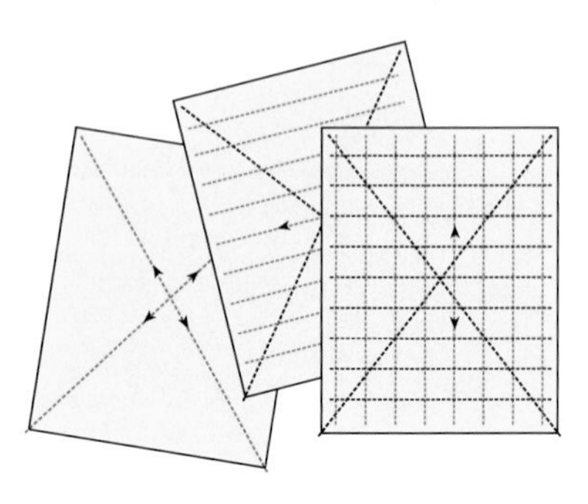

3 Beginning at the centre, baste diagonal lines outwards to the corners, making your stitches about 3in (7.5cm) long. Then, again starting at the centre, baste horizontal and vertical lines out to the edges. Continue basting until you have basted a grid of lines about 4in (10cm) apart over the entire quilt.

4 For speed, when machine quilting, some quilters prefer to baste their quilt sandwich layers together using rust-proof safety pins, spaced at 4in (10cm) intervals over the entire quilt.

HAND QUILTING

This is best done with the quilt mounted on a quilting frame or hoop, but as long as you have basted the quilt well, a frame is not essential. With the quilt top facing upwards, begin at the centre of the quilt and make even running stitches following the design. It is more important to make even stitches on both sides of the quilt than to make small ones. Start and finish your stitching with back stitches and bury the ends of your threads in the batting.

MACHINE QUILTING

- For a flat looking quilt, always use a walking foot on your machine for stitching straight lines, and a darning foot for free–motion quilting.

- It is best to start your quilting at the centre of the quilt and work out towards the borders, doing the straight quilting lines first (stitch-in-the-ditch) followed by the free-motion quilting.

- When free motion-quilting stitch in a loose meandering style as shown in the diagrams. Do not stitch too closely as this will make the quilt feel stiff when finished. If you wish you can include floral themes or follow shapes on the printed fabrics for added interest.

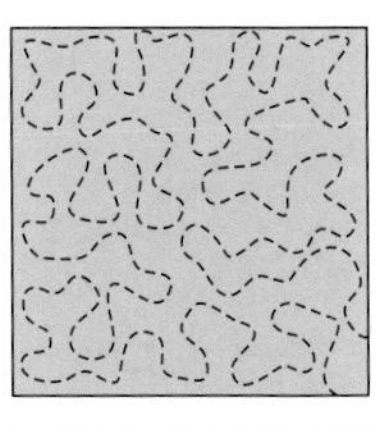

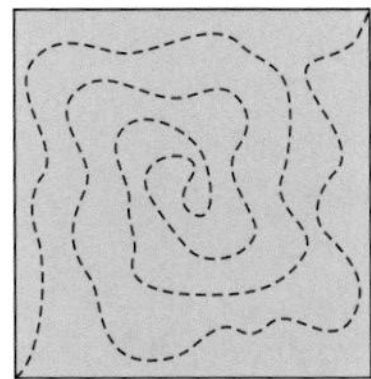

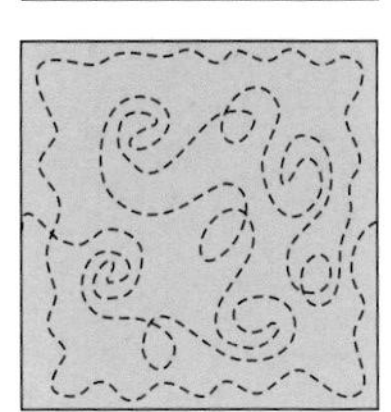

- Make it easier for yourself by handling the quilt properly. Roll up the excess quilt neatly to fit under your sewing machine arm, and use a table or chair to help support the weight of the quilt that hangs down the other side.

FINISHING

Preparing to bind the edges

Once you have quilted or tied your quilt sandwich together, remove all the basting stitches. Then, baste around the outer edge of the quilt ¼in (6mm) from the edge of the top patchwork layer. Trim the back and batting to the edge of the patchwork and straighten the edge of the patchwork if necessary.

Making the binding

1 Cut bias or straight grain strips the width required for your binding, making sure the grain-line is running the correct way on your straight grain strips. Cut enough strips until you have the required length to go around the edge of your quilt.

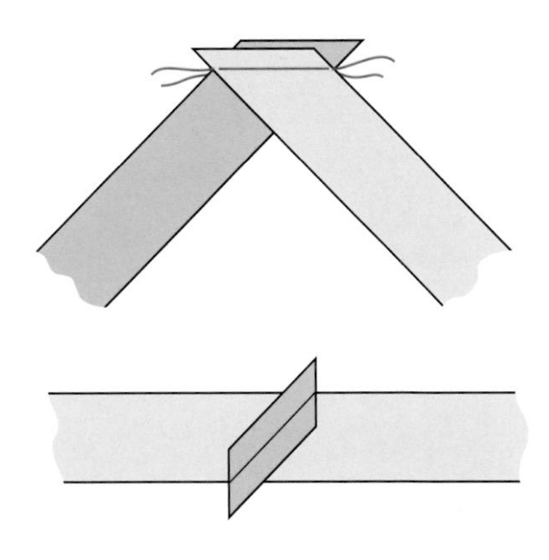

2 To join strips together, the two ends that are to be joined must be cut at a 45 degree angle, as above. Stitch right sides together, trim turnings and press seam open.

Binding the edges

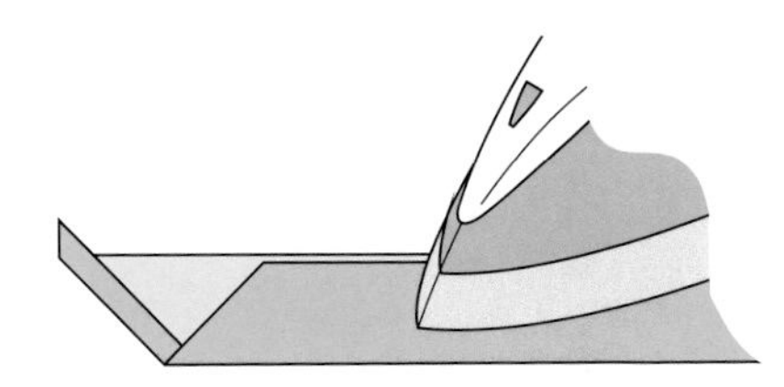

1 Cut the starting end of binding strip at a 45 degree angle, fold a ¼in (6mm) turning to wrong side along cut edge and press in place. With wrong sides together, fold strip in half lengthways, keeping raw edges level, and press.

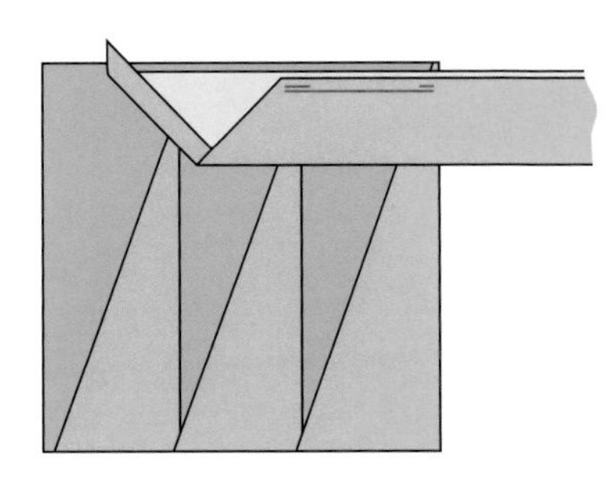

2 Starting at the centre of one of the long edges, place the doubled binding on to the right side of the quilt keeping raw edges level. Stitch the binding in place starting ¼in (6mm) in from the diagonal folded edge. Reverse stitch to secure, and work ¼in (6mm) in from edge of the quilt towards first corner of quilt. Stop ¼in (6mm) in from corner and work a few reverse stitches.

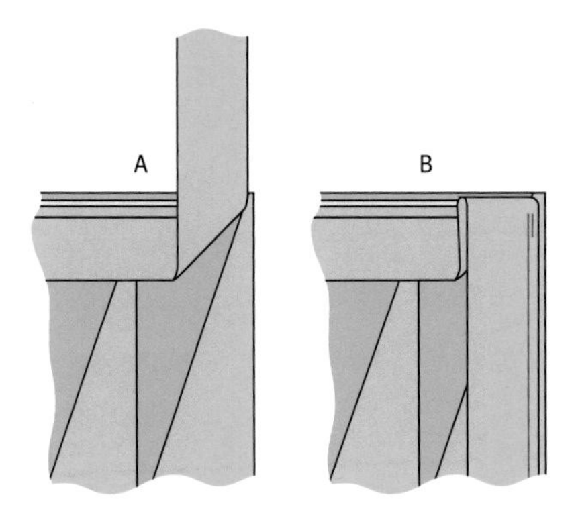

3 Fold the loose end of the binding up, making a 45 degree angle (see A). Keeping the diagonal fold in place, fold the binding back down, aligning the raw edges with the next side of the quilt. Starting at the point where the last stitch ended, stitch down the next side (see B).

4 Continue to stitch the binding in place around all the quilt edges in this way, tucking the finishing end of the binding inside the diagonal starting section.

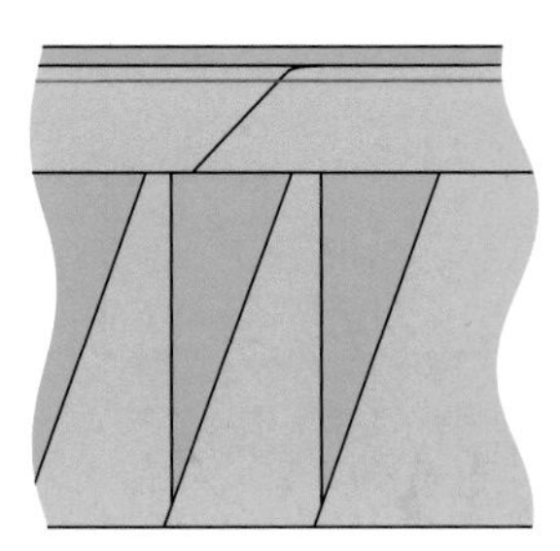

5 Turn the folded edge of the binding on to the back of the quilt. Hand stitch the folded edge in place just covering binding machine stitches, and folding a mitre at each corner

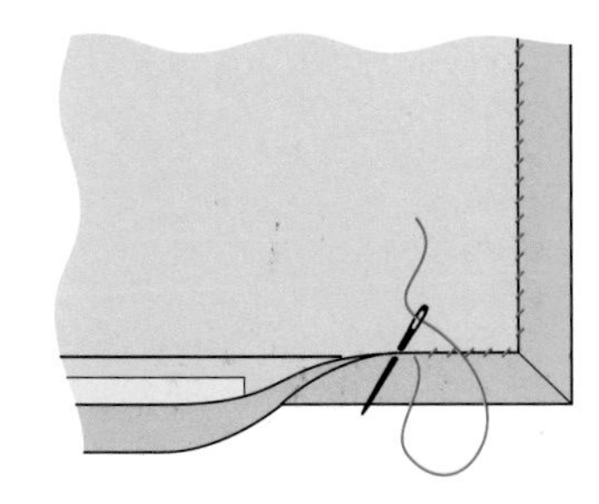

glossary of terms

Adhesive or fusible web This comes attached to a paper backing sheet and is used to bond appliqué motifs to a background fabric. There are 2 types of web available, the first keeps the pieces in place whilst they are stitched, the second permanently attaches the pieces so that no sewing is required.

Appliqué The technique of stitching fabric shapes on to a background to create a design. It can be applied either by hand or machine with a decorative embroidery stitch, such as buttonhole, or satin stitch.

Backing The bottom layer of a quilt sandwich. It is made of fabric pieced to the size of the quilt top with the addition of about 4in (10.25cm) all around to allow for quilting take-up.

Basting or tacking This is a means of holding two fabric layers or the layers of a quilt sandwich together temporarily with large hand stitches, or pins.

Batting or wadding This is the middle layer, or padding in a quilt. It can be made of cotton, wool, silk or synthetic fibres.

Bias The diagonal grain of a fabric. This is the direction which has the most give or stretch, making it ideal for bindings, especially on curved edges.

Binding A narrow strip of fabric used to finish off the edges of quilts or projects; it can be cut on the straight grain of a fabric or on the bias.

Block A single design unit that when stitched together with other blocks create the quilt top. It is most often a square, hexagon, or rectangle, but it can be any shape. It can be pieced or plain.

Border A frame of fabric stitched to the outer edges of the quilt top. Borders can be narrow or wide, pieced or plain. As well as making the quilt larger, they unify the overall design and draw attention to the central area.

Chalk pencils Available in various colours, they are used for marking lines, or spots on fabric.

Cutting mat Designed for use with a rotary cutter, it is made from a special 'self–healing' material that keeps your cutting blade sharp. Cutting mats come in various sizes and are usually marked with a grid to help you line up the edges of fabric and cut out larger pieces.

Design wall Used for laying out fabric patches before sewing. A large wall or folding board covered with flannel fabric or cotton batting in a neutral shade (dull beige or grey work well) will hold fabric in place so that an overall view can be taken of the placement.

Free-motion quilting Curved wavy quilting lines stitched in a random manner. Stitching diagrams are often given for you to follow as a loose guide.

Fussy cutting This is when a template is placed on a particular motif, or stripe, to obtain interesting effects. This method is not as efficient as strip cutting, but yields very interesting results.

Grain The direction in which the threads run in a woven fabric. In a vertical direction it is called the lengthwise grain, which has very little stretch. The horizontal direction, or crosswise grain is slightly stretchy, but diagonally the fabric has a lot of stretch. This grain is called the bias. Wherever possible the grain of a fabric should run in the same direction on a quilt block and borders.

Grain lines These are arrows printed on templates which should be aligned with the fabric grain.

Inset seams or setting-in A patchwork technique whereby one patch (or block) is stitched into a 'V' shape formed by the joining of two other patches (or blocks).

Patch A small shaped piece of fabric used in the making of a patchwork pattern.

Patchwork The technique of stitching small pieces of fabric (patches) together to create a larger piece of fabric, usually forming a design.

Pieced quilt A quilt composed of patches.

Quilting Traditionally done by hand with running stitches, but for speed modern quilts are often stitched by machine. The stitches are sewn through the top, wadding and backing to hold the three layers together. Quilting stitches are usually worked in some form of design, but they can be random.

Quilting hoop Consists of two wooden circular or oval rings with a screw adjuster on the outer ring. It stabilises the quilt layers, helping to create an even tension.

Reducing Glass Used for viewing the complete composition of a quilt at a glance. It works like a magnifier in reverse. A useful tool for checking fabric placement before piecing a quilt.

Rotary cutter A sharp circular blade attached to a handle for quick, accurate cutting. It is a device that can be used to cut several layers of fabric at one time. It must be used in conjunction with a 'self–healing' cutting mat and a thick plastic ruler.

Rotary ruler A thick, clear plastic ruler marked with lines in imperial or metric measurements. Sometimes they also have diagonal lines indicating 45 and 60 degree angles. A rotary ruler is used as a guide when cutting out fabric pieces using a rotary cutter.

Sashing A piece or pieced sections of fabric interspaced between blocks.

Sashing posts When blocks have sashing between them the corner squares are known as sashing posts.

Selvedges Also known as selvages, these are the firmly woven edges down each side of a fabric length. Selvedges should be trimmed off before cutting out your fabric, as they are more liable to shrink when the fabric is washed.

Stitch-in-the-ditch or Ditch quilting Also known as quilting-in-the-ditch. The quilting stitches are worked along the actual seam lines, to give a pieced quilt texture.

Template A pattern piece used as a guide for marking and cutting out fabric patches, or marking a quilting, or appliqué design. Usually made from plastic or strong card that can be reused many times. Templates for cutting fabric usually have marked grain lines which should be aligned with the fabric grain.

Threads One hundred percent cotton or cotton–covered polyester is best for hand and machine piecing. Choose a colour that matches your fabric. When sewing different colours and patterns together, choose a medium to light neutral colour, such as grey or ecru. Specialist quilting threads are available for hand and machine quilting.

Walking foot or Quilting foot This is a sewing machine foot with dual feed control. It is very helpful when quilting, as the fabric layers are fed evenly from the top and below, reducing the risk of slippage and puckering.

Yo-Yos A circle of fabric double the size of the finished puff is gathered up into a rosette shape.

ACKNOWLEDGMENTS
Very special thanks to all the people who contributed to making this book happen. We are particularly grateful to Antonio Rocco and his brothers for distributing our fabrics in Italy along with the help of Carlo Bosca, who introduced us to the tiny hillside villages Cinque Terre; to Luisa Fenoglio for sharing her beloved Santa Margherita and Portofino with us as the starting point to our creative journey; to Janet Haigh of Heart Space Studios, and her team of merry stitchers (Ilaria Padovani, Julie Harvey and Ceema McDowell), for her creative eye and their skills in making up our quilts, and to Liza Lucy for coordinating the American side for us. Last but not least to Debbie Patterson, our loyal friend and photographer for her unending patience, humour and sharp eye, and to Mr Mably for being both the donkey and the butler!

The fabric collection can be viewed online at
www.coatscrafts.co.uk *and* www.westminsterfabrics.com

Rowan 100% cotton premium thread, Anchor embroidery thread, and Prym sewing aids, distributed by
Coats Crafts UK, Green Lane Mill, Holmfirth, West Yorkshire, HD9 2DX.
Tel: +44 (0) 1484 681881 • Fax: +44 (0) 1484 687920

Rowan 100% cotton premium thread and Anchor embroidery thread distributed in the USA by
Westminster Fibers, 3430 Toringdon Way, Charlotte, North Carolina 28277.
Tel: 704 329 5800 • Fax: 704 329 5027

Prym productions distributed in the USA by
Prym-Dritz Corp, 950 Brisack Road, Spartanburg, SC 29303.
Tel: +1 864 576 5050 • Fax: +1 864 587 3353
email: pdmar@teleplex.net

OTHER TAUNTON TITLES AVAILABLE
Kaffe Fassett's Quilt Romance
Kaffe Fassett's Quilts en Provence
Kaffe Fassett's Quilts in Sweden
Kaffe Quilts Again
Kaffe Fassett's Quilt Grandeur
Kaffe Fassett's Quilts in Morocco
Kaffe Fassett's Heritage Quilts

The Taunton Press, Inc., 63 South Main Street,
P.O. Box 5506, Newtown, CT 06470-5506
Tel: 800-888-8286 • Email: tp@taunton.com
www.tauntonstore.com

Westminster Lifestyle Fabrics, 3430 Toringdon Way, Suite 301,
Charlotte, NC, U.S.A.
Tel: 704-329-5800 • Email: fabric@westminsterfibers.com
www.westminsterfabrics.com

distributors and stockists

Distributors of Rowan fabrics

EASTERN USA
Sales Manager
Beth Klar
704-519-6287
beth.klar@westminsterfibers.com

MN, SD, ND, IA, WI
1st MN Repping Company
Margaret Martin, Lori Evans
763-479-8966
margaret@mnrep.com
lori@mnrep.com

ME, NH, CT, MA, RI, VT
Gretchen Rath
207-475-6082
gretchen.rath@gmail.com

KS, NE, MO
Toni Steere
785-561-0225
quiltingtoni@gmail.com

NY, NJ
Liz Dougherty
908-442-5971
liz.dougherty@westminsterfibers.com

IL
Textiles Endeavors Inc.
Tammy Rice
847-309-1995
yourrep@isellfabric.com

FL
Brian Cox
407-257-0145
bjccotton@yahoo.com

MI, IN, OH
Kurt Myers
616-485-6223
ckmm527@comcast.net

VA, MD, DC, DE, PA
Jim Yourinson
302-528-0716
jyourinson@yahoo.com

TX, OK, AR, MS, LA
Bob Adams
214-704-9228
adamsrl@swbell.net

TX, OK, AR, MS, LA
Deb Otto
817-269-3362
crazy4quilting@hotmail.com

GA, W & Central TN, AL
Donnie Brandon
770-330-5543
donebran@aol.com

NC, SC, E TN
Tom Transou
336-209-7408
tptransou1@aol.com

WESTERN USA
Sales Manager
Jan Hurwitz
408-569-5671
jan.hurwitz@westminsterfibers.com

NM, AZ
Cathy Gormley
505-550-9385
cgormely9@msn.com

OR
Kathy Beal
541-504-5297
kathybealtextiles@gmail.com

WA
Jane Hager
425-503-0976
jane@jhager.net

UT, CO
Ron Garn
801-870-8289
rgfabtrimguy@gmail.com

Mid & South CA
Maureen Durnell
424-903-9652
maureendurnell@yahoo.com

North CA, NV, HI
Ron Zucker
650-799-1997
rzuck5@earthlink.net

AK
Kelly Meyer
907-232-5950
alaskafabrics@gmail.com

ID, MT, WY
Bob Gardner
307-248-1820
bgardner245@gmail.com

CANADA
Sales Manager
Norman Bagley
416-951-9059
norman.bagley@westminsterfibers.com

British Columbia (retail only) and Manitoba-all
Peter Daoussis
778-889-7015
peterdaoussis@msn.com

British Columbia (manufacturers only)
Patti Mills
604-575-2062
patty_millennium_textiles@shaw.ca

Toronto, N/SW ONT, Maritimes
Cal Cockburn
416-919-0157
cal.cockburn@hotmail.com

Toronto, SW ONT
Erika Barcza
416-998-6281
erikabarcza@rogers.ca

East Ontario
Kathy Angus
905-753-2598
kathy4035@gmail.com

QC
Mona Schmidt
514-794-8818
mona.strickt@gmail.com

Saskatchewan, Alberta
Carol Wammes
519-525-9608
cwammes@telus.net

North America Customer Service Dept
1-866-907-3305

INTERNATIONAL DISTRIBUTORS
Australia
XLN Fabrics
+ 61-2-9621-3066
allanmurphy@xln.com.au

Europe
MEZ GmbH
+ 49 (0) 7644-802-222
kenzingden.vertrieb@mezcrafts.com

Japan
Kiyohara & Co Ltd
+ 81-6-6251-7179
kazuo.fujii@kiyohara.co.jp

New Zealand
Fabco
+ 64-9-411-9996
melanie@fabco.co.nz

South Africa
Arthur Bales PTY Ltd
+ 27-11-888-2401
nicci@arthurbales.co.za

Sweden
Industrial Textiles A/S
+ 45-48-17-20-55
mail@indutex.dk

Taiwan
Long Teh Trading Company
+ 866-4-2247-7711
longteh.quilt@gmail.com

AFFILIATES
Brazil
Coats Corrente Ltd
+ 5511-3247-8000

China, Hong Kong, Taiwan, Macao
WanMei DIY China,
+86 13816681825
12178550@qq.com

Korea
Coats Korea
+ 81-2-521-6262

Mexico
Coats Mexico
+ 52 55 5227 1800
mercadotecnia@coats.com

United Kingdom
Coats Crafts UK
+ 44 (0) 1484 691544
ccuk.sales@coats.com
www.webshop.coats.com